HEALING THE MALE PSYCHE

Therapy as initiation

John Rowan

London and New York

First published 1997
by Routledge
11 New Fetter Lane, London EC4P 4EE

Simultaneously published in the USA and Canada
by Routledge
29 West 35th Street, New York, NY 10001

Routledge is an International Thomson Publishing company

© 1997 John Rowan

Typeset in Times by LaserScript, Mitcham, Surrey
Printed and bound in Great Britain by
Mackays of Chatham PLC, Chatham, Kent

British Library Cataloguing in Publication Data
A catalogue record for this book is available from the British Library

Library of Congress Cataloguing in Publication Data
A catalogue record for this book has been requested

ISBN 0–415–10048–8 (hbk)
ISBN 0–415–10049–5 (pbk)

HEALING THE MALE PSYCHE

Much of what was once taken for granted about gender roles has shifted, leaving a lack of desirable or achievable roles for men. John Rowan believes that the male psyche has been wounded by the new pressures of social uncertainty and needs to be healed. In *Healing the Male Psyche*, he explores the concept of masculinity using the work of Ken Wilber as a central guide and alchemy as a framework within which to discuss the processes of change.

The way this change happens is personal to each man and involves aspects of the body, emotions, rational understanding and soul. However, because the change required is so major, what is needed is a continuous process that sees the man through the ups and downs, contradictions and paradoxes along the way. The therapeutic relationship is ideally suited to this task. The efficacy of therapy cannot be taken for granted and the author explores how different sorts of therapeutic interventions can hinder as well as help the processes of change.

Addressed to men who are looking to understand their predicament as well as counsellors and psychotherapists working with men, the book is packed with useful exercises and supported by a wide range of references. It offers insights into the male condition which will be of value to therapist and client alike.

John Rowan is a Fellow of the British Psychological Society and psychotherapist. He is the author of *The Horned God: Feminism and Men as Wounding and Healing* and *The Transpersonal in Psychotherapy and Counselling*.

I have read a lot of books about gender, therapy and society but nothing to equal the intellectual, imaginative and humane scope of Rowan's comprehensive work. Not only does he bring together virtually every approach to masculinity (and indirectly to femininity) that one could think of, he does it in a way that does not marginalise anyone. Difference and diversity are respected even as the coherent argument evolves. Therapists have now got a superb resource to draw on, providing a responsible vision of personal therapy as capable of generating social, political and spiritual transformation. Equally important is the impact the book will have on the lives of all thoughtful men and women living in a frustrating and maddening world as they struggle with this problem of 'men' – who are, as Rowan puts it, certainly part of the problem but can also be part of any solution.

Andrew Samuels, author of *The Political Psyche*

The women's movement has made a powerful difference in understanding what it is like to be a woman today, and in how therapy must be reconceptualized for women. John Rowan has done this for men! You will learn from Rowan if this question piques you even a little bit: 'What is a powerful new way of understanding what it is to be male, a man, and in doing therapy with a man, in today's changing world?'

Alvin Mahrer, University of Ottawa

Healing the Male Psyche is specifically addressed to men and their therapists, but is a valuable compendium of information and approaches covering the broad range of gender issues. With his usual bracing clarity and compassionate touch, John Rowan guides us through the promises and the pitfalls of therapy, as well as the potentials and the perils of being a man in today's splintered world. A bold and comprehensive approach to this nightmare called men and women.

Ken Wilber, author of *A Brief History of Everything*

This book is dedicated to
Jocelyn Chaplin and the Immortal Serpent

CONTENTS

CONTENTS

Part I

MATERIA PRIMA AND NIGREDO

Right at the beginning you meet the 'dragon', the chthonic spirit, the 'devil' or, as the alchemists called it, the 'blackness', the Nigredo, and this encounter produces suffering

(Jaffe 1979)

1

INTRODUCTION

MASCULINITY AS PAIN

Being a man today hurts. The old certainties (which perhaps never were all that certain anyway) about who we are and what we are about have shifted radically. We cannot any more take it for granted that we have a job for life. We cannot any more take it for granted that we shall be husbands and fathers. We cannot any more take it for granted that the environment will stay stable and predictable. It seems that we are expected to carve out a future from unpromising materials. If we were free and responsible that would be all right; if we were unfree and irresponsible that would be acceptable too; if we were free and irresponsible that might be very nice for a while; but what we seem to be is unfree and responsible. And that is horribly uncomfortable. So it is not only the individual pains which come to every man which are an issue here: it is the social pain which comes from being a man in a society where strain has become normal.

PROBLEMATISING MEN AND THERAPY

This book is about men and therapy. It starts by saying that being a man is a problem today, and that therapy is a problem too. The reason why they are problematic is that both share a context of late crumbling patriarchy, and that patriarchy is itself problematic. (This is explained in detail in Chapter 2.) There is no assumption here that patriarchy is eternal or ahistorical – it is in process like any other social system – but it seems to be the major archetype of oppression in our time. It is the reason why any true postmodernism is impossible at the moment. Even though patriarchy has become unstable and unpredictable and fragmented in many ways, it still sets whatever standards there are left. It therefore needs to be taken seriously as the background to our whole investigation, and the source of many of the detailed problems in front of us.

PART OF THE PROBLEM AND PART OF THE SOLUTION

In the 1970s there was a saying 'If you're not part of the solution you are part of the problem' which was quite a guilt-inducing message and not really very helpful. Now in the mid-1990s we can see that men are part of the problem and also part of the solution. It is men who hold most of the power positions in society – and just for this reason it is men who have to be involved in any radical change which is to take place. The question that is often asked when we talk of radical change is 'Why should men give up their power?', but it is not really a question of giving up power but of transforming it. Chapter 6 is all about this question. Having power is a good thing, which is why many people go around talking about empowerment as desirable. It goes wrong only when it becomes compulsive and unaware, so that people do not realise that they are being oppressive and even deny it hotly. In a confusing society, it is normal to be confused.

MASCULINE ROLE AS COMPULSIVE

There is much about the masculine role which has become compulsive. In Chapter 4 we shall see why this should be so. Of course the whole notion of gender roles has been criticised: after all, we do not talk about class roles or race roles. There is a suggestion of intentionality about the concept of a role: normally we take up roles, we play roles; and gender roles are not like this, because they are given. But the powerful theory of gender role strain put forward by Pleck (1995) is so useful that it seems worth while to talk in these terms, so long as we realise the limitations involved. The whole point is that these roles are not taken up intentionally – they are imposed by a patriarchal society which still specifies them and enforces them in the family, in the school, in the peer group, in the media and in many other ways. We are all taught that certain ways of being masculine are normal, and others are not. But when anything has become unaware and compulsive, therapy is useful in undoing the compulsion. We shall work through an example of this process in Chapter 3.

THE SOFT MALE

It is not enough to reverse or oppose the expected masculine role to deal with the problems associated with it. This would be just as compulsive as the original role itself. If we feel that the current role involves being aggressive, it does not help to be resolutely unaggressive. If we feel that the role entails being dominant, it does not help to refuse all dominance. All that these manoeuvres achieve is a kind of soft male who is no better than his opposite – just more confusing. Confusing because the masculine role is so poorly specified that reversing the main aspects of it leaves all sorts of straggly remnants round the edges which have not been noticed, not been criticised. And so to the outside observer much of the 'old Adam' remains – the reversal is 'willed' rather than real, and hence inadequate and unconvincing. This is not a valid way of dealing with the problem, and we shall encounter something more useful and more usable in Chapter 9.

THE INITIATED MALE

For real change to take place in a man, what has to happen? I have struggled with this problem for many years now, ever since I joined my first men's group in 1972. In a previous book (Rowan 1987) I argued that he would have to work on three levels: the conscious, the unconscious and the transpersonal. But now I feel that a more useful way of putting it is to say that he has to be completely initiated into a new way of being, unique to him. By initiation I mean something that affects a person at every level, and offers an all-round opportunity for transformation. And it now seems to me inescapable that only therapy has the power to do this, because only therapy explores the nooks and crannies of a man's psychology in enough detail to leave nothing untouched in the end. But even then, not every type of therapy will do: and much of this book is about the variations within therapy – both individually and in groups – which make some types of it much more useful than others for the purposes of transformation.

THERAPY AS INITIATION

In Chapter 5 we shall see where psychotherapy came from, and how it developed. For therapy to be genuinely initiatory, it has to go beyond the adjustment favoured by the more medically oriented approaches. It has to go beyond the liberation favoured by the therapies of the 1960s. It has to deal with the soul. One of the main themes of this book is the male soul and how it is to be understood and approached and honoured.

> The dynamics of initiatory change can also be provoked by any unexpected, dramatic event: accident, divorce, abortion, the death of a loved one, the loss of a career, an eruption from nature that destroys the shape of a life. All severe separations in life evoke the sense of initiation in the psyche and open a person to psychological and mythical territories of unusual depth. Initiation is the psyche's response to mystery, great difficulties, and opportunities to change.
>
> (Meade 1993: 11)

It is a sad fact that many men, faced with such challenges, try to settle for a problem-solving approach which merely tries to put things back the way they were before. But in truth this is an opening, a way in to a new and different kind of life. In Chapter 8 we shall see exactly how this is done, and in Chapter 9 what comes out of the process.

Perhaps therapy is not the only way. It is a hard way to go. It would be nice if there were some other, easier way. But in spite of all my efforts over the years I have not yet found one. In this book we shall find therapy to be the great vision quest that is on every doorstep. It is the way of initiation that is available to all or most of us. And just because it is a way of initiation it is more demanding than we may at first imagine, as Joseph Jastrab tells us:

> On a journey of this sort, every decisive victory is born out of an equally decisive defeat. And paradox is more often the rule than the exception.
>
> (Jastrab 1994: 13)

He is talking about another kind of vision quest, but his words are relevant to us here. We wend our way through the opposites, the contradictions, the traps and the confusions with a sense of danger rather than a sense of safety. This book tries to offer guidance on the way through the labyrinth.

THERAPY AS A NEW SET OF SHACKLES

This means that we shall see, in a patriarchal context, that much of what passes for therapy in the world today is actually confirming the oppressive structure of society instead of questioning it. There are hidden pressures to conform within many forms of therapy today, and some of them are not so hidden. Instead of working towards initiation, which involves facing pain and dealing with it thoroughly, they avoid the pain, and instead try to close it off and deny it. As Alvin Mahrer puts it in his inimitable style:

> Virtually every helping approach assists the person in achieving the above goals [of avoidance] by shifting to another operating potential, and thereby helping the person maintain his self, reduce the burgeoning bad feelings, and push back down the rising deeper potential. These are the aims of supportive therapies, crisis therapies, suicide prevention centres, and the whole enterprise of chemotherapeutic drugs and pills. These are the aims of custodial treatment, behavior therapies, ego therapies, milieu therapies and social therapies. . . . Programs of desensitization and token economy and deconditioning are the allies of the person in working effectively toward these goals. The war cry of all these approaches is the same: control those impulses, push down the insides, reduce the bad feelings, stop the threat, maintain the ego, push away the threat to the self, deaden the tension, guard against the instincts.
>
> (Mahrer 1989a: 367)

We shall have to explore the alternatives to this and see whether some other possibility exists, and in particular which forms of therapy can become a genuine initiation for men. Chapter 7 is all about this.

TWO MAJOR CONTRADICTIONS

So there are two major contradictions which we shall be dealing with in this book. One is the contradiction between the oppressive nature of the masculine role and the transformational possibilities within every individual man. The other is the contradiction between the oppressive nature of much therapy and the transformational possibilities within therapy.

THE ALCHEMICAL PROCESS

In dealing with all these dangers and contradictions, the framework of medieval alchemy seems very useful. As Jung (1980) has shown at length, the work of the alchemists was not very convincing as chemistry, but can help us very much in understanding the process of personal growth. I am not a Jungian, although I have been in Jungian psychotherapy, but what he and some of his followers have demonstrated seems to me to make a lot of sense in this context.

An alchemical framework has been used in Chapter 8 to outline the process of psychotherapy; but it has also been used to lay out the book as a whole. In alchemy there are ups and downs, successes and failures, triumphs and setbacks, changes in colour, and a constant attention paid to paradox, opposites and contradictions. And in this book there are ups and downs and all the rest of that. More than once we shall meet the blackness of the *Nigredo*, and more than once we shall meet the beauty of the *Conjunctio*.

INDIVIDUAL AND GROUP

Most of this book is about individual therapy, and what comes out of it. In Chapters 10 and 11 we look at how going through the process of initiation affects men in the world of work and in their relationships. But men's groups are also very important, and Chapters 12 and 13 are devoted to an examination of what group work can and cannot do. It is in a group that all the social forces of the everyday world are reproduced and can be experienced in action. In the final chapters we shall look at all this from the point of view of how it affects therapists.

This book is primarily addressed to male psychotherapists and counsellors who work with men, though it is hoped that it will speak to men generally at many points. It is specifically designed to open up vistas of possibility for work with men which may not have been realised or appreciated before.

It seems necessary to establish what the background is against which all this takes place. We have to look at the nature of patriarchy. To do this we shall need some light from feminism, because it is feminists and profeminist men who have done most to analyse and understand the structure and functions of patriarchy, as it exists today. This is the subject of the next chapter.

COUNSELLING AND PSYCHOTHERAPY

It is necessary to say something about the difference between counselling and psychotherapy. This book is mostly about psychotherapy, but much of it applies just as much to counselling. I think the last word on the distinction was said over fifty years ago, by Carl Rogers. Here are his words:

> There has been a tendency to use the term counselling for more casual and superficial interviews, and to reserve the term psychotherapy for more intensive and long-continued contacts directed toward deeper reorganisation of the personality. While there may be some reason for this distinction, it is also plain that the most intensive and successful counselling is indistinguishable from intensive and successful psychotherapy.
>
> (Rogers 1942: 3)

In this book the word 'therapy' will be used to cover both, except where a statement is clearly about one and not the other.

2

LIGHT FROM FEMINISM

In this chapter we shall be considering the masculine role. This is a complex subject, and the details will emerge as we go along. The main point is that this role is imposed on men by society in a heavy-handed way which is hard to evade. If we want to understand why the masculine role is so compulsive and so universal, we have to go into the question of feminism. This is because it is feminism which has had the most illuminating things to say about the issue.

This takes us straight into the *Materia Prima*. In alchemy the *Materia Prima* is the material we are given at the beginning. It is where we start from. And it is frightening – the medieval alchemists talked about 'the terror of the *Materia Prima*'. Johannes Fabricius tells us:

> The alchemist's initial encounter with the prima materia is characterised by feelings of frustration, bewilderment, dissociation and disintegration.
> (Fabricius 1994: 20)

And the idea that there might be a deep question about masculinity, deep issues around maleness, a total absence of anything to be taken for granted about being a man – that is anxiety-provoking for men. It is not an easy idea to take on board. It is offputting and difficult. But if it is the *Materia Prima*, it is where we have to start from. The alchemists are clear about the fact that this basic stuff conceals the ultimate secret. We have to deal with it, because the answer is there right in the middle of it.

> It is found everywhere, which is a stone and no stone, contemptible and precious, hidden, concealed, and yet known to everyone.
> (Turba Philosophorum, quoted in Fabricius 1994: 12)

So here is where we start from, this is our base of operations. In this case the *Materia Prima* can be stated in one sentence.

There is a question about men. This is the basic feminist insight, which I think we have to take on board if we are to understand anything about the male psyche. Instead of taking men for granted, as representing the whole human race, we have to think of them as a minority group with particular

9

characteristics. These characteristics are partly genetic, partly social and partly created within the psyche of each individual man. What are they? This is a way of looking at men which takes nothing for granted: we have to really look and see, listen and hear, reach out and get in touch. Men are not the norm against which everything else is to be measured. Nothing is certain, nothing is sure, nothing is to be assumed.

In saying this, we as men may be entering into the *Nigredo*, the dark place in alchemy where things look black and we may tend to lose our confidence and lose our way. But this pain is a necessary part of the process. We cannot move on unless we do justice to the *Nigredo*.

SIX POSITIONS

When we problematise men in this way, there seem to be several different reactions which are possible for men to take up. There are at least these six, which Kenneth Clatterbaugh has named:

- the conservative perspective
- the profeminist perspective
- the men's rights perspective
- the spiritual perspective
- the socialist perspective
- the group-specific perspective

The conservative perspective

Here the reaction to the feminist insight is to say that certain roles and attitudes are natural, hard-wired. According to moral conservatives, masculinity is created by society in order to override man's natural antisocial tendencies, and turn them into fathers, protectors and providers. According to biological conservatives, virtually all social behaviour exhibits men's natural tendencies as selected through an evolutionary process. Feminism is wrong about men, and we must defend ourselves against it.

The profeminist perspective

Here the reaction is to agree with feminists, and to read their literature. Radical profeminists follow the lead of radical feminism in holding that hegemonic masculinity is committed to misogyny and violence against women, and that patriarchy is the social and political order in which this exists. (These terms will be explained fully later in this chapter.) Liberal profeminists follow the lead of liberal feminism in maintaining that masculinity is a set of limitations that are imposed on men, much as femininity is a set of limitations that are imposed on women. This is a nondefensive perspective which tries to learn from feminism rather than oppose it. It can sometimes lead to adopting, or trying to adopt, feminine characteristics, but as we shall see in Chapter 9, this is a mistake.

The men's rights perspective

Here the reaction is to emphasise that men are victims, just as much as women, and perhaps more so. Men's rights advocates draw particular attention to the oppression of men in divorce cases, the way in which men are success objects and disposable objects (e.g. Farrell 1993), and the way in which men's nurturance of women is denied and forgotten. This, they argue, is a new and largely unrecognised form of sexism. This is a highly defensive reaction to feminism, which includes quite a paranoid fringe: some men have actually redefined feminism as 'male-bashing' (Baumli 1985, Farrell 1990).

The spiritual perspective

Here the reaction is to say that masculinity derives from deep unconscious patterns, best revealed in myths and rituals. Female power cannot really be understood without reference to pre-patriarchal forms of thought and organisation. Nor can the male depths be properly respected without reference to universal images and symbols. In short, men need to reach down into the psyche and touch archetypal patterns from which they have been separated. They have to reach forward for the high archetypes which can draw them on and nourish their souls. This is closest to the point of view of this book. Again there are some strange variations on this, some of them quite reactionary, and again all this will become clearer as we go along.

The socialist perspective

The reaction here is to say that masculinity is a social reality, grounded in class. The male role is constructed to suit the ruling groups, who are mainly concerned with power and profit. Sex roles are constructed through and through: to detect them we have to understand the social context, which is patriarchal capitalism. Men have to organise together to dismantle the social system which is oppressive both to women and to men. This has been an important theme in the past, but since 1989 and the fall of the Berlin Wall, socialism has less credibility and draws less support, though it will always be there.

The group-specific perspective

The reaction here is to say that we also have to question the assumption that it is white men who are central. The gay experience is different, because gay men have experienced some of the same oppression that women have also had to contend with. Heterosexism is the oppression of gay people by heterosexual people, and feminists are no more immune from it than anyone else. The black, Asian, Latino experience likewise has oppression to contend with. Radical questions come from this perspective. (See Clatterbaugh (1986) for a much fuller discussion of all these points.)

PATRIARCHY

In this book I am coming from a profeminist and spiritual perspective. I believe patriarchy is the biggest problem of today. In a patriarchal system women are put down and oppressed, and everything female is devalued. The consciousness of men is distorted and limited. The diagram, which comes from Elizabeth Dodson Gray (1982), shows how this works.

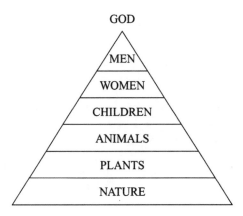

The rule is that each level is entitled and even expected to exploit each of the levels beneath it. They will not be criticised if they do. If you want to know what God thinks about this, you have to ask the men, because they are the closest to God in this system.

Of course a simple diagram like this does not do justice to the complexity of society – how could it? It is just a pointing finger, in this case pointing to a hierarchical way of looking at things, which applies very generally. Of course it is obvious that there is no place on this diagram for differences between men, or for gay experience, or for the dominant woman. But it does bear witness to a broad social pattern which is all-pervasive. And in the case of men themselves, we can as it were do a close-up of the top triangle, and find a small minority of men exploiting the vast majority of the other men. This is why most men feel relatively powerless, instead of as powerful as the diagram suggests at first.

Ultimately, we have to understand that patriarchy has two halves which are intimately related to each other. Patriarchy is a *dual* system, a system in

12

which men oppress women, and in which men oppress themselves and each other.

(Pleck 1989: 27)

One key word to keep in mind is vulnerability. Women are more vulnerable than men; blacks are more vulnerable than whites; children are more vulnerable than adults; animals are more vulnerable than children; people with learning disabilities are more vulnerable than people without; and each time a group is more vulnerable it will be exploited more, in such a system. Men are taught that they must not be vulnerable: Samuel Osherson, in his extensive research with men, found that admitting to their vulnerability was one of the hardest things for them:

> Our vulnerability and dependency became papered over by an instrumental, competent pose as adults or by focusing on what we do well: our ability to achieve in the work world.

(Osherson 1986: 13)

As we shall see, this reluctance to admit to vulnerability is one of the factors which works against men coming in to therapy, and against them coming forward for initiation.

Even amongst relatively enlightened and idealistic people, patriarchy is just as much of a problem. John Southgate once did a survey of 200 intentional communities – communities trying to question the values and structures of ordinary society – and found that 80 per cent of them had one charismatic male leader. The women usually took service roles, just as in the mainstream.

Even in humanistic psychology, which places so much emphasis on equality and genuine encounter and real meeting, it was once found that in the biggest and most important growth centre (Esalen), 80 per cent of the leaders were men, but 80 per cent of the participants were women.

Riane Eisler (1987) threw a lot of new light on to the whole question by suggesting that rather than use the word 'patriarchy', which arouses so many quibbles and peradventures, we talk about dominance cultures and partnership cultures. She went into 30,000 years of history and prehistory to show that there have been partnership cultures at intervals all through that time: periods of time, sometimes quite short and localised, when men and women worked together without having to set up structures of dominance and oppression.

It is important to realise that she is not talking about matriarchy: her terminology is specifically chosen to avoid any suggestion that women simply want to take over, in exactly the same way that men have taken over historically. She is talking about equality:

> The first, which I call the *dominator* model, is what is popularly called either patriarchy or matriarchy – the *ranking* of one half of humanity over the other. The second, in which social relations are primarily based on the principle of *linking* rather than ranking, may best be described as the

13

partnership model. In this model – beginning with the most fundamental difference in our species, between male and female – diversity is not equated with either inferiority or superiority.

(Eisler 1987: xvii)

For example, take the culture whose archaeological remains were dug up in the 1960s at Çatal Hüyük, where it seems clear that women were very highly regarded, and yet their houses and burial places are no larger than those of the men. Her vision, therefore, is one of partnership, where the male and female principles are equally honoured. We shall have more to say on this in Chapter 9.

HEGEMONIC MASCULINITY

However, one important modification needs to be made to her gender analysis. She indicates that the dominance pattern is a coercive one, kept in place by force. But in today's society there is not much show of force: what we have instead is a kind of power which has been called *hegemony*. With hegemony, there is no need for force, because the values of the society have been so thoroughly internalised that force is not necessary. Dominance at the point of a gun or by threats of imprisonment or torture are not hegemony: dominance which is embedded in religious doctrine and practice, mass media content, wage structures, the design of housing, welfare and taxation policies, the layout of supermarkets and so forth is hegemony.

The point is that the playing field is not level. Men are as it were playing downhill in relation to women, and have the wind behind them: women are playing uphill and have the wind against them. This is the basic patriarchal set-up of masculine hegemony, and it lies behind everything else we are talking about here. In this game we do not change sides at half-time. *In doing gender, men are doing dominance and women are doing deference.*

To the extent that therapy enables people to be more effective, to be less conflicted, to be more in touch with their resources, it will have the effect of enabling men to be more dominant. What is personally profitable may be socially deleterious. But as we shall see later, therapy with men can also do justice to connectedness, a value which complements the autonomy so often sought for.

It is clear, then, that there are pressures on men to be masculine. But this is not quite as simple a statement as it may seem. It has often been pointed out that we should speak of many masculinities rather than just one masculinity, because there are many ways of being a man, not just one. It is surprisingly hard to define what a man actually is.

A pair of the wiser men began to debate. One had said that 'masculinity is whatever you have to do to *look* like a man,' while the other thought that 'masculinity is whatever you have to do to *feel* like a man.'

(Pittman 1993: 8)

It seems to make more sense to speak, with Wittgenstein, of a 'family resemblance' than of distinguishing features. In a family, we can often see that the members look like each other, but there may be no one feature that they all have in common. Similarly, it may be possible to find all sorts of things that define men, but any one particular man may have some of them missing. Judith Lorber (1994) has put together a whole book of exceptions and difficult intermediate cases, which make it hard indeed to point to any one thing and say – 'This is what defines a man'. Even the favourite touchstone of the conservative man, testosterone, is not exempt from this. I remember a young man on the Oprah Winfrey show saying that when he was 15 he was 'a walking hormone' – meaning that he was perpetually randy. But it is not about hormones, it is about assumptions and expectations which are socially induced. Similarly with aggression and violence, which are popularly supposed to be the result of high levels of testosterone:

> A major problem with studies on the effect of hormones on aggression is that, as already mentioned for other animals, being aggressive or experiencing aggression also affects hormone levels. Thus correlations between, for example, testosterone and hostility ratings cannot reveal which is the cause and which the effect. There may be a change in production of the hormone following an experience of aggression rather than high hormone levels causing the aggression.
>
> (Turner 1994: 246)

Many men resist this knowledge, because they want to believe that their aggressive and sexual propensities are somehow natural, instinctive, biological, normal, justifiable. But as Andrew Samuels has discovered:

> Gerda Siann found that the evidence does not show any clear and unambiguous relationship between male hormones and the propensity to display violent behaviour or feel aggressive emotion. Siann points out that environmental and social variables have a good deal to do with the secretion of male hormones and also emphasizes evidence that discovered a role for female hormones in violent behaviour and aggressive emotion.
>
> (Samuels 1993: 156)

This chimes in well with what other researchers have found. One book which has a very thorough examination of the evidence, showing that very seldom is there any consistent story to be told, ends up by saying:

> As a postscript to this section it is worth noting that remarkably few studies have been done on men to investigate the relationship between their emotions, mental health and the not inconsiderable fluctuations in testosterone.
>
> (Hargreaves and Colley 1986: 260)

Again we are left with the knowledge that there are many masculinities, not just one, and that we cannot retreat to the certainty of hormones to bolster up a case.

However, it is still true, in the dominance system which we live in today, that there is one dominant masculinity, and many subordinate masculinities. The hegemonic pattern requires clarity and simplification to be effective. What this means in practice is that men are pressured into being masculine in just one way. To be a proper man, a man who is successfully masculine, is to be constrained into quite a narrow band of expectations. These expectations have been outlined well by Robert Brannon (1976), who has extracted four themes or dimensions that seem to be valid across all specific manifestations of hegemonic masculinity:

- *No sissy stuff* Anything feminine must be avoided. It is important not to be seen as feminine in any way. To do otherwise is to run the risk of being ridiculed or devalued by other men.

- *The big wheel* There is a need to be seen to be high in status, or to be connected directly to people or organisations with high status. It is important to be important.

- *The sturdy oak* One must be independent and self-reliant, and be ready to support others. This support may be physical or material: if it is emotional there is a risk of being seen as feminine.

- *Give 'em hell* Always be ready to respond to threat. Do not avoid violence if it is appropriate. Protect one's image and one's loved ones. Take risks and take the lead.

This research was done in the USA, but I believe that the same assumptions are found, with few variations, throughout the Western world, and in a good deal of the East as well. I once had a dream with the following image:

Think of a cartoon showing a huge piece of cardboard set up with props so that it stands by itself. In it is cut out the shape of a macho male. A boy is told that he cannot be accepted until and unless he can fit the cutout and pass through. So he adds armoured shoes to get the right height, body armour to get the right width and shape, and more armour to get the right arm length. He feels ridiculous and not himself, but he can now pass through the cutout with no gaps, and be accepted as a man.

What men want when they take up these images is a woman who will complement them. This woman will have what Bob Connell (1987) has called 'emphasized femininity' – that is, a corresponding pattern with the complementary values. Such a woman will want a manly man, will go for someone with social power (and possibly urge him on in his advancement), will behave in a dependent manner, not challenging the status of the man, and will praise a man for standing up to the various threats in the environment.

So in this kind of system, there will be pressure on men to conform to this pattern of masculinity, and on women to conform to this pattern of femininity. One result of this is that men die sooner than women do.

16

In 1900, life expectancy in the United States was 48.3 years for women and 46.3 years for men. In 1984, it was 78.2 years for women and 71.2 years for men . . . . A critical reading of presently available evidence confirms that male role socialization contributes to the higher mortality rate of men.

Waldron (1976) estimates that three-fourths of the difference in life expectancy can be accounted for by sex-role-related behaviours that contribute to the greater mortality of men. She estimates that one-third of the differences can be accounted for by smoking, another one-sixth by coronary prone behaviour, and the remainder by a variety of other causes.

(Harrison *et al.* 1989: 296 and 306)

The actual figures of course vary from year to year, but the higher mortality of men is constant throughout, as Sidney Jourard (1974) eloquently argued in the mid-1970s.

POWER

What we also have to take seriously is the real imbalance of power in patriarchal society. Warren Farrell (1993) tries to reduce power to a psychological question – 'Do you *feel* powerful?' – but it is much more than that. Men's real social power over women is described very fully in Bob Connell's work, or in an excellent compendium like Judith Lorber's (1994) book.

What we can look at psychologically is where men's need to control women comes from. There seem to be three possibilities, as Joseph Pleck (1989: 22–23) has suggested.

First, the male child perceives his mother and his predominantly female early school teachers as dominating and controlling him in a way he does not like. As a result, men feel a lifelong psychological need to free themselves from or prevent their domination by women. This argument is well put by Cynthia Adcock, in a striking essay. She has this to say:

The power, the immediate power over the infant, was female. We cannot help but live in fear, in dread, for any power on which we are so deeply dependent. In this fact, I think, lies the origin of sexism. Torn from the mother by birth, needy for her milk and love, we feel a terrified ambivalence toward her. This painful alienation dances maliciously, invisibly, throughout the rest of our lives.

(Adcock 1982: 213)

The argument is, in effect, that men oppress women as adults because they experienced women as oppressing them as children.

Second, the 'mother identification' theory holds that men develop a 'feminine' psychological identification because of their early attachment to their mothers. Men fear this internal feminine part of themselves, and try to control it by

17

controlling others, those who actually are female. This fits quite well with the Jungian notion of the *anima*, the internal unconscious female within every man. This is a source of strength or of disturbance, depending on how it is approached and understood. If this were so, men would project on to women all sorts of characteristics which they do not actually have. This can take the form of idealisation or of denigration, elevation or putdown – often both at the same time, which is pretty confusing for a woman. Here the theme is of men making and remaking women into images which fit with their needs, but which do not have much to do with the actual person involved.

Third, the 'mother socialisation' theory holds that since boys' fathers are relatively absent as sex-role models, the major route by which boys learn masculinity is through their mothers' behaviour in (a) rewarding masculine conduct and (b) punishing feminine conduct. Thus boys – and men too – associate women with punishment and pressure to be masculine. In some cases this can be done in a seductive way which in the extreme case may amount to a kind of emotional incest (Love 1990).

Of these, the first seems the most plausible and frequent to me, but there is probably some truth in all three. Of course men do not like to see themselves as controlling or powerful – that is too much in today's supposedly egalitarian world. From a man's point of view, it is often women who are the powerful ones, the unfair ones, the ones who hold all the aces.

The first power that men perceive women having over them is *expressive power*, the power to express feelings. Many men have learned to depend on women to help them express their feelings, and indeed to express their feelings for them. Many men are unable to experience anything like a live feeling except through relationships with women (Pleck 1989: 23–24).

A second form of power that men attribute to women is *masculinity-validating* power. In hegemonic masculinity, to experience oneself as masculine requires that women play their emphasised feminine role of doing the things that make men feel masculine. Frank Pittman points to this when he says:

> One man, who had recently reconciled with his wife and suddenly felt very much in love with her, said, 'Masculinity is doing what it takes to put a smile on a woman's face.'
>
> (Pittman 1993: 9)

It is unusual for men to be as honest as this, even if they sometimes think such thoughts, because it makes them seem not in control.

So the question of power is full of misperceptions, repressions, projections and most of the other types of ego defence. Joseph Pleck sums up some of this very well when he says:

> Thus, men's patriarchal competition with each other makes use of women as symbols of success, as mediators, as refuges, and as an underclass. In each of these roles, women are dominated by men in ways that derive

directly from men's struggle with each other. Men need to deal with the sexual politics of their relationships with each other if they are to deal fully with the sexual politics of their relationships with women.

(Pleck 1989: 27)

This is a crucial insight, and can be overlooked only at our peril. It shows that the patriarchal struggle for status in the hierarchy of power is never ending and dominates our whole culture.

In therapy we shall be interested in the ways in which men respond in their various ways to these pressures. Since the coming of the latest wave of feminism in the 1970s and 1980s, there has been much more confusion and uncertainty as to how to respond.

CURRENT FEMINISMS

This confusion has been made worse by the variety of feminisms which have been put forward at different times. We have to look at only a brief list to see how difficult it is for men who wish or need to question hegemonic masculinity. What is the alternative?

Anarchist feminism

The state and patriarchy are both to be questioned and dismantled. A woman's state would be no better than a man's state. We have to be completely radical, not partially so. Women's organisations must be completely non-hierarchical. The means used to change society must be models of the future society in themselves. Sometimes called anarcha-feminist.

Black feminism

All feminist theory must understand imperialism and challenge it. We cannot prioritise one aspect of our oppression to the exclusion of others. Many feminists are unconsciously racist, and need to challenge this. Some black theorists have developed the concept of womanism. 'Womanist is to feminist as purple is to lavender' (Alice Walker 1983).

Constructivist feminism

Gender is constructed socially, and we have to rethink in quite a radical way what ground we are standing on when we talk about it. Feminists tend to see constructivism in quite a critical way. Someone said 'When I hear that gender is constructed I want to know who has been awarded the contract.' This expresses a suspicion that those who have the power in other ways also have the power to construct whatever is constructed.

Cultural feminism

This wants to create a separate and radical women's culture. Because patriarchy is all-embracing, women will be free only in an alternative women's culture. A revised culture would be woman-centred. There is a need to develop a language which will genuinely represent the experience of being a woman. Womanculture stands for a wild zone, a woman's world which is free and fulfilling.

Eco-feminism

This stresses the connection between ecology, which gives real weight to the underside, the less obvious, the disregarded, and feminism, which gives real weight to the oppressed, the silenced and the degraded in society. Gives a central place to the connection between society and nature, and emphasises the side-effects of actions, not just the actions themselves.

Lesbian feminism

This contributes the idea that women are the sole source of female validity and women are the prime healers. The idea of woman-identified women was placed at the heart of feminism by these thinkers. Only a lesbian culture can be a true womanculture. One of the prime targets is heterosexism: the assumption that heterosexuality is superior and should always be dominant, which often leads to heterosexuality appearing to be compulsory. Many feminists are subject to heterosexism, without sometimes even realising it.

Marxist feminism

This identifies the sexual division of labour as a cause of oppression, and sets an agenda of economic change. The meanings of all the concepts involved in feminism have varied historically and cannot be treated as static or unified. The idea of patriarchy is a dangerous one insofar as it is ahistorical.

Radical feminism

This insists that the oppression of women is fundamental to all other forms of oppression. The patriarchal family precedes capitalism and can survive its demise. Radical feminism aims to destroy the sex–class system, where women form an inferior class on the basis of their gender. All forms of oppression are seen as expressions of male supremacy. The personal is political. Woman-centredness can be the basis of a future society.

Socialist feminism

This says that the roots of women's oppression lie in the total economic system of capitalism. Unlike radical feminism, socialist feminists refuse to treat economic oppression as secondary; unlike Marxist feminists they refuse to treat sexist oppression as secondary.

Spiritual feminism

Also called myth feminism, this involves the construction of cultural symbols, images, rituals and archetypes of power useful to women in opposing social oppression. It has created a theory of knowledge based on women's mystical experiences of connectedness with nonhuman nature and other women. It draws strength from outside the system. Spiritual feminists developed the concept of 'womanspirit' to develop tools such as meditation, personal mythology, natural healing, dreamwork, study of matricentric history and mythology. It tends to be quite political.

It can be seen quite easily from this list that any attempt to get it right with feminism is doomed to failure. What I am attempting in this book is to problematise men from a male point of view. But at the same time we have to problematise therapy and not take that for granted either.

This is why I have called this part the *Nigredo* – the blackness of the underworld, where we have to experience the pain of being caught up in the compulsions of a patriarchal society. It is no wonder that many men avoid this kind of a journey.

3

A CASE STUDY: THE MAN WHO HATED WOMEN

This is a fairly extended study of a client, a skilled manual worker aged 38 who entered counselling with anxiety, depression and a certain degree of paranoia. He was doing badly at work, had never had a relationship with a woman and was generally rather obsessive. It includes notes which he made at the time and has generously made available for publication. Certain details have been changed to avoid recognition, in agreement with the client.

Here we are still in the *Materia Prima*, still in the *Nigredo*. These are hard data about how bad things can be, and about how the secret stone is hidden within the bad stuff.

> Although of great inward value, the *prima materia* is vile in outer appearance and therefore despised, rejected, and thrown on the dung heap. . . . Psychologically, this means that the *prima materia* is found in the shadow, that part of the personality that is considered most despicable. Those aspects of ourselves most painful and most humiliating are the very ones to be brought forward and worked on.
>
> (Edinger 1985: 12)

In this case history we shall be starting from this sort of base.

The man, whom we shall call Tom, told a long tale of disappointment with therapists and doctors, and I thought at first that there was little chance of success with him. His problems had lasted for at least fourteen years, during which time he had had a brief 'nervous breakdown'. He was referred through a mutual friend involved with the local MIND (mental health agency). He worked in a technical capacity for the London Underground, repairing electrical problems on the track, and had been doing this for a number of years. He had recently moved out of the parental home into a flat nearby, where he lived alone, visiting his parents several times a week. He had a close, strong and mixed relationship with his mother, and a more distant and mutually critical relationship with his father. He had no sexual relationship, and no experience of any, though he had had one or two girlfriends for brief periods.

He had previously had therapy with a hypnotherapist some distance away for nine months, and had also been to National Health Service groups at the local hospital, but they had not helped. Nor had an analytic centre where he had two sessions.

His appearance was neat and organised, average height, average features, a steady and quite precise voice, nothing that would make him stand out in a crowd. From the start, he took the therapy seriously, and took notes on each weekly session. He then added to these during the week, from his further thoughts and ruminations. He insisted on reading out these notes at the beginning of each session, to make sure he had got the details right. This took up so much time (often half an hour or more) that the time for actual work was diminished. We agreed after a little experience of this to have sessions lasting one and a half hours, and this worked much better.

He had problems at work, mainly around the issue of relations with other workers, and especially his superiors. He experienced them as being very unfair and unsupportive, and as using his absences (due to the anxiety and depression) to make his attendance record look worse than it really was. We worked a good deal on this problem, and in a relatively short time he attained a much better sense of how to stick up for himself and hold his own. It was probably this success that made him stay with the therapy through the much more difficult material which followed.

It turned out that the main thing he wanted to talk about was women, for quite some time after we began. Because he kept these notes, and kindly allowed me to use them later, we can be quite precise as to what he was thinking. Here is an extract from the first session to which I have access, a month or two after the beginning of therapy.

I have severe difficulty in coping with sex and relationships. I have had many break-ups in my relationships, and have had virtually no sex life. The last time I broke up with a girlfriend nearly four years ago was the final straw. Psychologically these experiences with women have caused me so much damage that I find I can no longer form relationships at all. The prospect of asking anyone out creates so much fear and anxiety that I cannot take risks.

I feel that the whole scenario of broken relationships, anxiety and depression will repeat itself, should I become involved with women again. What is going to press this anxiety or panic button is the uncertainty and unpredictability I will be faced with. I can never tell how a woman is going to react, or what she will do. Therefore I am faced with a dilemma: should I avoid women altogether so that I can maintain my emotional health, but at the same time destroy any chances of finding a partner? Conversely should I take risks, and find myself in situations where this anxiety panic button is going to be pressed? How can you help me to sort out and resolve these frustrations and anxieties?

He obviously wanted an immediate solution, which he seemed to see as a kind of course of instruction in how to behave. But I did not want to take that course, as his problems seemed to go deeper, and to have quite a lot to do with his relationship with his mother. He explained that his mother was not a woman in the sense in which he was complaining about women. She did not have the faults he ascribed to all women: she had a different and quite distinct set. But let us come back to women in general. He wrote, again about the same time:

> Women behave as if it is their exclusive privilege and right to have a relationship. I feel as if they are saying to me 'Unless you come up to our expectations, or have a personality and behaviour which satisfies us, we do not want to know you.' They are telling me that I am inadequate, and must therefore change my personality to accommodate them.
>
> This makes me feel very angry and bitter, because they are treating me in a condescending manner. I also feel that women are in a far stronger position because they do not have to make much effort to attract a man, and can capriciously pick and choose their partners.
>
> As a man I am treated like an old football, kicked around. It is as if I am searching and scratching around for a relationship, while women show little tolerance and compassion for my feelings. How am I to keep any pride, dignity and respect for myself as a man? I want to feel more in control.

This is a very general pattern with men. They want to feel in control. If you put it to them that this is the case, however, they will often respond by saying that no, they don't want control, they just don't want to be controlled. But that is really the same thing. Adam Jukes remarks about the way in which many men find difficulty in achieving a genuinely intimate relationship:

> Such involvement represents a high degree of emotional maturity and integrity and the ability to surrender this integrity, secure in the knowledge of regaining it, and in the trust of the other. Most men are incapable of such relating, for the reasons I give in this book, yet they are sufficiently aware of their shortcomings to find them a continual source of guilt and frustration.
>
> (Jukes 1993: 220)

The guilt and frustration come out very clearly here, where Tom is admitting to feelings and experiences which most men are much more reticent about. Let us listen to just one more extract from this earlier period:

> How do I cope with women's hostility and the anxiety and fear it creates? I want to be a confident more effective person, but I do not want to distort my personality. I do not want to be something I am not – e.g. extraverted, loud, brash. I want to be myself, my true personality, and bring out the best qualities.

One of the favourite male tricks is shown here – the attribution of the problem to the other party. It is the women who have the job of carrying the hostility. But as we saw just now, the client did in fact admit to being angry: in his case, however, this was not considered to be hostility, but rather an inevitable consequence of the way he had been treated by women. Thus justified, his anger with women went deep, and was sometimes expressed in violent forms:

> I feel that if this goes on then my frustration and anger is going to get so bad that I will eventually start to seek my revenge. I swear that I am not just going to take all the shit that they throw at me unconditionally. . . .
> I want a way of fighting back. It feels as if I want to kill them for what they have done to me. Women would tend to treat my feelings as a big joke, as something to laugh at. I am going to get the last laugh.

These are quite serious statements. I did not believe he would act on them, simply because he was in therapy, and had therefore the opportunity to express these feelings rather than bottling them up. As Adam Jukes says:

> In the final analysis it is difficult to judge the exact contributions made by, on the one hand, paranoid projection and, on the other, reality in one's final perceptions because of the necessity of determining the enemy's intentions in the absence of unambiguous information. Often the only information available is one's own fantasies, and in conditions of uncertainty one's worst fantasies prevail.
>
> (Jukes 1993: 6)

This seems quite accurate to me, and quite applicable to the present case.

We did a lot of work on actual incidents of experience with women, and it turned out that in every case the woman's actions were understandable in terms of the way he had treated her. From seeing women as quite unpredictable and strange, he began to see how their actions could be understood as having some relation to his own. This was quite painful work, which he resisted all the way, but his persistence kept him at it.

We also tried an exercise which I have found useful. This is a visualisation, which because it is a fantasy must come entirely from within the client. He cannot blame someone else, because there is no one else involved:

> I was asked to picture a man and a woman in two boxes, and their reactions towards each other. I described how the man became frustrated and col-lapsed in a heap, while the woman remained aloof and indifferent.
> We then discussed the part that I had played in my past relationships. It was discovered that I had sabotaged many of them, thereby confirming my feelings about women. It was what you termed a self-fulfilling prophecy. It was hard to understand why I did this, but a clue was my close relationship with my mother. Because I trusted my mother and regarded all other wo-men as devious and unscrupulous, this relationship somehow excluded all other women.

His relationship with his mother was explored with the help of another exercise, of a different character. This was a piece of art work. I have found art work very useful in therapy, as it gives a piece of evidence which can be discussed again and again if necessary. This is how he experienced it:

> Next I was asked to draw two women, the good and the bad. I then wrote against those women their positive and negative attributes, e.g. clean, attractive, good personality. It was found that both women had good and bad qualities and that I basically mistrusted both types. The good woman I identified with my mother.

It was important for him to realise just how much he put his mother into quite a different category and reacted to her so strongly. We worked on incidents with his mother, and found that her putdowns of him were quite predictable, and related to her own problems.

By this time the therapy had started to work quite well on the level of his employment. He was experiencing less tension and dis-ease from this source:

> I keep having these doubts about therapy as to whether it is going to work. Certainly it is giving me more insight and self-knowledge. That in itself is useful and I can bring my fears into the open. On the work level it seems to have helped a lot.

But he was still perturbed about the efficacy of therapy in dealing with his main problems. It seemed to help somewhat when I gave him some references to research which had been carried out:

> We talked about personality development, and how changing one's attitudes brought about this breakthrough. I asked whether there was any scientific proof to back this up. You explained that an experiment was carried out on personal constructs, whereby points were taken before, during and after psychotherapy. Also a period of 2 years after treatment was measured. It was found that significant change and development had taken place with five subjects. Mathematically this could also be proved. I was reassured to find scientific fact to support this.

This refers to some research by Ninoska Marina (1982) which I had written about before. We went on to talk more about his father. His relationship with his father was also important. He experienced his father as very rough and ready, sometimes quite abusive and outspoken, and had long ago decided not to be like him. But this led to its own difficulties:

> To be more successful, I feel that I need to be assertive and confident, the very qualities my father has to a greater degree. Unfortunately being asser-

tive, confident and outspoken are the very attributes that I react against, because it is then being like my father. Therefore I tend to behave in a rather quiet and reserved manner.

So his self-image was partly formed in a negative way, by reference to a hostile reference figure. It was also formed in a positive way, by reference to an exemplar:

I was then asked to visualise a person who I thought had the qualities of a true man, someone who I admired and respected. This could be fictional or real. I chose Sherlock Holmes.

What an interesting choice! A detective, a cool mind, a keen observer, but not a great success with women, so far as we know. This turned out to be quite important in explaining many of this client's attributes. Of course, the reference to Sherlock Holmes might also have been a derivative of his dissatisfaction with me, as too much like a detective and not enough like a mentor. But the detective work was very interesting, and led to some memories coming back which had been repressed and warded off before:

I found that I had remembered an upsetting event which happened to me when I was about 9 or 10. I used to play with the girls next door to my grandmother, A– and B–. Because of a growing awareness of girls and sex, I had my first encounters with them. I took A– home to my parents' one day while they were out. I took her into my bedroom but could not have full sex. My cousin C– found out and told my uncle. I then got chastised by my uncle, and afterwards I felt extremely ashamed and guilty. That night I wept and felt nausea and tension. I felt so bad about myself that I confronted A– and told her what I thought of her. Fron then onwards I kept girls away from me.

Here we have sexual abuse being admitted, not from the receiving end, as is more usual, but from the angle of the perpetrator. Further details had emerged, of course, in the sessions themselves. And it can be seen how sexual abuse from this angle can be just as damaging as it is from the other and more usual standpoint. It seemed that this experience was actually very important in helping to form his ideas and feelings about females and how to handle them.

This made the work on women very slow. It did gradually move, especially in reference to situations where there was no chance of any sexual involvement:

I expressed that it was easier now to speak to women, and to feel more relaxed about myself. This was because of an increased awareness and openness, which was initiating this change.

27

This was progress, but it was not really in the area of most anxiety. It referred to the public sphere, rather than the private.

Let us now skip on to a period nine months later, when one might have expected some change to have taken place on the main issue. The problem was, however, that although the client was quite able to talk about feelings, he found it very hard to get in touch with them. He was also very inhibited physically, so that the idea of hitting a cushion, for example, was unacceptable. So the whole area of feelings remained in shadow. Here is what he was writing:

> I feel in such a state of anxiety about relationships because there are no guidelines or rules to follow. I like life to be neat and orderly, but relationships throw me into confusion because I cannot cope with uncertainty and risks. Women are unpredictable, and one never knows what they will do. It is is unexpected things that will cause panic and anxiety, and I do not know how to handle it. I cannot control women's behaviour or prevent myself from getting hurt – e.g. past experiences. Fear of women and what they can do to me still remains a difficult problem.
>
> It is a situation of being kept down and oppressed. I cannot get anything or anywhere in my job, or in my sexual or personal life. I face a constant struggle in my life to get anything at all. It almost seems as if I am being denied these things, or that they are being taken away. I face this paradox in that I work hard to strive for things but get absolutely nowhere. Why is it that I put in so much effort, but find that my endeavours are absolutely fruitless?

One might well feel a little disappointed that after this lapse of time not much more had happened to modify his attitudes. The client did in fact feel this himself. He wrote at the same time:

THERAPY PROBLEMS CONTINUED

> I feel that therapy is too academic and should be showing me a way out of my problems. I need more solid practical solutions. I need advice on how to lead my life so that I do not get into panic/anxiety states. Therapy is pointless unless I can prevent these problems from re-occurring. What specifically can I do about deeply entrenched attitudes, that are fixed? Why do I persist with these attitudes when they are not doing me any good and are counterproductive?
>
> What therapy is not doing is showing me how to handle my fears and anxieties. It is not telling me what I should be doing to overcome these problems. I feel angry towards you for not doing more for me. There is direction in therapy but not enough, and I do not quite know where it is all heading. What can I expect from therapy, and if I have not resolved these problems by Christmas or the New Year, what else can I pursue?

I do not want to finish therapy prematurely without having resolved these problems. I want these problems sorted out, I want to feel whole. Is there a solution? I have not changed my attitudes at the moment. I do not know how to change my attitudes or sort my problems out.

If I cannot resolve these problems, what is going to happen to me? Because I cannot cope with my sexual problems, it is putting my health under strain. Could I break down under this pressure?

At about this time he was doing something under his own steam which would have some effect. He started a men's group. He had picked up this idea from a magazine which I am involved with, called *Achilles Heel*. As issues come out, I have a habit of putting them on a table in my consulting room, and inviting my clients to look at them. I helped by providing a booklist of material which the group might find useful in their discussions.

But a few months later we had a very important breakthrough, which changed everything. What happened was that his grandmother died. He had been very close to her in his childhood, and in fact she had been better to him, he said, than his mother. He had very happy memories of her, and missed her very much. As he realised his loss, he burst into tears. I encouraged him to lie down and to give way to the feelings, carrying on like this for most of the session.

After this, a lot of things changed. He took over and moved into his grandmother's house, which was more distant from his parents' home, and visited his mother much less often. He made friends with a woman, and this became a sexual relationship which he appeared able to handle. His men's group came to an end, and he explained that he had become more and more at odds with the other men in the group, who seemed to want to spend all the time talking about the faults of women.

It was as if all the work we had done at a cognitive level had transferred itself, lock, stock and barrel, into the emotional level. Instead of intellectual insight, he had emotional understanding.

He left therapy soon after, and I heard later that he had acquired a regular girlfriend, and was having a sexual relationship with her. How this turned out would be another story, which would have to be told somewhere else.

Enough has been said, however, to point up some very interesting aspects of men's reactions to women. The views which he expressed are very common amongst teenagers, but they usually change in their twenties, because of greater maturity and also because of more experiences of success. In this case, for a number of reasons, they did not. So we have here a pure culture, so to speak, uncontaminated by successful experiences. I believe these feelings and ideas underlie much of what seems very different on the face of it; and it requires only one bad experience for them to be revived. So this case taught me a great deal about what lies behind the facade of many men, who are less explicit about what they are feeling.

POSTSCRIPT

After contacting Tom to get his permission for this case history to be published, I got the following reply:

> Thank you for your letter dated 9th Dec 1994. I have read the chapter on my case history, and would like to say that it is an accurate account of the various stages we went through in therapy. When I first consulted you I also thought at the time, that it would not work. I had as you stated a long history of disappointment with therapists and doctors, and thought at the time 'oh no not another therapist'. I was determined though to put everything into it, as I believed that it was my last chance.
>
> I can see that the work we did together was important, and a turning point in my life. Although therapy was painful, it went deeper than what I had experienced before. All aspects relating to my problem were discussed, and I understood it not only intellectually but more importantly emotionally. I did not force change it developed from within myself.
>
> Looking back in hindsight I can see how I have changed, and feel horrified to believe that I held such angry and bitter feelings. Therapy is not something I would like to go through again, but at the time it was necessary because of the seriousness of the problem. The [nationality] girlfriend I was dating a few years back, I married on the [date]. We spent our honeymoon in [place], and then moved into my grandmother's house, which we have been busily decorating for the past year.
>
> We are happily married and hope to spend Christmas Eve with friends in [another part of the city], and go to church at the Midnight Service.
>
> I hope you have a happy Christmas, and I give you my approval for the chapter which gives details of my case history. I hope that it will be of benefit to others.

This letter seemed worth including for its encouragement both for any clients or potential clients who might see it, and for any therapists who may be struggling with similar problems.

Part II

FERMENTATIO

The rising posture of the royal bodies testifies to the elevating power of the sown earth, i.e. to the swelling quality of the golden ferment.

(Fabricius 1994: 142)

4

DEVELOPMENTAL ISSUES

EARLY ORIGINS

The next stage in the alchemical process has to do with the chemistry of fermentation. The materials have now been sealed in the alchemical vessel, and are being heated. They are bubbling and changing. So in this chapter we shall be looking at how masculinity develops, and how a man becomes a man in this patriarchal context.

At the beginning, we do not distinguish ourselves very well from our mothers. We are not quite sure where our mother ends and we begin; there seems to be an overlap, which is quite large at first. We are not even sure that we want to be separate, or have the right to exist as separate.

> It is an 'oceanic' state without any boundaries where we do not differentiate between ourselves and the maternal organism or ourselves and the external world.
>
> (Grof 1992: 38)

All the strength, all the power, seems to be in the relation with the mother, the identity with the mother. Perhaps the mother and I are one. There may even be a feeling of omnipotence, of being all-powerful, because of this. Everything we do is right.

In order to move out of this unity, and become a separate body, something is necessary, and it is going to have to be something which threatens this power, this omnipotence. Harsh reality is going to have to tell us that we are not all-powerful, that we are not the mother, that we are little, and weak, and wrong.

Sometimes this is the trauma of birth (Janov 1983). Sometimes it is an earlier trauma, or a later one. Sometimes it is just the experience of not getting what we want, when we want it. Sometimes it is the feeling of being abandoned. It may be actual insult or injury. But whatever it is, and however violent it may seem, the broad effect is the same. We somehow split, in a primitive and almost instinctive way, into a hurt and vulnerable self that is hidden away, and a less sensitive self that is pushed forward.

The infant gets seduced into compliance, and a compliant False Self reacts to environmental demands and the infant seems to accept them. . . . The False Self has one positive and very important function: to hide the True Self, which it does by compliance with environmental demands.

(Winnicott 1958: 225)

Winnicott has a good description of this, with a useful diagram, but many other people have described it quite independently.

When this splitting takes place, a notice is put up, as it were, which says 'Do not enter; here be pain.' And so we carry on, improving the false self, and maybe even developing other false selves on the same model, to satisfy other, newer, situations. We do not go back. I have explained this at length elsewhere (Rowan 1990).

It may be that this is the crucial move that made us different from the animals. There is no evidence at all that the consciousness of an animal splits in this way. Poets and other writers down the ages have told us that the appealing thing about animals is that they are simpler than we are, more direct, less tortured. Perhaps it is this fatal split that makes us the complex creatures that we are – creatures with an inner life that is just as important as our outer life, and often harder to cope with.

Let us just go back to the trauma of birth. It is important to understand this, and in recent years much new information has come from research and clinical experience. The basic point is that the foetus is well developed and quite experienced before the birth process begins, as Verny (1982) has well described. It is a person who is being born, not a ball of flesh that later becomes a person.

One of the curious things is that even a person who has brought some quite fresh thinking to the question of the early origins of neurosis, Daniel Stern (1985), has nothing to say about birth or foetal experience. Like the psychoanalysts he is mainly addressing, he simply assumes that life starts at birth, and carries on from there. This could be regarded by some as quite extraordinary. Many years earlier, Winnicott (1958) had recognised and described some of the most important features of the birth trauma, as found in his clinical experience.

One of the best books to emerge about this is by David Chamberlain, an eminent researcher in the field. He says:

Perhaps the last big scientific barrier to full recognition of infants as persons will fall with acceptance of the possibility of complex personal memory at birth. Skeptical parents sometimes come to accept birth memory when they hear their two-year-olds spontaneously talking about it. Once we know that newborns are good at learning and that learning and memory go hand in hand, it is easier to accept birth memory. Some need no further convincing because they have discovered their own birth memories by one method or another. Others have discovered these memories under hypnosis or in a psychological breakthrough in therapy.

(Chamberlain 1988: xx)

One of Chamberlain's research projects was to correlate children's accounts of their birth with the mother's account of it. The mothers had to assure him that they had not spoken of their experience to the children. The children were aged between 9 and 23. He used open-ended questions and allowed the people to speak freely. Although there were one or two discrepancies, the vast majority of the descriptions tallied closely. In other words, the memories were on the whole extremely accurate.

The only reason more doctors and psychologists and counsellors and psychotherapists do not take this on board is that they are not aware of the burgeoning literature on infancy.

INFANCY

The word 'infant' comes from a Latin word meaning 'unable to speak', and so strictly speaking we should save the word for this period of life; but of course in ordinary speech it is often used more widely. What are the facts about what kinds of experiences infants are capable of? In psychotherapy and counselling we often find clients going back to these early times, and we sometimes wonder if babies so young can have such complex experiences as seem to be revealed in this process.

Since psychologists gave up doing all their experiments on rats, there has been a tremendous amount of research on infants, and much more is known now than before. Goren and co-workers found that infants with an average age of 9 minutes attended closest to a schematic face compared with a blank head shape, or one with scrambled features. Dziurawiec and Ellis found this hard to believe, and repeated the experiment with improved methodology, and got the same results. It seems that the purpose of this is to aid in bonding between the infant and the mother (Goren *et al.* 1975, Dziurawiec and Ellis 1986).

Wertheimer (1961) studied newborn babies actually in the delivery room, as soon as they were born. He worked only with those where there was no anaesthesia and no apparent trauma. He found that if he presented a series of sounds, placed randomly to left and to right, the baby looked in the direction of the sound source. There was no random looking about, just a direct look in the right direction.

Lipsitt (1969) did an experiment where newborn babies, just a few hours old, had to turn their heads to the right at the sound of a tone, and to the left at the sound of a buzzer. If they turned the right way they got a reward – a sweet taste in the mouth. It took them only a few trials to learn which way to turn their heads. Then the signals were reversed, and it took them only about ten trials to unlearn the old task and learn the new one.

So as early as the first month of life there is evidence that human infants participate in perception-action systems. Auditory and tactile sensations are perceived in relation to action from birth, and probably before. Infants only 3 months old can turn their eyes and head in the direction of a pleasing sound, but if the sound is intense, they turn their head in the opposite direction. These are not reflex actions: infants will visually scan around the room in which the sound source is located (Butterworth 1981). Even though newborn reaction times to the sound are rather slow compared to later in infancy, and even though the sound must be played for at least twenty seconds and in the middle range of audible frequencies (M.G. Clarkson *et al.* 1989), when newborns respond their actions are coordinated with their perceptions. Fogel (1993) notes that the hand and mouth of a newborn are especially sensitive. Infants will suck as if trying to get nutrition from a normally shaped nipple, but they will perform more exploratory movements of the tongue and lips when nipples have unusual shapes. They suck and touch differently depending on whether objects are hard or soft (Rochat 1987). Newborns will recoil from pain and curl snugly into the arms of a warm adult. Tom Bower says:

> The newborn can localize sounds. He can locate objects visually. He seems to know that when he hears a sound, there probably will be something for him to look at, and that when an object approaches him, it probably will be hard or tangible.

(Bower 1977: 24)

Visually, the baby has size constancy from birth onwards: also shape constancy, form and colour perception, movement detection, three-dimensional and depth perception (Slater *et al.* 1983). After two days a baby will show a preference for the mother's face when this is shown side by side with a stranger's face (Bushnell 1987).

The same things can be shown with the infant's ability to smell. Engen *et al.* (1963) found that infants only a few hours old will turn away from an unpleasant odour. MacFarlane (1975) placed 3 day olds on their backs and then placed breast pads from their mothers on one side of their heads. On the other side he placed breast pads from other nursing mothers. The newborns reliably turned their heads towards their own mothers' pads, regardless of which side the pads were.

Several investigators in the 1970s found that babies less than 1 week old will imitate other people. If we stick our tongue out at the baby, the baby will begin to stick the tongue out too. If we stop this, and begin to flutter our eyelashes, the baby will flutter the eyelashes back. If we then open and shut our mouths, the baby will match us at the same speed. If we use a TV split-screen technique, showing the adult face and the baby's face side by side, we find close matching of one to the other, which by 5 weeks old becomes very accurate and very quick, so that real two-way communication is taking place. Even at 42 minutes old, Meltzoff found the beginnings of this kind of response (Meltzoff and Moore 1983).

Smiling has been studied a good deal. Bower (1977) says that babies start to smile 46 weeks after conception, regardless of their age since birth. (Most babies are born 40 weeks after conception, but a range of 38 to 42 weeks is normal.) The research then shows that there are actually four different smiles: the relief smile, when the baby realises that an unexpected noise or movement is not threatening; the 'I want you to like me' social smile for strangers; the special smile for mother or other very close person; and the 'Got it, I've solved the problem' smile.

This last is the most surprising to many people. Papousek (1969) found that if he arranged the environment in such a way that certain specific movements of a baby could make things happen, babies smiled when they worked out how to make it happen. The smiling, in other words, showed an intellectual pleasure in discovery and control. The actual characteristics of the event the baby was producing were quite unimportant. What was important was that there be a relationship between a given action and a given event in the external world. At this point there was vigorous smiling and cooing which was not directed at the event in particular, but rather seemed to reflect some internal pleasure.

RESEARCH METHODS

How do we know these things? How are they studied? One way of studying visual preferences is to put the two stimuli reasonably well spaced to left and right, and then to measure the amount of time the infant spends looking at the one and looking at the other. This is done by means of corneal reflection, where infra-red light beams are shone into the eye, and their reflected images picked up by a television camera.

The rate at which the heart beats (as used for example in lie-detection machines) can be measured. Attention to something is accompanied by a drop in heart rate, and anxiety is accompanied by a rise in heart rate.

Tom Bower worked with a blind baby who, at the age of 8 weeks, had never been seen to smile. But when he was put into the experimental apparatus where he could produce sounds by kicking, he smiled for the first time. Prior to the experiment he had heard the same sounds and not smiled, so it was the sense of control over the sounds which produced the smile (Bower 1977: 45).

Spelke (1982) showed that babies of 4 months old do realise that an object can go partly out of sight and still remain a whole object, contrary to the earlier ideas of Piaget and others. Baillargeon et al. (1985) found that 5-month-old babies showed surprise if a screen moved up to hide an object and then appeared to move right through the space that the object had occupied. Keating et al. (1986) showed in a very ingenious experiment that babies of 6 months old are well aware that there is a world out there independent of their actions. Leslie (1984) conducted experiments to show that 7-month-old babies did understand causality not connected with their own bodies.

These research methods are very ingenious, and it seems that the more ingenious the experiments get, the more they discover about how remarkably competent the very young baby is. To sum up, all that we have been discovering in this chapter enables us to say that, while it is true that infants go through various phases of development, they are human throughout. They respond in a rational manner to what they meet, within the physical limitations of their abilities. They do not start to be human at some stage, out of being not human at some earlier stage.

TRAUMA

When something traumatic happens to the infant, therefore, whether during or after birth, there is a person present to experience and register it, and react to it.

Frank Lake (1980) argued that there are four levels of trauma, and what happens inside the individual depends very much on exactly what level of trauma is involved. He made no distinction between different causes of trauma. The first level is pain-free, and is the ideal state. The second level has to do with coping, and is where the stimulation is bearable and even perhaps strengthening, because it evokes effective and mostly non-neurotic defences. The third level involves opposition to the pain, but it is so strong that it cannot be coped with, and repression takes place. If the trauma happens in infancy or earlier, the defence will be splitting rather than repression, and some degree of dissociation will be experienced. The fourth level Lake calls transmarginal stress, and it is so powerful or so early, or both, that the person cuts off completely and may even turn against the self, wanting to die. Some work by Southgate and others suggests that many child accidents are in fact unconscious attempts at suicide, based on this fourth level of trauma (Southgate and Whiting 1987). If the trauma was actually a case of sexual or other abuse, and if the abuse is repeated or recreated somehow in later life, a real adult suicide may result, again possibly disguised as an accident. This has been seriously suspected in a number of cases.

Grof (1985) is clear that early trauma can be very real and very important, and relates it particularly to the process of birth. He distinguishes four stages of birth, and says that adult neurosis is very frequently based upon traumas suffered at one or other of these stages. Lake (1980), in one of his charts, brings out the way in which his four levels of trauma can be related to Grof's four stages of birth to make a matrix of sixteen cells which account between them for many of the origins of many of the neuroses. Again, of course, many of the drastic things which happen in the lives of adults may result from repetitions of the original trauma in some direct or disguised form.

Recent research has shown that strict diagnostic criteria of post-traumatic stress disorder can be applied to very young children (in their first, second and third years), and that when this is done it is found that:

> The clinical importance of these findings is that a posttraumatic syndrome does appear to exist in infants and children exposed to traumatic events. The sequelae can be severely debilitating and last for years if untreated. Any lingering notion that infants cannot be affected by trauma because of their limited perceptual or cognitive capacities ought to be dispelled by these empirical findings.
>
> (Scheeringa *et al.* 1995: 199)

What we learn from this is that there is a logic of trauma, which can be understood and applied to sexual and other forms of abuse later in childhood, and can also be applied to adult trauma through earthquakes, floods, war, etc. There is a direct link between the experience of the baby and the experience of the war veteran. This whole field is ripe for integration, and the primal work can help a great deal in understanding the phenomena of trauma generally.

SEPARATION

One of the first things the boy has to do, of course, is to separate from the mother. The early symbiotic relationship has to be broken. This first step, the one that the little boy takes in order to free himself from his symbiotic connection to his mother, Greenson (1968) refers to as *dis-identification*. The subsequent step, independent of the first, and which enables him positively to identify with his father, Greenson calls *counter-identification*. The first establishes the boy's separateness; the second, his maleness. Now this is something which does not happen to women in the same way at all. This process produces what has sometimes been called the male wound. The special interest of this wound is that it introduces a permanent element of dislocation into the lives of one sex, but not the other.

Adam Jukes has gone further and suggested that this breaking of the unconscious bond with the mother has even more serious consequences:

> The trauma of the birth of the individual subject, the self, in the separation from the primary object, the mother, leads to the development of what I think of as a gendered psychosis which is encapsulated by primitive internalized sado-masochistic objects. I believe this gendered psychosis is the source of male misogyny.
>
> (Jukes 1993: xxvi)

He also believes that the same process leads to 'the eroticization of dominance-heterosexuality' (Jukes 1993: 311). Now this is quite a mouthful, and he never explains exactly what he is talking about. What seems clear enough, however, is that he is again emphasising the pain of the rupture with the mother – the breaking of the symbiotic bond. When he speaks of these feelings being encapsulated, this seems to be just the sort of thing we are talking about in our notion of the false self, which also encapsulates the pain. These are all very early events in the life of the boy. But of course later events can be very important, too.

One of the classic findings in the clinical area is that the little boy competes with the father for the mother's affections. This, too, can lead to just this kind of pain, and the splitting that goes with it. Ethel Person puts it like this:

> As Freud suggests, the boy also withdraws his libidinal investment from his mother because he feels he does not have the genital endowment to compete with his father. His sense is that his mother rejects him in favour of his father because his penis is too small. Charles Brenner makes a

similar point, stressing both the narcissistic injury and the depressive affect that may be generated in the phallic-oedipal period and their connection to castration anxiety. Many men never recover from this literal sense of genital inadequacy. It appears that many men are therefore destined to suffer lifelong penis envy.

(Person 1993: 39)

To the extent that this is true, it accounts for the anxiety about penis size which is so characteristic of many men. The picture we are building up is of trauma producing a split between a true self (hidden and remote) and a false self (presented to the world). This false self basically thinks of itself as not-OK, and hence has to be protected from any real or fantasised attack. This then is the male ego.

THE FALSE SELF

How do we arrive at adulthood carrying around this enormous burden – this public relations self that has to be protected and improved at all costs, kept up and made bigger and better each year that passes?

Why is it that this self-image is so vulnerable? Why is it that we spend all our time boosting and building up this ego, and still someone can shatter it with a word? For it does seem to be true that, no matter how much we surround our public relations self with successes and confirmations and proofs, it does not take much to spoil it. A famous actor said that he had to see only one sour face in a large happy audience, and he felt he was no good, and should really give up acting for ever.

Sometimes it is hard to understand that a handsome and successful man, admired and imitated and loved and pursued and idolised, can still be reduced to nothing by a rejection. Yet we have only to mention the name of the great actor John Barrymore to know that this can be true.

We can see from all this that the origins of the false self can go back much farther than is normally understood, and may be associated with many of the ordinary childhood traumas. In women this takes one form, and in men another.

And so the mask begins. It is as if we were saying somehow 'I am not OK; but I will give you something good enough to please you if I can.' This is how we learn to be what we are not. And this is why we are always uncertain about our self-image, as to whether it is really good enough. It is because it is built on these foundations. It is because we do not really have inside ourselves any sense of having the right to judge. It is other people who have all the rights, all the power.

We look to others to know what is right, how things should be. We look for leaders and exemplars and people who can protect us. When they let us down, as they inevitably do sooner or later, we feel depleted and exhausted. We pick ourselves up after a while and look for another one, who this time will be perfect for ever.

Or we may rebel. We can see what other people want, and go and do just the opposite. We still have to notice and observe what they want, what they require of us, but now instead of systematically saying Yes, we equally systematically say No. This is a choice.

Or we may get cynical, and decide that there is no answer, that the dreadful has already happened, that life is a burden and a shame. So all we can do is to survive, and withdraw, and not get too involved with anybody or anything. That is another choice.

HOW SOCIALISATION HAPPENS

So how does all this take place? How is it that men are burdened with these characteristics, which are so limiting and can even be lethal? Where does this apparent need for certainty come from?

> Jack Sprat could eat no fat;
> His wife could eat no lean;
> And so, between the two of them,
> They licked the platter clean.

When we come to talk to Jack Sprat, we find that it is not just a matter of taste: he has an image of himself as someone who does not eat fat. It is a self-definition that he maintains in action and in conversation.

These self-definitions are very common. Few of us can escape from having one or more of them. 'I am a teacher.' 'I am a pessimist.' 'I am a Protestant.' 'I am a student.' 'I am a father.' 'I am a man.'

We carry around with us a large and complex self-image, made up of all these self-definitions, all of which we feel are us. 'What I always say is . . . ' They seem to be true, inescapable, factual. 'I just couldn't do that.' They are aspects of our ego.

If you want to predict what someone is going to do next, look for that action which is most likely to preserve and enhance their self-image. Don thinks of himself as a nice person; you know that if you ask him to do something, he will say Yes. If you want to manipulate someone, simply talk to them in terms that will boost their ego. John thinks of himself as someone who is good with computers. Ask him if he can type up a short program, and he will agree; it flatters him that you should think him capable of such a thing. It is really very patronising when you tell him you trust him to do it, and would not trust Terry to do it, but he eats it up.

It is sad but true that most of us, most of the time, go around collecting things that are going to shore up our self-image, make things safe for that precious ego. 'Your car says something about you, don't you think?' We collect compliments, we collect evidence that we are capable and good. 'I feel so much better now that we have moved to a good address.' Even a new purchase that we can not really afford makes us feel good. 'This really suits me, don't you think?' And this makes us very predictable, very manipulable.

41

RESEARCH STUDIES

If we are interested in the roots of all this, they are easy enough to find. Several research studies show that in the kindergarten boys experience pressure to be boys and not sissy. This happens earlier and with more pressure than the similar demands on girls. Boys do not understand exactly what this is all about, but they are impressed with the danger of going against the norms. It makes it all the harder that what they are supposed to do is not defined positively – they are just supposed to avoid the negative. This induces anxiety. There soon appears virtual panic about being caught doing anything traditionally defined as feminine (Martin 1989, 1990).

Another source of pressure and anxiety is the fact that the father is often not at home, and that even when he is, he is not doing the work that earns him a living, nor is he interacting with male friends. This means that the boy has hardly any examples of what men are supposed to be like or to do. Research shows that men resemble their fathers much less than women resemble their mothers. There is so little for boys to identify with. The books in school reinforce existing sex-role stereotypes (Purcell and Stewart 1990). Fathers in general seem often, when present, to be punishing or controlling or shaming (Osherson 1986).

So peer pressure becomes doubly important for boys. The models which are at hand are peer models. But since the peers are just as much in the dark as the boy himself, it is a case of the blind leading the blind. The injunctions become quite arbitrary and absolute – we know what we have to be because we decide what we have to be. And the images on television reinforce all this over again (Signorielli 1989).

All this comes out quite clearly in the playground. The sex cleavage undergoes a qualitative change at about 5 years of age, when the peer group differentiates into a boys' group and a girls' group. Nurturance is almost absent in boy/boy dyads, but progressively increases in girl/girl dyads, and is in full bloom at 5 years old. At the same time teasing and rough-and-tumble play reaches a peak among 5–year-old boys. Researchers got children to tell stories:

> Girls told many more stories of personal relationships, especially of families. Boys' tales had more themes of violence and destruction involving objects or nonhuman forces.
>
> Subsequent studies by other scholars have supported the findings about sex differences documented by these studies.
>
> (Pitcher and Schultz 1983: 2)

By 6 years old, girls learn to inhibit aggression, boys to avoid intimate attachments.

The twist of the knife is that a boy is in most cases brought up by women: his mother and his early teachers are likely to be women. So the very thing he is supposed to avoid – the feminine – is the only thing he sees as examples of correct behaviour. He often feels that women do not like boys very much – they praise and favour girls, who are easier to manage. He clings to the self-image which is forming and which is all he has, with a desperation caused by so much pressure.

So not only is he taught a precarious and over-sharp definition of masculinity by his peers, but also he is made to defend it against the quite different pressures of the women around him. He develops a narcissistic shell – a defensive self-image designed to make him feel good in the face of all this confusion.

But this is not a smooth process. It is painful to go through. It arises out of a deep feeling of rejection. We feel acutely that we are not accepted for what we are – that what we are is somehow bad and condemned. It is the covering up of our badness that leads to the adoption of a false self that will be good. Because we are boys, we know that what we are supposed to be is big and good, strong and masculine. So this false self has to be narcissistic, in the sense of putting our best foot forward. And this does not happen just once: it happens over and over again, time after time.

It is the division that hurts. It is the division between the real self, which is hidden away as unacceptable, and the false self, which is propped up and held in place by a variety of means, specifically to be good enough to satisfy other people.

There is so much effort involved. It is really an effort to be what we are not. What we really are is set aside, put away in a drawer: and what we are not is dressed up to take its place. It fools everyone; very often it fools us too, and we really believe that this is all there is. But the energy that has to be expended in avoiding what is real and holding on to what is not real is enormous. No wonder we feel tired so much of the time.

And so we go through life holding up this mask, improving it from time to time, hiding behind it, hoping it will be good enough, and accepting other people's judgements as to whether it is good enough or not.

THE ADOLESCENT MALE

Adolescence is an important area, because many of the later patterns get laid down here, particularly in regard to identity and personality. Adolescence centres around puberty – the arrival of adult sexual functioning – and often brings a crisis of ego revaluation (Ausubel 1954). There is much emphasis on the self and the symbols of self. The adolescent may begin to keep a diary. The adolescent phase can end as late as 20 years old, in physical terms, with late maturing boys. One large survey (Tanner 1978) suggested these phases:

- *infantile* infantile genitals, no pubic or axillary hair, voice unbroken
- *early signs* intermediate between advanced and infantile
- *advanced* genitals assessed as mature, but one of the other maturity signs absent
- *mature* fully broken voice, hair under arms, profuse pubic hair, mature genitals

At the age of 15 boys may be at any one of these stages and still be normal.

One of the most useful things a therapist can say is 'Young man, you are normal!'

DEVELOPMENTAL TASKS

Adolescence presents certain developmental tasks (Havighurst 1953), which are midway between an individual need and a societal demand. These four tasks are

- achieving some adequate sexual identity
- becoming emotionally independent of parents
- becoming responsible for self
- finding a job in life

Chickering (1969) extended these to seven:

- developing competence
- managing emotions
- developing autonomy
- establishing identity
- freeing interpersonal relationships
- clarifying purpose
- developing integrity

Good and May (1987) suggest that all of these may or may not help in the development of a more androgynous male identity, with wider choices.

But in today's world, which because of feminism is very different from the world of 1953 when Havighurst wrote, the task of 'achieving some adequate sexual identity' is not so simple. We are really in the *Fermentatio* here. If the old certainties have gone, as we have been seeing all along, what is masculinity today? It seems that we have to talk in terms of masculinities, plural, rather than one thing called masculinity (Brod 1987).

Furthermore, there is an unconscious development as well as a conscious one. In terms of the conventional gender stereotypes, as measured by projective tests, there are four possibilities for a man. He can be consciously masculine and unconsciously masculine (MM); consciously masculine and unconsciously feminine (FM); consciously feminine and unconsciously masculine (MF); or consciously feminine and unconsciously feminine (FF).

In a fascinating piece of research, Nevitt Sanford used this fourfold classification to see how these combinations correlated with intellectual productivity and creativity in a sample of postwar male Berkeley graduate students.

He expected the unconscious-feminine/conscious-masculine (FM) pattern in men to have a great potential cost in the cognitive rigidity necessitated by the repression of inner femininity. But the main conclusion of his study

44

was, interestingly, not the problems of the FM males, but the unusual creativity and intellectual strength of the reverse male pattern: unconscious-masculine/conscious-feminine (MF).

(Pleck 1987: 32)

Already things look much less straightforward than they did before.

GENDER CONFUSION

It may even be the case, as Andrew Samuels (1989) has suggested, that gender confusion is a good thing. In an era where we are moving away from one model, and no alternative model is yet available, perhaps those who are not gender-confused are just unaware of what is going on. Gender certainty, he says, is dangerous because it emphasises patriarchal patterns. It inevitably uses the standard stereotypes of the available culture. And it is not necessary. He says: 'In future, we will all become even more confused about gender.' He believes that a flight into androgyny is just as suspect as a flight into gender certainty.

Androgynous people are probably nicer and more effective than gender-stereotyped people, and in a non-patriarchal society it would be easier to be androgynous, but it seems clear to me that in itself it means very little on a social scale. Joan Baez once said: 'I remember the first thought I ever had about women's lib was that if women could teach men to cry, maybe we wouldn't have to go to war.' I do not know how she feels now about that statement, but what I believe is that men can cry and cry, and still pull the trigger; can tremble with fear and still drop the bomb; can go into paroxysms of guilt and still push the button. Just as women can be strong and fearless, and still let a man walk all over them. Androgyny is just another kind of certainty, and it is certainty which I am questioning. But more is to come. Andrew Samuels actually suggests that gender confusion is on the increase. He points out that these stereotypes of masculinity and femininity are part of the problem: they offer a spurious certainty which is comforting and familiar, but which may not have a lot to do with the real world and real experience. If we want to live in the real world, we may have to let go of these illusory certainties and live with the uncertainty of gender confusion. Indeed, to push the argument even further, gender confusion may actually be a good thing.

> Gender confusions may have as important a role to play as gender certainties. They contribute something imaginative to social and political reform and change. . . . *'Gender confusion' is a necessary antidote to gender certainty* and has its own creative contribution to make.
>
> (Samuels 1989: 95 and 97)

Whatever the truth of this may be, it can be seen how this sort of thing can make things harder for the adolescent. It was bad enough having to measure up to a phoney standard: it is perhaps harder still to lose any standard at all. It is no

45

wonder that we find the proliferation of styles which we shall be looking at in a later section of this chapter (pp. 47–48).

But it goes further. We can actually find another fourfold classification. A man may be consciously gender-certain and unconsciously gender-certain; or consciously gender-certain and unconsciously gender-confused; or consciously gender-confused and unconsciously gender-certain; or consciously gender-confused and unconsciously gender-confused. In the past, all the emphasis in psychotherapy has been on the second of these, where the task has been seen as bringing the unconscious gender confusion to the surface and dealing with it constructively. But nowadays we can see that the third of these may also be very important.

> The recognition of unconscious gender certainty lying behind apparent gender confusion is a radical revising of conventional kinds of psychodynamic formulations. These are usually content to reach the unconscious gender confusion that lies behind apparent gender certainty.
>
> (Samuels 1993: 131)

If it is true, as we shall see in Chapter 6, that the Patripsych inhabits us all, there will be an unconscious assumption of the values of hegemonic masculinity. Our apparent confusion may make it seem as if this is not operative any more, but as we shall see over and over again, it certainly is. So this whole area of gender is problematic, and raises difficulties for the adolescent trying to discover what being a man really is.

One of the stepping-stones towards the achievement of these objectives is the like-sexed peer group. This is one of the routes to desatellisation – breaking free from what Mahrer (1989a) has called the 'primitive personality field' of the family. Newman (1982) notes four main functions of the peer group:

- to be a setting for the development of increased autonomy
- to offer a place for experimenting with new values and to help in resisting established family or cultural views
- to allow for a sense of belonging or affection outside of the nuclear family
- to be a source of regulation and direction of individual behaviour.

Adolescents especially need to feel that they belong and are valued. So the choice of peer group is very important.

Adolescence is often complicated by the fact that the parents may be going through a crisis too. Many males in our culture, at the age of 40 or so, come to the realisation that they have not 'made it' in their own terms, and that they are virtually stuck in a rut for the rest of their lives; they may be getting less satisfaction from sex with their wives, but for one reason or another do not go out and look for it anywhere else. So they are in a state of defensive and rather passive frustration – just the sort of combination which can result in aggression towards the less powerful. Women, too, may have their own frustrations at this time, as feminists have pointed out, often feeling that they have become just a drudge or a servant for the benefit of others, and not getting their own needs met at all. In such a case it is obviously less painful and difficult for her to gang up with her husband to pick on the adolescent than to challenge or work out things with the husband. So the adolescent may become the scapegoat, taking criticism which the parents really need to direct at each other. This means that 'the adolescent problem' should often be renamed 'the middle-age problem'.

For the adolescent, one route to the achievement of the four (or seven) tasks is through inflation of the self-concept. Adolescence is a time when the individual is preoccupied with self and the symbols of self. 'Who am I?' is the universal question. This can become such a pressing problem that it may seem better to have a negative identity than no identity at all. But this is very dangerous, because it can mean cutting oneself off from social support, which is necessary at this stage. As Eric Erikson well said:

> At any rate, many a sick or desperate late adolescent, if faced with continuing conflict, would rather be nobody or somebody totally bad or, indeed, dead – and this by free choice – than be not-quite-somebody.
>
> (E.H. Erikson 1966)

In adopting a negative identity, the person comes to get greatest emotional satisfaction from activities that are the most disturbing to those whose support is essential to him or her. Peter Madison says of one of his students: 'She knew she was destroying herself in the process, but satisfying her hatred was more important than protecting her own welfare' (Madison 1969: 454). This can then lead to the psychiatric problems mentioned below.

IDENTITY PROBLEMS

All the problems of identity become more difficult if the adults have identity problems too. In recent years there has been a collective search for identity which has become very difficult for many parents. Many of the old landmarks have gone, and there is uncertainty for everyone. There is little role consensus today.

There seem to be about seven groups (Mays 1969, Rowan 1973, 1990) with whom the adolescent can identify:

- *the roughs* rejected and rejecting – petty aggression and petty crime
- *the fixers and wanglers* non-violent, but involved in activities around the edges of the law
- *low-level conformists* have an acute sense of their own limitations, and often wish to impose limitations on others
- *fancy dressers* a mixture of seekers, retreatists, risk-takers, withdrawers, positive and negative identities, united by a common rejection of convention and some of the new romanticism
- *the political* leftist, humanitarian, emotionally extremely sore and sensitive – often both intelligent and creative

- *the cowboys* often working-class, positively oriented towards an affluent society, interested in fashion and possessions, but more conformist than the fancy dressers
- *high-level conformists* on the way to being the so-called yuppies – often not very clear as to what they are trying to conform to

The fancy dressers seem to draw all the publicity, because they do offer somewhere to go for the adolescent who is totally confused. It is a genuinely non-elitist group, which has no mechanism for ejecting or excluding anyone. Parents need to understand it, or risk losing those children who get into it.

PSYCHIATRIC PROBLEMS OF ADOLESCENCE

While most of the problems of adolescence are within the normal range of variation, there are some which may actually take the adolescent into psychiatric care. These are defined in the standard diagnostic classification manual as the *conduct disorders* which go far beyond the normal level of antisocial behaviour – the usual pranks and insensitivities (or oversensitivities) of growing up.

In the *aggressive and undersocialised type* of conduct disorder, youths show a consistent disregard for the feelings of others, bully smaller children and have few friends. They usually do not have any feelings of responsibility or guilt, and tend to be uncooperative and provocative to adults. They come across as consistently hostile, verbally abusive, defiant and negativistic.

In the *unaggressive and undersocialised type*, youths are adept at manipulating people, and also have a lack of concern for the feelings of others. Generally, they show one of two patterns of behaviour. In the first, they are timid, unassertive and whiney, and often report being rejected and mistreated; they may sometimes be victimised, most often sexually. In the other pattern, youths may be less timid and more able to exploit and manipulate others. Under pressure, they will show deviousness and guile rather than aggression.

In the *aggressive and socialised type*, there will be violent episodes, robbery, drug-selling and so forth, but youths will be able to hold a friendship for six months or more, and may even accept punishment on behalf of friends rather than inform on them. They are more likely to be members of a group or gang, and may be quite charming until challenged in any way.

In the *unaggressive and socialised type* of conduct disorder, youths are equally rebellious, and their actions may often be mistaken for ordinary pranks, but because of the regularity and persistence of the behaviour, this type usually gets into serious trouble, even though not being violent.

The most successful treatment found so far for adolescents in these difficult groups is a combination of residential treatment and family therapy. The youngster spends weekdays in a home, and the weekends with the family. At the same time the family is seen in ongoing family therapy (Nowicki 1983).

One important problem posed by adolescents is running away from home.

This is usually because the relationship with parents has become impossible, for whatever reason. Those who do tend to be insecure, unhappy and impulsive, have low self-esteem and feel out of control (Duke and Nowicki 1986). Runaways generally have problems in school, seem to need to search for adventure and meaning, and suffer from boredom. Often the whole family is disturbed, and the adolescent gets picked on to be the problem. The great majority of them return home safely, but unless some family therapy can be undertaken, the problems are likely to recur. Families of runaways more often appear to be organised around punishment and negativism and seem unable to support one another in crises.

Another important problem in adolescence is *suicide*. Suicide is an important cause of death in the age group 14–19, and also for the next ten years. The main precipitating factors are family conflicts, difficulties with partners and school problems. In other words, perceived failure at the developmental tasks outlined earlier.

HIGH COSTS OF CONFORMITY

From here we can look back at the days when we depended so much on our false self and its definitions. The false self, the safe healthy social mask, which has such insecure foundations, always needs bracing and supporting with struts and crutches. Ian Harris (1995) has a terrible catalogue of the various images and ideals which men go for, based on the messages they hear from their parents, from peers, from the media, from work, and so on:

Adventurer: Men take risks and have adventures. They are brave and courageous . . .
Be the Best You Can: Do your best. Do not accept being second. 'I can't' is unacceptable.
Breadwinner: Men provide for and protect family members. Fathering means bringing home the bacon, not necessarily nurturing.
Control: Men are in control of their relationships, emotions, and job . . .
Playboy: Men should be sexually aggressive, attractive and muscular.
President: Men pursue power and status. They strive for success . . .
Sportsman: Men enjoy playing sports, where they learn the thrill of victory and how to compete.
Stoic: Ignore pain in your body. Achieve even though it hurts. Do not admit weakness . . .

(Harris 1995: 12–13)

And so it goes on. We can see how high were the costs of needing appreciation, needing boosts, needing to be right, needing everything to go right, needing to be reassured, needing to be perfect, needing to smile all the time, needing to be noticed and attended to, needing to fulfil all the expectations of the list above. The costs are giving ourselves up, not being, except on their terms.

Or rebelling, being different, being in total opposition – equally exhausting, and equally dependent on what the others think and want.

Or being cynical and withdrawing, not really committing ourselves in any way, making the most of what is there without any expectations of it turning out well.

Who wants to live like that, if there is an alternative? Who wants to live at such high cost?

But to escape from this pressure is not easy. The argument of this book is that it takes a complete initiation to do it. But how do we get up the determination to tackle such a problem by going into therapy? Often it takes some crisis to take us into psychotherapy, or into personal growth, or into counselling. But in reality we do have the right to go to a growth group, or anything else we need to go to, at any time we like. We do not have to wait for a crisis. We do not have to be desperate. We can just say 'I am fed up with being what I am not. I would rather be who I am.'

If we can contrast roles with the real self, as I think we have to do in humanistic psychology, we can see the real self as put down by social pressures. What we develop instead is the false self, the persona, the mask (or a set of them). This is a form of self-concealment, and this hiding of the self is normal in a patriarchal society. So unless individuals have worked consciously and often painfully at exploring and discovering their real self, they will automatically be alienated and shut off from their innermost core of being. In other words, to be alienated is to have developed normally. To be non-alienated means a conscious interference with 'normal' development. As we shall see later, most men steer clear of psychotherapy because they do not want to expose their vulnerability.

So to the extent that therapy works at all, it has the effect of making the man less automatic about his role, and more able to choose his actions. But here we come back to the point made much earlier: even if the man is freed from all the absurdities of the male role, his choices are still made in the context of a patriarchal society. Unless this social fact is faced and questioned, the man is just going to be a better oppressor. How do we tackle this?

I believe it is not enough to say, as we used to in the past, that getting rid of neurosis automatically made a person better morally and politically. I have seen too many exceptions to this to believe it any more. It does require specific attention to the political context in which all our actions take place. Therapy can get us to the position where we can make real choices in our lives, but it cannot make those choices wise. We shall have more to say about politics in Chapter 6.

FATHERS AND FATHERING

A difficult area, which has had a lot of attention in recent years, is the question of how all this affects men as fathers. The traditional role of the father is to be the economic provider and firm disciplinarian. This has been undergoing change, for two main reasons: first, the job market is such that one person cannot earn enough to provide for a family; and second, the whole idea of firm discipline has been much challenged and disputed. So the role of father is much more ambiguous than it used to be, and instead of being supported by a socially determined structure, each family has to create its own structure, its own norms. Samuel Osherson says that hardly any men feel close to their fathers: the fathers are physically absent, psychologically absent or even dangerous. Father hunger, paternal deprivation – these are common phrases today.

> Many of us strive to be different from our fathers while also unconsciously trying to live up to their image.
>
> (Osherson 1986: 8)

As we saw earlier, we live in a patriarchal society, but it is one which is crumbling fast, and in quite unpredictable ways. This places a great deal of stress on the role of father, which is different from the stress of past years. In the past, the stress came from earning, or not being able to earn, enough to keep the family. In the present, it comes just as much from not being sure what the role entails. For example, does the role entail waiting around in a corridor while my wife gives birth in a properly appointed hospital, or does the role entail being in the room while my partner gives birth, and giving her emotional and possibly physical support?

In relation to birth the position has changed since the early 1970s. Fathers being present at the birth increased from 27 per cent in 1973 to 79 per cent in 1983. This indicates a greater degree of involvement with the partner, and a greater interest in children. How big a change of role is this?

The idea of the 'New Man' who changes nappies and spends time with his children has penetrated the public consciousness, and research shows that such behaviour does benefit the children. For example, Radin (1982) studied a group of children in the United States, aged from 3 to 6 years, and was able to compare those whose fathers were very much involved with their care as against those who were not. A correlation was found between father involvement and cognitive ability, particularly in the verbal area. In other words, these children were sharper and more articulate. There was also an important link between father involvement and 'internal locus of control': this is based on a psychological test of either seeing oneself as at the mercy of outside forces, or seeing oneself as having an important influence on one's surroundings. The children with high father involvement felt more in charge of their own lives. A third result was that children of the less involved fathers had more fixed and stereotyped perceptions of parental roles. In other words, the children of the more involved fathers had more flexible ideas about what fathers and mothers should do. Sagi (1982) did much the same research in Israel, and got similar results.

However, many men have a great resistance to adopting these more nurturing roles. They see involvement with children as feminine. We have already seen that femininity is deeply threatening to the male who subscribes to hegemonic masculinity. A second reason for avoiding such involvement is a fear of failure. This is closely allied to fears of making mistakes and making a fool of oneself, and being criticised for this. The internal critic can also come into play about this, convincing the man that he had better leave the children alone, and let the mother take all the responsibility. The scares about sexual abuse which have been so prominent in recent years also make men much more nervous about touching their children, in case such touching may be misunderstood. It requires a confident man to persevere in such circumstances. Such a man may also come into contact with the Patripsych, which at an unconscious level convinces him that such activities are not for men. In the latter case, a man may well be quite unaware of his own avoidance, and get very defensive if anyone points it out.

Lack of involvement is a kind of neglect, and even if the father is not in any way negative towards the children, they will perceive it as indicating that there is something wrong with them. So by doing 'nothing' the father is in effect doing something negative. If a child has two parents, and is in effect rejected by one of them, the fact that the other one is quite reliable may not be enough to protect the child from negative self-images.

If, instead of neglect, the father gives stern discipline, this too can have bad results. The reason for this is that in today's climate, where the norms are so indistinct and vague, social support cannot be depended on for any enforcement of norms. In other words, the father is likely to be seen as a bully rather than as a fair disciplinarian, and resisted accordingly. Conflict instead of correction will then result.

Another mistake the father can make is to set up a link with the child which is based on an agreement to criticise the mother. This most often seems to be a father–daughter coalition. This actually puts the child into a false position which is ultimately hurtful.

Possibly the worst relationship which can be set up in the family is one of sexual relations between a father and daughter or stepdaughter. Research has shown that abusive fathers are most often rigidly traditional, authoritarian men with low self-esteem, low frustration tolerance and poor impulse control (Tyler 1986). Sexually abusive fathers usually manifest a very high degree of denial, even when confronted with overwhelming evidence that they have been abusive (Jukes 1993). This may be rationalised by saying that the relationship was affectionate. The question to be asked of any man who claims that sexual relations with children are mutually affectionate is – what happens when the child ceases to be a child? Abusers of children drop them like hot potatoes when they reach puberty.

TRUST THE PROCESS

What do we find when we get into therapy? Getting in touch with the real self is not easy. Often it takes a form which seems scary – something weak, or something absent, even just a black hole, or something ugly. But by staying with it, and identifying with it, we can re-own it and redeem it. We have to trust the process, and trust the therapist, enough to stay with it and enter into it fully. Sometimes this is a cathartic experience, which feels like a breakthrough; sometimes it just feels disconcerting and unfamiliar. One of the most unfamiliar and unexpected things about it is that there is no fear there, once we really get in. Usually, however, this experience of the real self does not last for long, and then we are back to the familiar routine.

But we have had a glimpse of the truth, enough to encourage us to try again. Sometimes it is not even necessary to try again; there may just be more and more spontaneous occasions when we get the same sense back again, that sense of being real, and without the familiar fears.

And so we gradually find our own centre. We little by little manage to get rid of that old ego, that old false self that we do not need any more. Very often it is not a question of losing it, but rather of redefining it as a useful servant, rather than as a dominant boss.

When our ego gets triggered off by some rejection, some mistake, we can just notice it. We have the power to stand back from it, and laugh at how seriously the ego takes such things. So much self-importance, so much desperate need for everything to be right!

This may seem a simple view of therapy, but it seems important to me to have some sense of what we are aiming at. More will be said in Chapters 8 and 9 to fill out the complex details of the process. All we are looking at here is a preliminary vision of what is possible.

THE REAL I

If we want to change this situation, and lead our own lives, there is a way to do it. We do not have to be at the mercy of other people's needs and requirements and definitions. We do not have to play roles all our lives. We do not have to be what we are not.

If we can go back and somehow get in touch with the real self, the one that got covered over in the socialisation process, then we can decide differently this time round, and live differently on the basis of this new decision. We can get in touch with that real self who was left behind and covered up. We can go behind the mask, the roles, the images, and find the person that we really are. This is the initiation we need.

Philosophically minded people sometimes criticise the notion of the real self, saying that it is conceptually incoherent. But this is to miss the point entirely. The real self is not a theoretical construct, it is an experience. The experience of contacting the real self is self-confirming and self-validating. It is often ecstatic. I believe it is a mystical experience, and have laid out that argument at length elsewhere (Rowan 1993a).

This means finding a centre that is really ours, that does not belong to someone else. It means that we can see out of our own eyes, instead of seeing ourselves out of everyone else's eyes. It means that I can be who I am, and not just what someone else wants me to be.

And it is not so hard to know how to do this. Every time we feel at a disadvantage, every time we feel that we are not OK, is a clue to what we need to do, and where we need to go. As James Hillman has said many times, symptoms are the gateway to soul.

All we have to do is to follow the trail of our bad feelings, and they will lead us back to where we need to go.

But because the original covering-up was associated with pain, we find it harder and harder as we get nearer and nearer. We need someone to be there to encourage us, to say to us, 'Keep going; you are nearly there.'

The point is that, no matter how much we felt at the time that we were going to die, we did not in fact die; we did survive. So whatever happened can in principle be handled and faced. We just need to have our hand held, so to speak, to be able to get up the courage to face it.

That is where a therapist comes in. Therapists are people who have faced these things in their own lives, and who are therefore not afraid to accompany someone else along that seemingly dangerous path. A therapist can go with us, and when we reach the notice-board saying 'Here be pain: do not enter', can help us to take it down and move on in.

Here I think we have to take on board the necessity for a further level of development beyond 'the fully functioning person' we find at the end of our therapy. There is a kind of spirituality, which develops and deepens the soul, not just the psyche. Ken Wilber (1980) calls it the subtle level, James Hillman (1983) calls it the level of soul, and so does Thomas Moore (1992). This kind of spirituality makes us lower our boundaries and admit our connectedness with other people and with nature. This will be spelt out in detail in Chapter 7. Out of it emerges a natural form of ecological concern:

> Biocentric equality is intimately related to the all-inclusive Self-realization in the sense that if we harm the rest of Nature then we are harming ourselves. There are no boundaries and everything is interrelated.
>
> (Devall and Sessions 1985: 244)

This is a politics of inclusion, where we see the real needs of all as reconcilable. Conflicting interests can be integrated, if we are creative enough, and willing to spend the time on negotiation (Graham 1995).

THE HORNED GOD

I believe it is not enough to say that the man will automatically be more politically enlightened after initiation. I do not know of any evidence for this. Specific attention needs to be paid to this question. And the key point, in my own view of this, is that we lack male models for how to be and behave. The so-called New Man is not the answer – he is a media creation who is not to be found in the real world. Even if he did exist, my belief is that he would degenerate into the New Lad all too easily.

Robert Bly (1990) speaks to us of the archetype of the Wildman. He is the deep masculine, the hairy man who lives in the depth of men's soul. Bly's work is often deeply original, sparking off insight after insight in a sparkling way. He has opened up a treasure chest of new ideas in the field of men's studies. But as I have argued elsewhere at some length (Rowan 1987), his work is curiously limited because of its weakness in the area of the feminine. The Wildman has no visible connection to the female in any form. Bly is fine on the father, but weak on any version of the feminine. As an archetype to help in critiquing a patriarchal society, therefore, the Wildman seems to be lacking.

Robert Moore and Douglas Gillette (1990) give us four archetypes – the king, the warrior, the magician and the lover – and say that men have to learn the mature forms of these figures, and then all will be well. This seems quite a narrow selection to choose from. What about the trickster, the shadow, the child, the orphan, and all the rest? More importantly and relevantly here, how are any of these going to struggle with a patriarchal system? There is no hint here.

Someone else who has tried to give some kind of a usable model is Sam Keen (1991). He does at least have the merit of admitting that women exist, and that men might want to relate to them. But in the end, what all this amounts to is mutual adjustment on a level playing field, and this is not what patriarchy is like. There is nothing here about power, nothing about oppression.

But I agree with Bly and the others that we have to move into different territory if we are to find a fresh model of men. We have to move into the territory of the imagination, of the mythopoetic. What I have found is a great deal of inspiration from the mythic figure of the Horned God. The Horned God has many names, but in Britain he is best known as the Green Man.

The Green Man does not fit in to the usual stereotypes at all. He is gentle, tender and comforting, but he is also the hunter. He is the dying god, but his death is always in the service of the life force. As Starhawk says:

> He is untamed sexuality – but sexuality as a deep, holy, connecting power.
> He is the power of feeling, and the image of what men could be if they
> were liberated from the constraints of patriarchal culture.
>
> (Starhawk 1989: 108)

But when we come to examine the source of the power of the Green Man, we find that it comes from the Great Goddess. The Goddess too has many names, but in Britain she is best known as Mother Earth. So when we say that the Green Man embodies the power of feeling, this feeling is contained within the orbit of the Goddess; his power is always directed toward the service of life. This is the world-view of paganism, which so far as we can tell has always existed in the life and experience of human beings. The very oldest sculptures identifiable as such are statuettes of the Goddess.

The Green Man can help us to relate to women if we remember his role in paganism, which is to be the guardian and student of the female. His creativity is in the service of the Goddess at all times, and does not try to be separate and independent. He knows where he stands, and can teach us where we stand too. I have said much more about this previously (Rowan 1987).

> The relationship between men and women is at the heart of our culture. It is the basis for life for straight men and women. It affects the thoughts and emotions of lesbians and gay men, because it is a pattern of life that they can either accept or reject. The relationship between men and women is one of the most injured, dysfunctional aspects of our society.
>
> (Klein 1993: 98)

If we want to change this, it is hard to find good models in the same culture. We have to go outside it. This is where the Horned God can help us most. How does this work out in practice? In answering this, I have taken the liberty of adopting an irreverent and freewheeling approach. Some may find it out of place. It is important not to be always too serious and academic, it seems to me. Here are some hints and tips from the Horned God:

- Always ask – where is the energy now? Go with the flow, don't try to make things happen.
- Creative energy doesn't do the same thing the same way twice – let each time be new.
- Penetration is OK, but it is not what it is all about.
- When you use a condom, introduce your partner to the idea of putting it on you, either by hand or mouth. Let it be a real part of the event, not something offstage.
- Imagine the side-effects of your actions – adopt an ecological type of imagination. What else is going to happen if you get what you want? Power is OK if it is 'power-with'.
- If you are with a woman, be with her totally, don't look over her shoulder at other women. Really be there. The Horned God doesn't mess about.
- Be interested in what she wants, but don't expect her to make all the decisions. Put forward alternatives, different choices she might like, all of which you like.
- When you have a problem, share it with her. Combined energies are better than isolated energies. A burden shared is a burden halved.
- If you say you'll do something, do it within a week. If you really don't want to do it, refuse nicely, and offer to do something else instead.
- Keep in contact. Use letters, telephones, faxes, telegrams, carrier pigeons or whatever is necessary. Don't go absent.
- When she has a problem, listen to it carefully, but resist the temptation to try and solve it for her. The Green Man is close to the animals and the trees, and animals and trees don't try to solve problems.
- The Green Man is happy with green stuff, like leaves and money, and knows that there is plenty more where that came from, in due season.

- The Green Man sees sex everywhere, and is continually horny. He can get erotically involved with food, drink, women, men, animals, trees, rivers, oceans, cars and computers. There is no end to it all.

That is perhaps a little light-hearted and not to be taken too seriously, but I think it captures something of the right atmosphere. We shall come back to this later. But it is time now to move out of the *Fermentatio* stage, and into the stage of the *Separatio*. This is where we separate out two things which were getting intertwined – men and therapy. It is time to look at therapy as such and in itself.

Part III

SEPARATIO

Separate the earth from the fire, the subtle from the dense, gently, and with great ingenuity.

(Edinger 1995: 159)

5

WHAT IS IT WITH THERAPY?

Up to now, we have been speaking of psychotherapy as if we could take it for granted, and as if we knew what it was and what it did. It is now time to go into it more thoroughly. If it is to perform all the tasks we need it to, it must have all the requisite qualities. But does it? And is there, indeed, just one thing called therapy? Or do we have to separate it into different areas, and treat each area differently?

WHERE DOES PSYCHOTHERAPY COME FROM?

The word comes from two roots meaning 'soul' and 'healing'. The first therapists of ancient Greece were temple helpers who sat with people and prepared them for the spiritual experiences which would transform their illnesses, either by curing them, or by enabling them to see a purpose in them, or by making death less frightening. Often there was a suggestion of initiation, of the person being helped through a process of renewal.

Then later, in what is now Israel, there was an Essene sect of therapeutes, a rather mysterious group who dedicated themselves to others who were suffering. Again there seems to have been this emphasis on self-transformation, and seeing the meaning in the pain, rather than on correcting a fault or mending a machine.

Today there are some vociferous critics of psychotherapy, who see it as nothing but a powerful means of exploiting vulnerable patients. Of course it can be this, as we shall see later in this chapter, but it can also be a genuine attempt on the part of two people to work together for the self-transformation of one of them, and the payment of a fee (directly or indirectly) to the other.

There is a healing process within the person which can be trusted, in the field of the mind just as much as within the field of the body. Just as a doctor relies on the basic urge to health in the body to do much of the work, so the psychotherapist relies on the basic urge to health in the mind.

Traditionally, psychotherapy has been an individual thing. It is true that there has been couple therapy, group therapy, family therapy, milieu therapy and community action, but for the most part what goes on is individual therapy. We can confidently assume that this will continue, because simply from a logistic point of view, it is the easiest to engage in. It is easier to get two people together than it is to get a larger number, simply from the point of view of getting the appointments set up.

EARLY DAYS

Psychotherapy has a history and a tradition which is quite specific. Over the centuries there have been many attempts to deal with mental distress of one kind and another, from the physical to the spiritual. But the one stream with which we are concerned here is psychotherapy. The word 'psycho-therapeutic' was first recorded by the *Oxford English Dictionary* in 1887 to mean the treatment of disease by psychic, that is, hypnotic, means. It did not take long for the new discipline to catch on. By coincidence, the celebrations of the centenary of the French Revolution enabled large numbers of foreigners to come together in one place, and for the public to see the great names on the platform, and for the media to get excited about it all.

The International Congress on Hypnotism took place in Paris in 1889, at the time of the Universal Exhibition in honour of the hundredth anniversary of the French Revolution. It attracted huge crowds and was attended by journalists from 31 countries. Among the participants were Azam, Babinski, Binet, Delboeuf, Dessoir, Freud, James, Ladame, Lombroso, Myers, de Rochas, Van Eeden and Van Renterghem. These latter two described the Clinic of Suggestive Psychotherapy they had opened in Amsterdam two years earlier. This may have been the first time the word 'psychotherapy' was used in a congress (see Ellenberger 1970: 757).

By 1891 Bernheim (in Nancy, France) made less and less use of hypnotism, contending that the effects that could be obtained by this means could also be obtained by suggestion in the ordinary waking state. This he called 'psychotherapeutics'.

In England this term was introduced by Hack Tuke, who defined it as 'the cure of the body by the mind, aided by the impulse of one mind to another'. At the same time Van Eeden in the Netherlands was saying that treatment of the psychic functions should be called Psycho-Therapy. The ferment was spreading to more countries at the same time.

Between 1894 and 1896 the word 'psychotherapy' was catching on and taking the place of the vaguer word 'suggestion'. By 1897 all that pertained to hysteria, hypnosis and suggestion was becoming increasingly suspect, and the word 'psychotherapy' was now the accepted term for all methods of healing through the mind. A typical instance of the attitude of this time is to be found in Lowenfeld's textbook of psychotherapy, where he explains psychic gymnastics, hypnotic and suggestive treatment, Breuer-Freud's method, emotion therapy and faith healing. It is fascinating to see the new discipline, with its emphasis on science, and its association with medicine, gradually emerging from its surroundings, and acquiring increased respectability as it did so, together with medicine itself.

The London Psycho-Therapeutic Society was formed in 1902 for the study of mesmerism, hypnotism and other psychic phenomena and their adaptation to the cure and prevention of disease. In 1903 Dr W. Stekel was described as a psychotherapist in the *Daily Mail*.

The field of psychotherapy was quickly dominated by psychoanalysis, so much so that even today people tend to think of psychotherapy as essentially psychoanalytic. 'On the couch' is a way of working which has been used by cartoonists for many years now to indicate a therapist at work. The growth of psychoanalysis was helped by the fact that Freud consistently worked to make it respectable and organised. One of the distinguishing features of psychoanalysis is the way in which it has always been seen as a unified structure, even when it has been riven by schisms. We speak of 'classic' psychoanalysis as if there were a core, a heartland, from which Adler, Jung, Horney, Fromm, Klein and others have split off in specialised ways – even though some of such people have seen themselves as part of the mainland after all.

It is not often realised, however, what an interesting part the First World War had in the development of psychotherapy. Immediately before then, all madness or hysteria had been included within medicine, and put down to genetically inherited degeneracy – a medical and moral problem. But the war threw up a new phenomenon – shellshock. Perfectly ordinary healthy men, both officers and other ranks, were finding themselves behaving very strangely, and feeling totally unfamiliar feelings, and finding themselves unable to work as normal. These mental breakdowns would have aroused much controversy, were it not for the fact that it was considered unpatriotic to question the credentials of these individuals (Stone 1985). So they became legitimate targets for unusual types of therapy. Correspondingly, the prestige of psychiatrists went down, depending as they still did on the old notions of degenerative disease. It stayed down for several years after the war, and not a single psychiatrist was appointed to the Royal Commission on Lunacy and Mental Disorder in 1924.

When the Second World War came along, psychoanalysts were treated as advisers and contributed to the war effort in a number of ways. It must not be forgotten that the work of Bion on groups originated in Army groups set up by the War Office (Pines 1992).

Although there had been attempts to apply humanistic ideas to counselling and psychotherapy before the Second World War, notably in the work of Jacob Moreno (Marineau 1989), and behavioural ideas through people like Watson, Jones, Kantorovich and Max (Chambless and Goldstein 1979), neither of these came to any prominence until after the war. So psychoanalysis had a pretty clear field until the 1950s. But starting in the 1940s and 1950s and bursting forth in the 1960s and 1970s, an enormous burgeoning of humanistic forms of counselling and psychotherapy took place.

The most recent development has been the emergence of cognitive-behavioural therapies (Dryden and Golden 1986) and the resurgence of hypnosis, particularly under the aegis of Milton Erickson (Rossi 1980).

All evolution is a process of differentiation and integration, and we have seen since the 1960s an enormous differentiation and proliferation of psychotherapies. The fat book edited by Herink (1980) contains details of more than 250 different therapies: of these approximately 34 per cent come from the 1970s, 36 per cent from the 1960s, 17 per cent from the 1950s, 6 per cent from the 1940s, 5 per cent from the 1930s, and 2 per cent from before 1930. This shows the remarkable increase over the twenty years from 1960 to 1980. If a similar book were produced today, my belief is that the growth would have slowed down considerably. Today we are in a period, I believe, of integration rather than differentiation.

In the 1980s and 1990s the speed of development has slowed down considerably, and instead we have had a period of consolidation. One result of this is that it is now easier to see how the different psychotherapies relate to one another.

THE STRUCTURE OF PSYCHOTHERAPY

One of the worst things about psychotherapy is the way in which it tends to be very parochial and very ignorant. Each school tends to know very little about the other schools, and where it does acknowledge their existence, puts them down in very unfair ways. This is probably because each therapist has been through her or his own therapy, and the lessons of this very personal process are more powerful than any theory or clinical experience with clients. This results in books like Joel Kovel's (1978) *A complete guide to psychotherapy*, which purports to be an objective tour round various therapies, but which in fact boosts psychoanalysis and puts down everyone else. In a better book, Dryden (1984) did attempt to overcome this by drawing up a set of dimensions on which therapies could be compared and contrasted. This brought about a great deal of clarification, but at the cost of producing a chart at the end which was hard to look at and understand. It is possible, however, to adopt a different approach, which is to use two dimensions, and to range all the therapies in the space so created. In Table 5.1 may be found all the best known approaches which help to define this space. Here is the *Separatio* in full force.

The first dimension is arrived at by saying that some therapies work at the level of conscious awareness and rarely or never mention the unconscious, while others are continually referring to that which is unconscious and not present to awareness. This is a fairly obvious one, because one of the main controversies in the field has always been between psychoanalysis and behaviourism, and this is the main bone of contention between them. But existential therapy also denies the importance of the unconscious in the way in which it arises in Freudian theory, and so do some of the other approaches to therapy, so it is not just about behaviourism. Orthodox biologically oriented psychiatry goes even further than modern behaviourism in this respect, almost denying that there is anything mental about mental illness.

64

Table 5.1 The therapeutic space

	Mental ego		Real self		Subtle self
Everyday operating potentials (conscious mind) ↑	Psychiatry		Existential		Basic meditation
	Behaviour modification				
	Behaviour therapy		Focusing		
	Cognitive therapy		Some TA		
	Rational-emotive behaviour therapy		Personal-centred therapy		
	Family therapy		Gestalt therapy		Enlightenment intensive
	Personal constructs		Psychodrama		
	Transactional analysis (some)		Encounter		
			Co-counselling		
Attention explicitly paid to	Hypnotherapy		Feminist (some)		Psychosynthesis
	Neuro-linguistic programming			Bioenergetics	Transpersonal psychotherapy
		Reichian		Biosynthesis	
		Horney		Primal integration	
		Primal therapy			Jung
		Object relations therapy			
↓	Freudian				
Deeper potentials (unconscious mind)	Kohut				
	Klein				
	Lacan		Mahrer		Hillman
	Mental ego		Real self		Subtle self

Source: Psychospiritual development dimension from Ken Wilber (1981) model

At the other end of this scale, it is not only psychoanalysis which lays great stress on the unconscious. Mahrer (1989a), in his very important contribution to humanistic theory, also deals in central detail with what he calls 'deeper potentials' occupying very much the same region as Freud's unconscious, and the various approaches to body-oriented therapy also use such a concept a great deal, as do the primal approaches which are close to them in many respects. So this conscious/unconscious dimension does separate out the therapies quite well, though approaches such as encounter and co-counselling are very variable, ranging at different times all over the dimension in question, so we have to put them in the middle. This, then, gives us our vertical dimension in the figure.

But what are we to use as the other dimension? It is really very difficult to find a suitable continuum, and many ideas have been tried in the past, but the best answer so far discovered seems to be the dimension outlined by Ken Wilber in his many books. This is a dimension of psychospiritual development. In his book *No boundary*, which is specifically addressed to therapists, Wilber (1981) distinguishes between three broad levels on which therapists can work. The first of these, he says, is the Persona level; here we are helping the client to adjust to his or her role in life, and one of the main tasks in this is to deal with the Shadow. Wilber says that one of the main therapies at this level is transactional analysis, though others are rational-emotive therapy, reality therapy and of course psychoanalysis itself.

The second one he mentions is what he calls the Centaur level. Here we are helping the client to find his or her own existential self, and one of the main tasks in this is to re-own the body. At this level we have to question almost everything which comes under the heading of ego, or role; and indeed the ego is now seen to be almost exclusively concerned with roles. At this level we are concerned with self-actualisation, autonomy and meaning in life. Wilber says that the therapies at this level may include hatha yoga, Gestalt therapy, focusing and bioenergetics.

The third level he mentions is the Transpersonal. Here what we are about is going beyond the existential self, going beyond authenticity, going beyond 'meaning in my life'. Jung was the great pioneer of this territory, but in recent times Roberto Assagioli and Stanislav Grof have been the clearest practitioners working in it. Wilber recommends as therapy at this level Progoff's journal approach, psychosynthesis, vipassana meditation and some Jungian therapy.

These are discrete levels, but the process of development joining them is a continuous one, so that it is appropriate to regard the dimension as a continuum. This is what has been done in Table 5.1, and it can be seen from this that the various forms of psychotherapy spread out rather well over the space formed by the two dimensions. This in itself is reassuring, because it seems from many accounts of psychotherapy that there are just two categories – those which are right and those which are wrong. Also the therapies which we intuitively regard as close to one another do come out close to each other on the map, so this tends to assure us that the approach here does make sense.

The only therapy which does not relate very well to this schema is feminist therapy, because here a political dimension comes in which very rarely appears in most other forms of therapy. This makes it very distinctive; it is perhaps as if we should have a third (vertical) dimension, running perhaps from conservatism to radicalism. If we did this, we should see the whole of the middle part of the chart rising into the air, and the edges moving downwards. We should get a sort of arch or tunnel. Co-counselling, encounter, the person-centred approach and Gestalt have historically been associated with radical groups and political awareness. Mahrer pays lengthy and explicit attention to social factors. The existentialists have always had a political streak. Transactional analysis (TA), too, has made some moves in this direction. But feminist therapy goes further than any of them, it seems, in very centrally relating therapy to the social context.

It has been suggested that the therapist is more like a homeopathic doctor than like an allopathic doctor. An allopathic doctor often tries to kill germs by using some natural enemy of the germ, which will be stronger than the germ and will overcome it. A homeopathic doctor will work with the germ – or whatever else may be the trouble – using its own strength against itself, pushing it to the point where it overcomes itself. So therapy is more like aikido than it is like boxing.

Therapy can be conducted on a one-to-one basis, in couples, with families and in groups. Each of these is different and has slightly different rules and different atmospheres.

One of the most interesting things that has happened today is that the earlier ideas about therapy, healing and spirituality are being revived, so that psychotherapy can be seen as a psychospiritual discipline of the self instead of just as a way of getting people back to work, or improving their relationships.

Because of the proliferation of therapies, referred to already, there are many disagreements between therapists of different persuasions. Some would even disagree with the very basic comments made above. But as the years have gone by, and each therapy has met with the same problems as have faced the previous ones, therapists of all persuasions have learned humility. They are not so prone as they once were to praise their own and denigrate all the others.

This has made it possible for psychotherapists to get together and act in concert to create a proper profession, where there can be a proper complaints procedure and proper accountability and proper accreditation. In such a structure different schools can respect and get to know one another. If a federal structure is adopted, this can be done without unrealistic attempts at uniformity or harmonisation. This is the mission of the UK Council for Psychotherapy.

One point which needs to be made is that counselling is not very different from psychotherapy. Many books on counselling might just as well be about psychotherapy, and many books on psychotherapy might just as well be about counselling. Counselling is not exactly the same as psychotherapy, either historically or practically, but there is a huge area of overlap, and all the schools of psychotherapy are represented within counselling.

CRITIQUES OF PSYCHOTHERAPY

However, down the years certain criticisms of psychotherapy have surfaced, and they need to be looked at carefully before we can proceed. It is not the case that psychotherapy is universally acclaimed and appreciated. Five criticisms are as follows:

- psychotherapy does not work
- outcome research is very difficult
- process research is very difficult
- psychotherapy ignores medical facts
- psychotherapy ignores social systems

Let us now examine some of the counter-arguments which have been put forward. Here we have another aspect of the *Separatio*.

Psychotherapy does not work

In 1952 Eysenck produced a paper in which he tried to show that two-thirds of the patients treated by various methods of psychotherapy got better, and that two-thirds of those not treated but simply placed on waiting lists also got better. He concluded that psychotherapy was an expensive waste of time. Since then there have been a number of successful attempts to prove this wrong. The most notable of these have been M.L. Smith *et al.* (1980) and Shapiro and Shapiro (1982), which showed that good therapy had an 80 per cent success rate, while bad therapy could actually make people worse.

The curious thing is that Eysenck has never retracted his views, and has often gone on record as saying that they have never been disproved (Eysenck 1992: 103). But they have. McNeilly and Howard (1991), in an almost ideal comeuppance paper, used Eysenck's own figures to show that improvement was directly related to length of therapy. Of course, Eysenck and his friends never quote or refer to this paper. Eysenck has a reputation for failing to mention research which goes against his own views: his reply to Garfield (1992) is particularly obtuse.

Every now and then, people try once again to prove that psychotherapy does not work – usually people from the biomedical camp – but really the consensus does seem now that it does. Not only that, but all the research published so far indicates that no one therapeutic approach can claim better success than any other. The behavioural and cognitive people continually publish papers which purport to show that their approach is the best, but the vast majority of these studies are either extremely brief or extremely trivial, or both. Most researchers discount these attempts to prove superiority, and go along with what the Dodo said – 'All have won and all must have prizes!' This is really a very surprising result, and it seems clear enough that in the years to come more will be discovered about which approach works best in certain cases. There is a good discussion of all these matters in Barkham (1992).

Outcome research is very difficult

It is hard to arrive at the truth of these matters, because there are so many factors involved, and because they interact in such a dynamic way. The more precise the research becomes, the further from real life and real problems it seems to get. Here is a typical set of criteria for outcome research:

1 Survival – simply not dying
2 Effective reproduction and parenting – survival of the culture the person represents
3 Decreased vulnerability to inner and outer sources of stress
4 Increased competence in one's role
5 Feeling better – satisfaction, wellbeing, happiness

6 The person can make the system better in which he or she operates
7 A reorganised personal world, and increased personal awareness

It can be seen how difficult most of these are to test, and then there is the problem of telling how much of the effect was due to the therapist, how much to the client and how much to the other circumstances prevailing at the time. Leslie Greenberg, one of the best researchers in the field, put it succinctly:

> After decades of research the amount of well established knowledge about what affects therapeutic outcomes is disappointingly meagre. Research of the sort done in the last decade, although approaching clinical relevance, still has not offered much to practising clinicians.
>
> (Greenberg 1981: 31)

If we take as our exemplar the standard work on outcome research, Garfield and Bergin (1986), and look at the chapter on therapist variables in outcome research, we find a very interesting state of affairs. The chapter is neatly divided into four sections, according to whether the research was about matters external or internal to the therapist, and external or internal to psychotherapy as such. But the interesting thing is – and I did not believe this myself until I went through it line by line – is that every single piece of research turns out to be minimally revealing. In each case, whatever variable one looks at, the answer seems to be the same – either there is no effect, or the effect is very small, or the answers are confused in some way. No clear results emerge at all. And the best-controlled studies tell us virtually nothing about psychotherapy as ordinarily practised. What conclusions do our authors come to themselves? Here is one quotation from the section marked Conclusions:

> With the awareness that unidirectional studies have produced largely weak and inconclusive results, increasing attention is being directed to understanding complex interactions between the therapist, the intervention, the patient and the nature of outcome.
>
> (Beutler *et al.* 1986: 298)

This seems to be saying that we cannot do something relatively easy, so let us try something more difficult instead. These are unimpressive results indeed, and I can believe in the end only that the methodology of this kind of research is fundamentally flawed.

This calm acceptance of the unacceptable becomes quite unbelievable at times. The standard volume on process research (Greenberg and Pinsof 1986) makes the excellent and totally valid point that process research and outcome research are mutually necessary. Basing outcome research on ascribed or alleged orientations without actual verification is equivalent to giving blue and green pills to patients in a drug study without knowing the content of the pills. Similarly, process research which pays no attention to outcome is inadequate and one-sided in its complementary way: for instance, to know that certain behaviour therapists convey high levels of warmth and support to their patients during desensitisation is interesting, but did their high level of warmth and support make any kind of meaningful difference?

Well, that all makes sense and leads in to the rest of the book, with its detailed examinations of many different systems of measuring or describing the process of psychotherapy. But 720 pages later, Greenberg is saying this:

> A study of the relationship between the three variables therapist intervention (T), client process (C) and outcome (O), however, poses a difficult 'three-variable' problem for traditional experimental designs. Although it is possible to study the relationship between any two in both correlational and experimental designs, the task of relating all three at the same time is difficult . . . unless T is shown to cause C and cause O at the same time, the nature of the *direction* of the causal relationship between T and C always remains in doubt and one never knows whether it is T or C which leads to O. [To research this problem adequately] appears beyond the capabilities of current research procedures.
>
> (Greenberg and Pinsof 1986: 726)

So after all the work has been done, and all the research surveyed, all that the authors can do in the end is to throw up their hands, and say in effect – let the next generation do it.

Now this kind of research has been going on for over a hundred years now, and the old paradigm is wearing thin and running out of excuses. I think we have to move to a new paradigm of research which does not even attempt to talk about variables, but which talks instead about people, and to people, and with people. This is not the place to go into all that, which has been fully described and discussed elsewhere (Reason and Rowan 1981, Lincoln and Guba 1985, Mahrer 1985).

For all these reasons, it is very important to scrutinise closely the way in which each piece of research was done. One recent piece of research, for example, claimed to find better outcomes associated with directive than with non-directive counselling for Asian clients. What one found out only by reading the details was that the participants in this study were role-playing, not real clients; the whole research was based on only one interview with each person; and that the clients came from four or five quite different cultures, and ranged in age from 18 to 44. This is not serious research at all. I do not want to give the reference to this, because it is only an illustration of a general point, and I would not want to embarrass the authors.

Process research is very difficult

This is where we try to find out exactly what the therapist was doing, and whether one approach is any different in practice from another. What actually goes on between therapist and patient? The main thing which emerges from this research is that therapists of different schools are quite similar in what they actually do. Again this is very hard to sort out in detail, and the more precise the measurements become, the further from reality or any useful information we seem to get. As we have just seen, a 700-page book on process research (Greenberg and Pinsof 1986) says that really adequate research to relate process to outcome 'appears beyond the capabilities of current research procedures'. In other words, there is no proof that it is the process which produces the outcome.

This again shows how hard it is to do research in this area, and how crazy it is to ask for quantitative proof of things which perhaps are not susceptible to that kind of proof. I have argued elsewhere (Reason and Rowan 1981) that we need a new style of research altogether for this kind of work.

Psychotherapy ignores medical facts

Psychiatrists often say that all forms of psychotherapy seem to operate as if there were no medical problems to be taken care of. The typical psychotherapist seems to consider that it is all a mental matter or a behavioural matter. But when it comes to psychosis, psychotherapy has been notoriously ineffectual, and this area is in practice largely left to the medical profession. If psychotherapy really works, why does it not work with the difficult cases? It is very suspicious that it deals mainly with the YAVIS patient – Young, Attractive, Verbal, Intelligent and Successful.

It is true that psychotherapists generally stick to neurotic and borderline clients. But there are some very interesting case histories where psychotherapists have taken on and had some success with psychotic patients. One of these was fictionalised into a famous book called *I never promised you a rose garden* (Green 1964). The basic point is that most psychotherapists are in private practice, though some do work in hospitals. To come to a psychotherapist in private practice the client has to get to the therapy room once, twice or three times a week, arrive on time, leave on time, pay fees on time and so forth. This requires a degree of control that the person diagnosed as psychotic generally does not have, because to be psychotic is to be to some degree out of touch with reality. So on the whole the psychotic client needs residential treatment, and the majority of psychotherapists cannot offer that. It is therefore wise and prudent for the client not to be taken on unless the proper care can be offered.

Much the same points apply to counsellors, though more counsellors work for agencies and organisations. Counselling is more 'front-line' than psychotherapy, and clients often arrive and are seen almost immediately. Counsellors have to be very clear about when to refer clients on to someone else.

There is also the problem that vague feelings of depression and so forth, which may be taken to psychotherapists or counsellors, may actually be due to allergies or other medical conditions. The practitioner should therefore be aware of this, and refer any client for a medical check should this be suspected.

Psychotherapy ignores social systems

All forms of one-to-one therapy and nearly all forms of group therapy seem to pretend that the person is a social isolate. If the therapy succeeds in making internal changes inside the person, psychotherapy assumes that those changes will persist regardless of circumstances. This is absurd, because 'no man is an island' – we are all parts of social systems and behave very largely in terms of the roles and expectations offered to us within those systems. It is no good people changing their attitudes if they are going to go back into a system where old attitudes are rewarded and new ones punished.

This criticism comes from the family therapists, who of course have a lot to offer in terms of a systems approach. However, in practice it is not always possible to get a family in all together; it is quite hard in many cases to get even a couple to come together, never mind a whole family. Even when a couple does come in, they may resist all the efforts of the therapist to get them to explore their relationship, as in the following example:

> Admittedly the marital therapist was having a hard time, since whenever he asked us to do something – like posing towards one another in a way that would reveal our respective attitudes – my wife, being a sensible woman, would say 'I'm not doing that: it's silly', and I would say 'Give me five references to show that that helps.'
>
> (Sutherland 1992: 175)

So merely seeing a couple or a family instead of an individual does not necessarily help.

It does seem crazy when you find, as a group of trainees did once, that four members of the group were seeing four members of the same family separately. But in this case when family therapy was offered, it was turned down. This is perhaps only anecdotal, but there is a vast literature on family therapy which bears out the points made. In fact, there are at least six different styles of family therapy:

- the communication style (Satir 1988)
- the structural style (Minuchin 1974)
- the strategic style (Haley 1976)
- the behavioural style (Peine and Howarth 1975)
- the psychodynamic style (Bowen 1978)
- the network style (Reuveni 1979)

There is a good discussion of all these matters in Manor (1984).

Other critiques

David Smail (1987) has said that 'psychological distress occurs for reasons which make it incurable by therapy', and urges instead that the way to alleviate

72

and mitigate distress is 'for us *to take care of* the world and the other people in it, not to *treat* them'. This seems to me so sweeping and cavalier as not to be worth answering, except in the sense that this whole book is some kind of answer. How could we, in all conscience, ignore the need for skill in dealing with mental distress? Love is not enough.

Peter Lomas (1987) offers a critique, more specifically directed against psychoanalysis. I think he also downplays the necessity for theory and technique too much, and this again is something which will come up again and again in this book. Let me give just one example of what I mean. There is a book by Ann France called *Consuming psychotherapy*, which is the story of her experiences with three different therapists, one of them apparently trained by Peter Lomas. This book made me angry, because at the beginning of the book the author is suffering from severe and recurrent depressions, which take her to the brink of suicide, and at the end of the book the author is still suffering from severe and recurrent depressions, which take her to the brink of suicide. The only difference is that, somewhere around the middle of the process, her strong negative transference to one of the therapists led her into a continuous depression which did not lift for two years.

It is true that there are some positive things. The author is no longer frightened of spiders. She did have a good period of six years after the first three and a half years of therapy. But on the other hand she was not very frightened of spiders in the first place, and the six years did come to an end with another crisis, which further therapy did little to resolve.

At the end of the book the author says that the best she could do was to erect once again the defences she had had at the start, and which she had learned in her early years. Here is a quotation from near the end of the book:

> While in therapy, my previous defences had been broken down, revealed as false strategies. But I do not think that newer, more effective ways of coping took their place, as the textbooks suggest they do. I simply changed my view that I was neurotic not to cope *all* the time (although I usually did) for the view that I was actually stronger than many because I did in fact continue to function in situations which most people would find unacceptable. This restored some self-respect; I no longer felt quite so unworthy or inadequate. But it did not stop depression from engulfing me at times of crisis.

> (France 1988: 248)

I think anyone reading this book and trying to decide whether to go for psychotherapy would stay away, would run a mile if they had any sense. If this author's experience is anything to go by, psychotherapy is an expensive failure.

The woman who wrote this book not only had the three therapists, but also had a Samaritan who visited her; she also had a psychiatrist who was helpful from time to time, she also had a number of friends she could call on, but it seems to me that they all failed her in the end. Why?

Obviously none of us really knows. My own best guess would be that none of them went far enough back into the origins of the depression. There are some hints in one of the chapters that some very early stuff about symbiosis was involved, and none of the therapists was competent to handle such material. It just did not fit with their model, their training or their experience. Nobody told her this, nobody alerted her to the possibility. She defends herself against such a possibility at one point, by making the dark hint that stories about people *really* getting better are usually written by therapists, rather than being written by clients.

The author herself lays great stress upon authenticity and genuineness as being the most healing thing about the therapists. To the extent that they listened to their texts and their training rather than to the consulter, to the extent that they removed themselves from the real interaction, they did a bad job and did not succeed with this particular person at any rate. But it seems crystal clear from this book that authenticity and genuineness are not enough. The therapist also has to have a good enough training that they are able to go with the consulter into the places where that person needs to go. One of Ann France's therapists told her at one point that she was coming up against her limitations; it is not enough for therapists to be aware of their limitations – it is their responsibility and their duty to question those limitations, to work with them and on them, and to grow further at the instigation of the person they are supposed to be working with. That is how therapists grow, or how they avoid growing. In this book, they avoided it.

After writing those words in a review, I later heard that 'Ann France' (a pseudonym) had committed suicide. This shows, I think, that authenticity, genuineness and love are not enough. The therapist also needs sufficient skills to do what is necessary for a particular client. More on this theme will be found in the interview published in Dryden (1992).

Then again there is Jeffrey Masson (1990) and his extraordinary diatribe against therapy in all its forms. It starts off well, with a genuine concern about the abuse of power which can take place in psychotherapy. But in the end this seems to me a wildly biased book, and I cannot take it seriously, because it is much too general and indiscriminate. Masson even goes so far as to try to attack Carl Rogers. He acknowledges that Rogers was a benevolent person who impressed everyone who met him, and on the whole had a benign influence on many aspects of counselling and therapy. About the worst thing he can find to say about him is that he put up with the oppression of a state mental hospital in order to do research there. This seems to me to be clutching at straws, and to show that he is determined to find fault with everything. This impression is reinforced when he also attacks feminist therapy, incest-survivor therapy and radical therapy.

Another critic is James Hillman, who with Michael Ventura wrote a book with the striking title *We've had a hundred years of psychotherapy and the world's getting worse* (Hillman and Ventura 1992), which even the dustcover called 'furious, trenchant and audacious' – a broad hint that it is way over the top. This is indeed so: a book which can say things like these must be a bit strange:

The puzzle in therapy is not how did I get this way, but what does my angel want with me?

The attention to child abuse in the culture is serving the culture's puritanism.

The 'inner child' is a fiction, a fad in psychotherapy.

Making the child purely innocent makes childhood purely Hell.

Therapy kills our craziness and makes therapists boring.

People go to therapy to be cured of having a psyche.

We want to control all the things which make life worth living.

The recovery movement is about recovery from spontaneity and individuality.

(Hillman and Ventura 1992 *passim*)

I really enjoyed reading this, because it is so stirring and alive. It covers a huge range of different points – even making some interesting points about answering machines at one stage – but it is not a serious critique of psychotherapy.

Much more serious is the book by Spinelli (1994) which first of all criticises psychoanalysis for a mystifying notion of the unconscious, too much reliance upon a notion of linear causality, an enormous reliance on the dubious notions of transference and countertransference and a largely unsupported belief in the importance of interpretations. He goes on to criticise the cognitive-behavioural model for assuming the possibility of objectivity, the way in which it turns the therapist into a normative judge of what is rational and what is irrational and a technicised view of the therapeutic relationship. He then criticises the humanistic model for its belief in self-actualisation, its emphasis on change, its unaware conditionality, its belief in the self as a distinct and separate entity and its tendency to turn its heroes into gurus. There is a very brief criticism of transpersonal therapy. All this is done from a position of the author's own which he calls the existential-phenomenological model. He does not explain what this is or where it comes from in this book, though he does in a previous volume (Spinelli 1989). What was said there, however, is so general that in reality it seems safest to say that when Spinelli says 'existential-phenomenological model' he really means 'my model'.

His critique of the humanistic approach suffers from being too narrow. He seems to think that Carl Rogers (Kirschenbaum and Henderson 1990) is about the only humanistic therapist who matters, and quotes Corey (1991) very often in support of his points. I do not know when Gerald Corey became an authority on humanistic psychology. What I do know is that it is a mistake to ignore people like James Bugental, Rollo May and Alvin Mahrer, who have just as much right to be considered part of the heartland of humanistic psychotherapy as does Carl Rogers. Hardly any of Spinelli's critique applies to them, and in fact all three of them work in a way which is close to Spinelli's own. The separation he makes between the humanistic and the existential-phenomenological is not quite real. But in general this book raises important issues, and is well worth attention.

A final critical book is *The case against psychotherapy registration* by Richard Mowbray (1995). This takes each of the arguments in favour of the statutory registration of psychotherapists, and systematically demolishes them, one by one. It quotes a good deal from Hogan (1979), who says at one point: 'The harmful side-effects of licensing laws usually outweigh their supposed benefits' (vol. 1: 238). This is not so much against psychotherapy itself, but rather against its institutionalisation: but again it is well worth the attention of anyone affected by these matters.

THE FEMINIST CRITIQUE OF PSYCHOTHERAPY

All these books criticise psychotherapy for one defect or another, sometimes more specifically, sometimes more generally. One of the most wide-ranging critiques, however, comes from the feminist analysis. First of all they ask about the basic set-up in psychotherapy, which seems quite clear. There are two people in a room. One of them is healthy, the other sick. One of them is autonomous, the other is trying to become so. One of them is an authority figure, and frequently stands in for other authority figures the other person has met in the past; the other is one-down, often feeling like a child. One is relatively silent, the other does most of the talking. One is the helper, the other is the helped. One gets paid, the other does not. One sets the times and places, the other agrees to them. One has the responsibility for starting and finishing on time, the other does not.

This is all much more obvious in co-counselling, where the two people take it in turns to be counsellor and client. Each switches into the appropriate role at the appropriate time, and each behaves differently when in the other role (Evison and Horobin 1988).

Normally, of course, there is no such switching. The therapist goes on being a therapist, and the client goes on being a client. What is wrong with this is well stated by Rachel Perkins:

> No matter how feminist a therapy purports to be, it essentially transforms the political into personal, individual and pathological terms. Therapy implies that something is wrong with the individual or that she is in some way functioning less well than she might. By offering therapy to lesbians experiencing distress and difficulties, whether these be a direct consequence of anti-lesbianism or not, clinical psychologists and therapists locate the cause of problems, and their solution, firmly within the individual concerned.
>
> (Perkins 1991: 331)

This seems to be not quite true, as we shall see later. But it has enough truth in it to be taken seriously. So what we have in therapy is a double form of oppression: firstly the patriarchal relations of superior and inferior are reproduced in the consulting room, and secondly all problems are made into individual problems, to be solved at an individual level. As Perkins says, again:

Consciousness-raising was the process of making the personal political. By contrast, therapy renders the political personal, and individual.

(Perkins 1992: 260)

The case against therapy, then, from this point of view, is that whatever its content, its form is basically oppressive, taking for granted the individualism and hierarchy which is so characteristic of patriarchy.

For many years there have been accusations of psychoanalysis in particular for putting women down – asserting that women's attempts to gain social power in the wider world represent penis envy, and so forth. The marvellous work of Christiane Olivier (1989) has summarised and questioned all that very well.

More recently, Ruth Waterhouse has accused the humanistic approach too, and that of Carl Rogers in particular, of being too individualistic and too optimistic about relationships between women and men:

By contrast to 'humanistic approaches', feminist approaches problematise the nature of 'self-hood', 'person-hood' and 'subjectivity' within the context of gender relationships. In contrast to Rogers' harmonic view of human relationships, feminists point to the many examples of gender inequality which create profound conflicts of interest between women and men.

(Waterhouse 1993: 61)

She goes further, and suggests that the humanistic approach, which lays so much stress on the individual taking responsibility, is oppressive in another way too:

I would suggest that in failing to address the structural and interpersonal constraints on women's lives the person-centred approach can at times collude with a very subtle form of 'victim-blaming', in which the victim of rape is made responsible for her failure to be sufficiently active in striving to move on from victim to survivor to thriver.

(Waterhouse 1993: 63)

These are quite heavy political accusations, and they have to be answered if we are to go on using psychotherapy with a clear conscience.

The whole question of autonomy is very important here. Many men are attracted to therapy because they think it will increase their autonomy. And this is indeed one of the promises of therapy, as we saw in Chapter 4. But the idea of autonomy can also be a dangerous illusion for men.

There is no self without an other, and the challenge is to integrate autonomy and connection. One reason a man can look so enviably strong and separate is because women are playing out the other side for him.

(Goodrich et al. 1988: 19)

What men have to learn in therapy is that integration means joining these two things, not separating them even further.

In the next chapter we shall see how these important political points can be met.

Note: An important addition to the feminist critique outlined here is to be found in the book by Betty McLellan entitled *Beyond Psychoppression: A Feminist Alternative Therapy* (Spinifex Press, North Melbourne, 1995).

6

THE PERSONAL/POLITICAL

THE PERSONAL AND THE POLITICAL

What exactly is the relation between the personal and the political? I seem to have met a lot of people recently who have been reading the political critiques of psychotherapy and have been quite worried by them. After all, they do purport to show that therapy of whatever persuasion is highly dubious, and a lot of the things that therapists say are nonsense. My own response was to reconsider the whole relationship between the personal and the social – personal change and social change. Every now and then in various magazines (and particularly the more radical ones) there is an article chasing after and eventually killing psychotherapy. It seems quite an exciting pursuit, though the quarry seems to keep on coming back to life after being shot down yet once again.

What one does not expect is to see the same sort of thing in the pages of the official publications of the British Psychological Society (the orthodox large body representing academic psychology in the UK). Yet the articles forming the special Psychotherapy Section in the February 1991 issue of *The Psychologist* are exactly of this kind. So whether we look at the feminists, or whether we look at the radical Jungians, or whether we look at the regular psychologists, we seem to be facing the same argument.

What we are seeing here is another aspect of the *Separatio*. The personal has become separated from the political. The I, the We and the It have flown apart. There is a fragmentation which has become quite pathological. Everywhere we look there is a loosening of the old ties, of the old expectations. What are we to make of this?

What I believe is that the political activist and the psychotherapist are pursuing the same activity, one in a third-person way and one in a first-person way. They are both (we are both) in the business of liberation, one at the level of social forces and impersonal pressures, the other at the level of inner tumult and self-oppression. Both are necessary and both are flourishing. Both of them find it necessary to organise in order to make their work more effective; and I think if anything the psychotherapists are more careful not to do more harm than good.

FIRST PERSON OR THIRD PERSON

A dilemma often arises for any counsellor or therapist around the issue of the personal versus the political: how much of what a client is going through is due to what is outside the person, and how much of it is due to what is inside the person?

Usually this is resolved by the practitioner settling for the personal, and saying that what we are concerned with is not so much what actually happened (or is happening now) but rather with what the client makes of it. The person does have a choice as to take it in one way or to take it in another. Mahrer (1989a) has a very good discussion of this question under the heading of 'Modes of construction of an external world'.

However, the more political person will say that we are continually at the mercy of social forces which press on us from every angle. If we think we are independent of our genes, of our early family set-up, of the schools in which we were educated, of the media which surround us, of the economic structure within which we live, we are crazy. If we think we have much choice as to what to make of it, we are deceived.

Where is the pain machine located? And what do we have to do to switch it off? Is it somewhere within the person, as the practitioner hopes, or is it outside the person, as the more socially oriented critic maintains?

The social psychologists have taken up this problem under the heading of person versus situation, and have performed many experiments to show that people are partly determined from inside and partly from outside. But I want to argue that this is to miss the point, and in any case to do something which the practitioner cannot make use of. I want to suggest a completely different way of looking at this question, which does genuinely resolve the matter once and for all.

If we say to the client in effect that we are assuming that he or she is responsible for everything they do, then that is encouraging the client to take up a first-person ('I') attitude. This is a crucial move in all forms of counselling and psychotherapy. If clients can take up a first-person stance to the world, seeing the world through their own eyes rather than seeing it all the time through other people's eyes, this puts them in a position to do something about themselves and their situation. This applies even to the most abused and damaged people, who perhaps have never in their lives known a decent environment or real love (Hampden-Turner 1976). This move, to a first-person stance, is something which can very often be a turning point in the therapy, the point where the person takes hope.

If on the other hand we take up, or encourage the client to take up, a third-person attitude, talking about what 'he', 'she', 'it' or 'they' do, what we are saying is social and potentially political. We are turning our attention outwards, and saying that something out there needs changing. This is an absolutely essential move if we want to change the environment, change the rules, change the organisation or whatever. From this point of view, turning the attention inward is a diversion, a luxury which can perhaps be postponed.

Now the first-person view is necessary: without it we should be pawns, one-dimensional, powerless. And the third-person view is necessary: without it we should be victims, exploited, mystified. We can equally well and equally legitimately take up either stance. In fact, we have to switch between them if we are to make any sense of our world at all. We have to be able to go from one to the other, and not get stuck exclusively in either one of them.

There is no contradiction between them. It is not that the first-person view accounts for some percentage of the way things are, and that the third-person view accounts for the other percentage. The first-person view accounts for 100 per cent of the way things are, looked at from that position. The third-person view accounts for 100 per cent of the way things are, looked at from that position. They are different positions, and different views of the whole, not of part only. We do not have to choose between them, or allocate percentages to them: we must have both.

Perhaps, as Gandhi once said, the personal and the political are the two legs on which we walk.

RESPONSIBILITY

One key area in which we can apply our analysis is to the question of responsibility. One of the important things which therapy can be about is autonomy, the ability to take charge of one's own life. When clients can take responsibility for their own actions, can own up to their own intentionality, the therapy is over. Charles Hampden-Turner describes a project for dealing with some of the most damaged and difficult people in society, most with considerable jail experience. He says that the project was very successful for those who were able to grasp the key point:

> The system made you what you are, but if you want to change the system, you have to accept the responsibility for what you let the system do to you.
> (Hampden-Turner 1976: 289)

Those who got this point made it, those who did not, did not. But the key to understanding this correctly is to note that it is couched in first-person terms. In other words, it worked only if the person said '*I* take responsibility for what *I* let the system do to me'. This first-person use is self-empowering. It enables the person to find the necessary and stable fulcrum to move their world. It leads the person to say something like 'I create my world' and there is a very solid ring to that at this stage.

The terrible mistake we can make is to use the same approach in a third-person way. This difference between the first-person use and the third-person use is crucial. If we say '*They* create *their* world', that is not empowering at all. It can become punitive and oppressive. It turns into something like 'Pull yourself together', or 'Stand on your own two feet', or 'Don't expect any handouts from me, buster'. This then loses all sense of community or fellow-feeling, never

81

mind any sense of solidarity or mutual support. And these are things we all need, too.

If the difference between the first-person use and the third-person use of the idea of responsibility is so crucial, what about the second-person use? What happens if we say '*You* create *your* world' to someone? Here it is a question of trust. If we have a good relationship with the person, such that they take what we say seriously – take it on board, as we say – it may be very valuable and strengthening. It will then come across very much as an invitation to first-person use. This is particularly so if we offer to stay with them and work out with them the implications. But if, on the other hand, there is no trust, it is simply seen as an unsympathetic rejection, just as with the third-person use. So trust is terribly important in this area, and where the idea of responsibility goes wrong, it is usually over some question involving mutual trust.

The point is that *you alone can do it, but you don't have to do it alone*. Both sides of the statement are true, and they must not be separated from each other. In fact, sometimes you cannot do it alone even in principle. Autonomy is important, but love and mutual support and nourishment are important too.

There is a nice diagram in Paul (1985), which shows the sequence of personal development as dependent (passive supporter), leading to counterdependent (angry, rebellious), leading to independent (competitive, aloof), leading to interdependent (involved achieving team member). This is within an organisation, but it can also apply to small groups and couple relationships, and to the individual. We all start off at mother's knee in total dependency. We may then progress to adolescent rebellion (counterdependence), where we use the peer group as a stepping-stone towards leaving the family, as we saw in Chapter 4. If personal development then continues, we eventually arrive at independence, the kind of autonomy of which we have been speaking, and which for some therapists is the end of the road. But this is not the end: we can go on to interdependence, where we can have genuine relationships with other people, letting them in to our world and cooperating with them in such a way as to empower us both. This mutual empowerment is even stronger and more effective than the original autonomy which seemed – and was – so important at the time. We shall come back to this point in later chapters.

Let us look at this again, in a slightly different way, but again seeing how the internal view and the external view relate to one another.

BEHIND OR WITHIN

Sociology, social psychology and group dynamics – and politics – are interested in *the person behind the person*. They see, when a person comes into a room and sits down at the conference table or whatever, a whole great invisible backpack extending out behind, consisting of social class interests, identifications, reference groups, membership groups, affinities and commitments, nationality, gender, working role, ethnic identification, religious identification, ideological identification, heroes or heroines and so on. All these are right there in the room, even if invisible and unacknowledged. And the person carries those around all the time, whether liking it or not, and whether knowing it or not.

Psychotherapy, counselling and personal growth, on the other hand, are interested in *the person within the person*. They notice, when a person comes into the room, a whole set of complexities hiding within, consisting of instincts and needs, Parent–Adult–Child, ego–superego–id, animus or anima, internal objects, complexes, archetypes, inner conflicts, subpersonalities, attitudes and opinions, traits, character armour, transpersonal self, and so on. All these are right there inside, even if invisible and unacknowledged. And the person carries those around all the time, whether liking it or not, and whether knowing it or not.

What I want to say is that the person behind the person *IS* the person within the person. Equally, the person within the person *IS* the person behind the person.

Seeing it as *behind* gives us sociological insights. Seeing it as *within* gives us psychological insights. Seeing it as a *unity* (of behind and within) gives us the dialectical insight. Seeing it as a unity gives us a meta-perspective which is beyond sociology and psychology.

The practical move which emerges from this analysis is to use the *same* language for both our political analysis and our psychological analysis. One way of doing this is to look at the question of the Patripsych.

THE PATRIPSYCH

In an attempt to pursue this analysis, some writers have been using the notion of the Patripsych – an internal constellation of patriarchal patterns. This is a structure inside, which corresponds to oppressive structures outside, each supporting the other. The internal structure arises out of a set of movements towards, against and away from a symbolic patriarchal figure or set of figures, and is held out of consciousness by the usual defence mechanisms, this time in the cultural unconscious. The tendency for men is to have unconscious *against* patterns, with idealised glorified images of aggressive mastery; and the tendency for women is to have unconscious *towards* patterns, with the glorification of morbid dependency as love, motherhood, etc.; while the tendency for both may be to have unconscious *away from* patterns, glorified as private living, religions of withdrawal, etc. All these unconscious patterns would then be seen as defences against messages coming from the Patripsych.

Now if we see one of the key political issues as patriarchy (or to put it more generally, dominance cultures), and one of the key psychological issues as the Patripsych, anything we do on one level will feed into whatever we do on another. Patriarchy forms a good lead in to all the problems of domination and submission in our social system; I have spelt this out in some detail elsewhere (Rowan 1987). The Patripsych forms a good lead in to all the problems of internal self-oppression which affect us most inwardly. This is similar to what

Hogie Wyckoff (1975) has called the Pig Parent – an internalised form of cultural oppression. Most importantly, the insights we get on one level can be applied directly to the other level.

We can do serious work on the Patripsych using the group workshop methods of psychotherapy as outlined by Hogie Wyckoff (1975), Sheila Ernst and Lucy Goodison (1981) and others, and in this way can get a lot of feeling for the kind of work we are going to have to do to change patriarchy on a large scale. We shall get a much better sense of what is possible, what is important, what works and what does not. As we do this, we can start to find new ways of working, which do more justice to the fact that the person within the person IS the person behind the person. I have done a lot of work with men on male consciousness, which bears directly on these points (see Chapter 13). There is no reason why we cannot think of many new ways of working, once we have the basic insight. The whole thing opens up. As the feminist Laura Brown succinctly puts it:

> I do not see it as either a- or anti-political to attend to internal, non-conscious manifestations of oppressive phenomena.
>
> (Brown 1992: 244)

Similarly, we can start to look at other things in the same way. We can look at situations, and see from a dialectical point of view that in order to understand the situation, we have to look at the situation behind the situation – history, class interests, alliances, power structures, economic resources, etc. – and at the situation within the situation – interpersonal relations, norms, shared experience, attitudes, etc. – and then see that the situation behind the situation IS the situation within the situation. But this would take us too far away from our central concerns here.

A WAY FORWARD

It is no good criticising psychotherapy as if somehow it could be wished away, or even diminished. It is here to stay for good reasons. But we certainly do not want a psychotherapy which is socially illiterate. To speak more positively, any decent training in psychotherapy needs to do justice to the social point of view as well as the personal point of view. And then there is the whole question of spiritual realities, which I have written about at length (Rowan 1993a). Perhaps this is the way to go, rather than abandoning all that we have learned over the years.

Psychotherapy is not necessarily anything much to do with patriarchy, as we shall be seeing in detail in the next chapter, but if it is not to reproduce the characteristics of patriarchy, we have to pay more attention than most have done in the past to the way in which it is carried out.

There is such a thing as feminist therapy. There is also such a thing as nonsexist therapy. And there is also such a thing as profeminist therapy. Someone who has written with great clarity about this is Anne Ganley.

Feminist therapy involves the resocialization of women and of men. It uses the androgynous model of mental health for both men and women to assist clients in identifying goals for therapy. This is a model of health, growth, and development rather than one based on illness. . . . The feminist therapist employs psychoeducational approaches, choosing to incorporate strategies from radical psychiatry, humanistic psychology, cognitive behavioural approaches, etc. Some even attempt to use psychoanalysis within the feminist conceptual framework. In sex role analysis, the external and internal constraints to change are identified. While feminist therapy stresses individual responsibility for change, it deals with the issues of choice, control and power within the current social structures. . . . Furthermore, feminist therapy is recognized as not being solely a change process for an individual, since it calls upon both client and therapist to change society's institutions, including the structures of psychotherapy itself.

(Ganley 1988: 189)

Now we may not all agree on some of this, but it is at least clear and unambiguous. Such a definition of feminist therapy distinguishes it from two closely related approaches to therapy: nonsexist therapy by male and female therapists, and profeminist therapy by male therapists.

In nonsexist therapy we may well find the use of sex role analysis and the androgynous model of the mentally healthy adult. However, little attention is given to the need to restructure social institutions, either by the therapist or the client. Nonsexist therapy practice may at times reflect traditional methods and procedures; little attempt is made by the therapist to be accessible to varieties of persons or to empower clients both in therapy and in their communities. Inclusive language may be used, traditional sex roles challenged, and individual change supported, but these nonsexist approaches may focus solely on the progress of individuals to the exclusion of social change. This is of course the point which the feminist writers we have already met are intent on putting across. The primary difference between feminist therapy and nonsexist approaches is that the nonsexist approach addresses the personal but overlooks the political.

Profeminist therapy is similar to feminist therapy in most respects, including the analysis of power and the concern with social change. The difference between the two rests solely in the gender of the therapist. In feminist therapy the therapist is a female who uses her phenomenological experiences as a woman to understand her clients and to enrich her therapeutic strategies. In profeminist therapy the therapist is male. Since he does not have the phenomenological experience of being female, he uses his experiences as a male and particularly a male whose understanding of himself, of all men, and of women has been transformed by feminist analysis.

In this book what we are exploring, all the way through, is profeminist therapy. And what we are saying is that the personal is political. Not that the personal ought to be political, nor that the personal ought to be more political, nor that the personal ought to have more links with the political, nor that the political is more important than the personal – all of which seem to have been meanings which have sometimes been added on to the original elegant statement of Carol Hamisch (1969) – but just simply that the personal already has the political contained within it, and that what we can then do is to recognise it and be aware of this. We said that alchemy was full of oppositions, contradictions and paradoxes. Here is one of them. This complete integration of the personal and political is part of the separation process, enabling us to proceed on our way. If this sounds paradoxical, that is the way things are.

7

WHAT IS THERAPY ABOUT?

There is endless discussion about the aims of psychotherapy and counselling. What are they really all about? What I would like to suggest here is that there are at least three quite different approaches to this question, based on different notions of the self. This is another aspect of the *Separatio* which we need to consider at this point. In order to focus this discussion, let us look at Table 7.1. Creation by *Separatio* is often described by the alchemists as division into four, as Edinger (1985) points out.

A MAP OF THE REALM

This is based on the work of Ken Wilber (1980), though he is in no way responsible for my application here. He says that there is a process of psychospiritual development which we all go through, though most of us do not go all the way with it. This process starts before birth, and there are definite way-stations as we go on from there. In early childhood we have a body self, which is very much attached to our experiences of being a body, or being in a body. In later childhood we have a membership self, which is very much attached to our experience of being a family member. We see ourselves as part of a family, and identified with that. In adolescence, we move out of this conception of the self, often with the help of the peer group as a stepping-stone, as we saw in Chapter 4, and eventually end up with a mental ego. This is where we have got to in the first column of our chart. There is plenty of research and plenty of support from developmental psychology for the story so far (Craig 1992).

The point Wilber makes, however, is one which is not often found in the standard texts: it is that the whole notion of the self changes with each of these transitions. It is not just a smooth process: we have to abandon the previous stage in order to go on to the next one. Each of these transitions feels risky and dangerous, not just automatic. Perhaps the most obvious example of this is adolescence, where there is often a quite traumatic breakaway from the family, which is sometimes not completed until years later. As we saw in Chapter 3, it is possible to find a man in his late thirties who has still not snapped the cord joining him to his mother.

Table 7.1 A comparison of four positions in personal development

	One Persona/Shadow Mental ego	Two Centaur Real self	Three Subtle self Soul	Four Causal self Spirit
Wilber level Rowan position				
Self	I am defined by others	I define who I am	I am defined by the Other(s)	I am not defined
Motivation	Need	Choice	Allowing	Surrender
Personal goal	Adjustment	Self-actualisation	Contacting	Union
Social goal	Socialisation	Liberation	Extending	Salvation
Process	Healing – Ego-building	Development – Ego-extending	Opening – Ego-reduction	Enlightenment
Traditional role of helper	Physician Analyst	Growth facilitator	Advanced guide	Priest(ess) Sage
Representative approaches	Hospital treatment	Primal integration	Psychosynthesis	Mystical Buddhism
	Chemotherapy	Gestalt therapy	Some Jungians	Raja Yoga
	Psychoanalysis	Open encounter	Some pagans	Taoism
	Directive	Psychodrama	Transpersonal	Monasticism
	Behaviour modification	Neo-Freudians	Voice Dialogue	Da Avabhasa
	Cognitive-behavioural	Bodywork therapies	Some Wicca or Magic	Christian mysticism
	Some TA	Some TA	Kabbalah	Sufi
	Crisis work	Person-centred	Some astrology	Goddess mystics
	REBT	Co-counselling	Some Tantra	Some Judaism
	Brief therapy	Regression	Shamanism	Advaita
Focus	Individual and group	Group and individual	Supportive community	Ideal community
Representative names	Freud	Maslow	Jung	Eckhart
	Ellis	Rogers	Hillman	Shankara
	Meichenbaum	Mahrer	Starhawk	Dante
	Beck	Perls	Assagioli	Tauler
	Eysenck	Lowen	Gordon-Brown	Suso
	Skinner	Schutz	Mary Watkins	Ruysbroeck
	Lazarus	Moreno	Jean Houston	Nagarjuna
	Watzlawick	Stevens	Bolen	Lao Tzu
	Wessler	Argyris	Grof	George Fox
	Haley	Bugental	Boorstein	Julian of Norwich
Research methods	Qualitative	Collaborative	Transformative	None
Questions	Dare you face the challenge of the unconscious?	Dare you face the challenge of freedom?	Dare you face the loss of your boundaries?	Dare you face the loss of all your symbols?
Key issues	Acceptability Respect	Autonomy Authenticity	Openness Vision	Devotion Commitment

THE MENTAL EGO LEVEL: ADJUSTMENT

Although it is perhaps clear enough from the chart, there are some points to be made about the mental ego stage of development. It is a very important achievement, which most of us do reach some time in our twenties or thirties. It is the stage of being able to play our social roles effectively, and to carry them off well enough to make us acceptable workers, husbands, fathers, and so forth. Its most characteristic feature is that it entails looking to others to define us. That is, we get our basic esteem from other people. (See Maslow 1987, Loevinger 1976 and Kohlberg 1981 for details of what they call the *conventional* stage.)

When we first enter this stage, we may want everyone to like us. As we get more mature within this stage, however, we become more discriminating, and pay more attention to the views of some than to those of others. We want to be respected by those we respect. In this process of development, society helps us to grow. Society continually tells us, in many ways at every level – yes, this is how you should be. It gives out rewards to those who think like this, and withholds rewards from those who have not yet reached this point.

I use the word 'we' here, as elsewhere in this book, to represent 'most men, including me'. It seems that any other word would be less accurate than this. For 'most men' I rely on research, for the most part, certainly at this early stage, but later to indicate what I have picked up, rightly or wrongly, as the general consensus on the subject.

Over a period of some years, then, we build up this ability to play our social roles, and we may even get mature enough to play with our roles, and wear them quite lightly (Goffman 1961). In this way we build up a world which may seem, at least in reasonably stable times, to be safe and secure and predictable. In less stable times, we may have to work a lot harder at it, but this is still the aim. And so we become respect-able.

Let us now begin to see how all this mapmaking applies to psychotherapy. It will be useful here to apply the ideas to all the existing forms of psychotherapy, to see where they fit in to Wilber's schema. We have already come across some of these ideas in Chapter 5.

It can be seen that there are four columns in Table 7.1. Column one is labelled persona/shadow or mental ego. This is the level at which most counselling and psychotherapy is carried out. It has to do with adjustment to consensus reality. The client at this stage is going through some very unpleasant emotional experiences, and wants to get back to the status quo. Or perhaps the client has been experiencing incapacitating feelings for a long time, and just wants to be able to love and to work. The client may be presenting with depression, eating disorders, anxiety, shyness, bereavement, exam nerves, being made redundant, fear of flying, loss of a partner, persistent headaches, any one of the thousand symptoms and problems which plague our daily life.

Virtually all practitioners are able to handle this level of work, because virtually all practitioners are familiar with this level of development in their own experience. Probably the vast majority of the work done in this field is at this level, and the vast majority of the research carried out is also at this level. Language is extremely important for this kind of work, because language embodies the consensus reality which the person wants to get back to.

Psychoanalysis is included in this column because classical Freudian psychoanalysis explicitly says that it is restricted to this level. There are of course some neo-Freudians and groups who are not so restricted, such as Horney, Fromm, Guntrip, Balint, Fairbairn, Winnicott and so forth, and they are actually highly relevant to our search.

This is very much the level of symptom removal, and of working directly on the problem in a focused way. But we are not aiming at liberation, and may indeed at this stage regard it as something dangerous:

> Indeed, it is clear to me that society needs men to have unresolved Oedipus complexes; that we continue to live with the fear of the father (the Law). A truly free man would represent a real threat to social organisation.
>
> (Jukes 1993: 114)

There is a fear here, a fear of social disorganisation. If the boundaries of control were broken, all kinds of bad things might happen. It is catastrophic expectations on the part of the therapist which make them restrict their work to what is safe and unexceptionable. One of the favourite slogans at this stage is 'We don't pretend to know better than the client. We let the client set the agenda and the aims.' This assumes, of course, that there is just one client – the rational one who makes the contract.

But perhaps it is sometimes the irrational one, the neurotic one, who makes the contract, with the rational one nowhere to be seen? This sort of suggestion is often resisted, at this stage, with a sort of robust common sense, which says things like:

> When the going got tough [in restricting his rituals], George typically suggested that it might be better for us to explore the meaning behind his symptoms. I would react, using my 'tough army sergeant stance' by pointing out that he had devoted six years of his life to exploring meanings and dynamics to no avail.
>
> (Lazarus 1989: 234)

It may be surprising to some to find psychoanalysis in the same group as all this, but of course since the 1960s there has been a good deal of exploration of brief psychodynamic psychotherapy, as well as a more eclectic approach by many psychodynamic psychotherapists. Some of the most interesting developments have been the integration of psychoanalysis and behaviour therapy by Wachtel (1977, 1982), and the integration of cognitive and dynamic therapy by Schwartz (1993). But even in the most orthodox and central Freudian tradition, Freud himself always warned against high-flown aims of any kind, and played down the possible outcomes of psychoanalysis. When he talked about aims at all, it was in such terms as enabling people 'to love and to work' or 'exchanging hysterical misery for common unhappiness'.

THE CENTAUR LEVEL: LIBERATION AND THE REAL SELF

Now the movement from column one to column two, from the mental ego to the centaur or real self, is another of the wrenching moves mentioned earlier. It is the first initiation. It very often starts as a result of some crisis, such as a partner leaving, loss of a valued job, death of a loved one, and so forth, which brings us into therapy. This very often happens about the age of 30, but it may be considerably later.

It is the stage where we say in effect: 'I know how to play my roles very well, and to get esteem from others to quite a reasonable estate, but it all seems to be about playing a part: how about me? How about the person behind all the roles? I know all about playing parts in other people's dramas: how about writing my own dramas?' Usually this thought does not occur at the beginning – at the start we are very often lost in some problem which seems overwhelming – but it starts to dawn as the journey progresses.

But the movement does not have to start like that. Nowadays it can start in a much more positive way, where we say in effect: 'I know I can do my stuff adequately, but maybe I can do more than that. I am able, but maybe I can be more able.' This is the line of personal growth, rather than of problem-solving. It can also be linked with starting to take a training in counselling or psychotherapy, and finding that one's own therapy is obligatory. But however it starts, the movement is away from role-playing and towards authenticity.

Column two is the one which has been of most interest to humanistic practitioners (although most of them work most of the time in column one, just like everyone else). At this level, the emphasis is on freedom and liberation. There is a great deal of the humanistic literature, which I have tried to sum up elsewhere (Rowan 1988), saying that we go from the realm of deficiency (where all the motivation is to repair some deficit) to the realm of abundance (where the motivation comes from a positive urge to explore, create and grow). Some people talk about the move from an emphasis on doing and having to an emphasis on being.

It is very important to note, however, that this centaur, this real self, is still regarded as single and bounded. It has definite limits, a habitation and a name. People at this level often talk about community, but their actions are in fact very individualistic. Wallis (1985) in a sociological analysis, describes this whole way of looking at the world as epistemological individualism – that is, treating our whole way of knowing as essentially an individual and private matter.

What is also important to note is that no one can bring someone else to this level who has not reached it themselves. This is an amplification and extension of Freud's original statement that the therapist can move the patient only to the limit of the therapist's own resistances. What we are now having to go on to say is that as well as resistances, the therapist also has contractions. These contractions are drawings-back, avoidances, distortions of growth. But individuals who have never contacted their own real self, because of this kind of contraction, cannot enable other people to contact their own real self. In fact, they can effectively obstruct it.

This is a crucially important point. Each of the Wilber steps requires a move to a new definition of self, and this is a very central and involving move. It affects the whole person in a radical way. It is not something which the intellect can put on and take off. In fact, it is the intellect which does most of the contracting and avoidance which prevents movement further along the scale.

The actual experience of the real self is, I have argued, a mystical experience. This is the feeling of being in touch with my own centre, my inner identity, my true self, my authenticity – that self which lies behind or beyond all self-images, self-concepts or subpersonalities. It is what Assagioli (1975) calls the 'I', the centre point of the personality. It is what Wilber (1980) calls the 'Centaur', the complete bodymind unity. The discovery of this self often happens in primal work, whether individual or group, but it can also happen in many other ways. It is a developmental step, principally discontinuous, involving step-jump rather than gradual form (Pedler and Boydell 1981). We can now say 'I am I', and it means something to us. The existential tradition has a great deal to say about how it works. Martin Buber quotes from the tales of the Hasidim:

> Before his death, Rabbi Zusya said: 'In the coming world, they will not ask me: 'Why were you not Moses?' They will ask me: "Why were you not Zusya?"'
>
> (Buber 1975: 251)

This is the classic existential insight, that we are responsible for being ourselves, and this is a high and deep responsibility indeed. If we take responsibility for ourselves, we are fully human. This is why we have to call it an initiation.

When I was exploring this level for the first time, one of the most helpful texts I found was the Carl Rogers and Barry Stevens book *Person to person: The problem of being human* (Stevens and Rogers 1967). It spoke to me very directly about being a real human being, in such stories as this:

> He [Herbert Talehaftewa, a Hopi Indian] was working as a carpenter on a construction job where I was office manager. Cab, the owner and boss, was a Boston snob who looked down on *everyone*, belittled them to the point where most people who were subjected to it went to pieces and had to pull themselves together again. One day I saw this man look at and speak to the Hopi in this way. Cab was a small man, and the Hopi was quite tall and broad, but Cab still managed to look down on the Hopi. I saw the Hopi look at Cab so *equally* that he drew Cab down to his own level – precisely, and not one bit lower – so that they seemed to be two people eye-to-eye. I

was so impressed by this that I looked up to the Hopi as though he were some sort of god. The Hopi turned to me with that same strong *equalness* in his gaze, and I felt myself being drawn *up* until we were on the same plane. Through him I knew that all men are equal if only we will regard them so.

(Stevens and Rogers 1967: 35)

This is the view of humanity which is very characteristic of this stage, where the ordinary and the spiritually valuable seem to go together in quite a striking way.

This seems to me a very important step in psychospiritual development, because it is a gateway to the realisation that we *must have spiritual experiences for ourselves*, we cannot get them from someone else. This is the basic attitude of the mystic in all religious traditions – to get inside one's own experience, to commit oneself to one's own experience, to trust one's own experience.

At this stage, too, comes the typical breakthrough experience. It often involves some sense of death and rebirth: as Perls used to say, 'To experience one's death and be reborn is not easy' (Perls 1969). Death and rebirth are crucial concepts here, as Stanislav Grof has shown at great length and in some detail (Grof 1988). At each point where we leave the level of the mental ego for a higher or deeper or more inclusive state of consciousness, we experience a breakthrough, a peak experience where we suddenly seem to be in contact with the Truth. It is like a kind of initiation. All the previous effort now seems dust and ashes, quite irrelevant or even handicapping. Everything now seems clear and true, and there is no fear any more. Alvin Mahrer, the great theorist of this level, says:

The following words apply to the nature and content of the good feelings of experiential actualization: aliveness, vitality, physical-body lightness, tingling, buoyancy, 'high', excitement, exhilaration, ecstasy, joy, happiness, satisfaction, pleasure, power, force, energy. Each word is to be taken as referring to events of the physical body.

(Mahrer 1989a: 585)

This often happens after a cathartic experience. John Heron, a British humanistic and transpersonal therapist (Heron 1977), has argued that this kind of catharsis makes possible these five things:

1 spontaneous insight
2 celebration of personal being
3 break-up of distorted behaviour
4 living in abundant time
5 synchronous events

This suggests at least the foothills of spirituality.

The phrase which often comes in at this stage is: 'I create my world'. This is the stage where we start to take responsibility for our own development, rather than allowing ourselves to be moved on as if up an escalator. Symbols may be used deliberately for growth. This is the highest point in the existential realm. Blissful states or peak experiences may be experienced. Fritz Perls, who specialised in working at this level, talked of the 'mini-satori', which is quite explicitly a mystical experience. Again, however, as before, it may be very scary to move on from the previous stage, with all its certainties and all its familiarity.

This is an extraordinarily important step, and the concept of the centaur stage is one of Wilber's most important contributions. No other map of psychospiritual development seems to include it at all. It represents at one time the end of the process of individual development within the confines, so to speak, of one's own skin; and the beginning of the process of transpersonal development, because it breaks the mould of the mental ego. It is very hard to get to the centaur stage without going through the process of psychotherapy (or the best kind of long-term counselling), because it entails working through the unfinished business of the past, and bringing everything into the present. Only in this way can a genuine existential consciousness be achieved. We cannot have the authenticity which is so crucial at this stage unless there is a whole person there to be authentic.

This is a particularly paradoxical stage, because of this quality of being the end of one process and the beginning of another. It is a spiritual stage which may be totally atheistic.

THE SUBTLE LEVEL: THE SOUL

Let us now look at column three in Table 7.1, labelled subtle self or soul. This is the area worked in so thoroughly by James Hillman and many other Jungians, and by Assagioli and his followers. This is a level which now clearly deserves the term transpersonal. Here we are concerned with problems which, as Jung pointed out, often come more in the second half of life, though it is perfectly possible for them to arise at any time.

There is more than one spiritual experience, and some of these are very different one from another. One of the most common of these, I suppose, after contacting the real self, is contacting what used to be called the higher self. This is the sense of being in touch with my transpersonal self, my deep self. This often comes about in transpersonal therapy or groups, or in psychosynthesis therapy or groups, but again it can happen in many other ways (see Ferrucci 1982, Vaughan 1985, Starhawk 1982). At first it appears to be outside of us, and may even appear to have a three-dimensional reality. Essentially it has a touch of the divine: it is a symbolic representation of the sacred. This is a second initiation. There are many synonyms for the transpersonal self, depending on the belief system of the participants. In the years to come I think we shall see much more discrimination and differentiation in this area.

My own view is that the transpersonal self is best represented, in most cases, by a person. But it does not have to be so. I have known cases where the transpersonal self was represented by a dome, or flowing water, or a jewel, or a flower, or a light. For example, Emmons (1978) quotes the example of a 20–year-old woman in a therapy session who said this:

> It was as if there were a bright light encompassing my whole body. My body seemed to inflate and balloon out and 'I', the 'me-ness' of my body, seemed to be filled and carried with this light. . . . The light then narrowed into a stream of an intensity I would imagine a laser beam to have and focussed deep down somewhere, no place physical that I can point to, just deep in my 'me-ness'. . . . After awhile the light seemed to be focussed on the lump in my throat where I'd tried to hold down my tears . . . The lump in my throat dissolved . . . I feel great.
>
> (Emmons 1978: 111–112)

This symbol of the laser-beam was used in later sessions as a guide, helping to awaken more of the client's potential. This again does seem like an initiation into a mystical experience of some kind.

After having had such an experience I may follow it up in various ways: I may take religious advice and instruction, and most mystics do (Moss 1981), but even so, I have to decide which instruction and advice to take and which to follow, and there is no way I can put the reponsibility for this outside myself. Even if I say that it is a voice inside me, I still have the responsibility for which voice to listen to. Jon Klimo (1988) has a good discussion of this point in his book on channelling.

I do not want to say much more about the deeper self, because I think it is familiar to most of us, but I just want to underline that it is a spiritual experience. One of the symbolic entities one may encounter at this level is a high archetype. A typical high archetype which affects many men is the anima. Jung says:

> It is always the *a priori* element in his moods, reactions, impulses, and whatever else is spontaneous in psychic life. It is something that lives of itself, that makes us live; it is a life behind consciousness that cannot be completely integrated with it, but from which, on the contrary, consciousness arises.
>
> (Jung 1968: CW9, i, §57)

So these archetypes can be very deep and very important in our psychic life. They can also be very important in psychotherapy. As Jung puts it:

> It is as though, at the climax of the illness, the destructive powers were converted into healing forces. This is brought about by the archetypes awakening to independent life and taking over the guidance of the psychic personality, thus supplanting the ego with its futile willing and striving . . . the psyche has awakened to spontaneous activity . . . something that is not his ego and is therefore beyond the reach of his personal will. He has regained access to the sources of psychic life, and this marks the beginning of the cure.
>
> (Jung 1969: CW11, §534)

95

Another person who has spoken of high archetypes is Jean Shinoda Bolen. In her book on men she says:

> Based on the pantheon of Greek deities, this psychology reflects the richness of our human nature and hints at the divinity we experience when what we do comes out of our depths and we sense the sacred dimension to our lives.
>
> (Bolen 1989: 16)

Whether she does full justice to this or not, there is a clear statement here that in her view these high archetypes are directly related to the divine. But it is the divine seen as multiple, not the one deity we may be familiar with if we have been brought up as Christians, Jews or Muslims.

The visions we may have at this stage are not visions of unity but of multiplicity; even in the case of Christian mystics, they run to many angels:

> I saw in [the angel's] hand a long spear of gold, and at the iron's point seemed to be a little fire. He appeared to me to be thrusting it at times into my heart, and to pierce my very entrails; when he drew it out, he seemed to draw them out also and to leave me all on fire with a great love of God.
>
> (St Teresa of Avila, quoted in Underhill 1961: 292)

Many of her trances, raptures and ecstasies are full of symbolic representations of different aspects of the Divine, and other mystics, such as Hildegard of Bingen, go much further in this direction. Yet all this is limited by the fact that these people are basically wedded to monotheism, and therefore bound to downgrade and discount such experiences.

So we go to someone like Starhawk, a powerful writer on this stage and its rituals, who says:

> Power, the subtle force that shapes reality, is raised through chanting or dancing and may be directed through a symbol or visualization. With the raising of the cone of power comes ecstasy, which may then lead to a trance state in which visions are seen and insights gained.
>
> (Starhawk 1989: 28)

Here is someone with a real feeling for the Subtle. She goes on to expound even more the sense of the universe which lies behind this experience:

> The world of separate things is the reflection of the One, the One is the reflection of the myriad separate things of the world. We are all 'swirls' of the same energy, yet each swirl is unique in its own form and pattern. The Goddess falls in love with Herself, drawing forth her own emanation, which takes on a life of its own. Love of self for self is the creative force of the universe. Desire is the primal energy, and that energy is erotic: the attraction of lover to beloved, of planet to star, the lust of electron for proton.
>
> (Starhawk 1989: 39)

96

She speaks eloquently of the male and the female, and how they can relate together in a new way, which we shall also be meeting in a later chapter:

> Divine ecstasy becomes the fountain of creation, and creation is an orgasmic process. Ecstasy is at the heart of Witchcraft – in ritual, we turn paradox inside out and become the Goddess, sharing in the primal throbbing joy of union.
>
> (Starhawk 1989: 39)

She points out that witchcraft is a shamanistic religion, and the spiritual value placed on ecstasy is high. This makes the link to shamanism, which is one of the few expressions of the Subtle which ever gets into the pages of the *Journal of Transpersonal Psychology.*

Roger Walsh (1993) speaks well, if briefly, about the shamanic stage of consciousness, characterised by 'Organised, coherent imagery determined by shamanic cosmology and purpose of journey'. He says shamans go in for controlled ecstasy:

> For example, the shaman seeing power animals, the Christian contemplative envisioning angels, and the Hindu practitioner merging with her *Ishta deva* are all clearly having different experiences. Yet at a deep structural level they are all seeing archetypal spiritual figures . . . . the mental phenomena of these subtle stages may take specific forms such as the archetypal images previously described.
>
> (Walsh 1993: 127–128)

In the same journal, in an earlier essay, more is said about the actual details of shamanism. Of course many men have been involved in sweat lodges and other shamanistic practices. Larry Peters says:

> The house, tent, or yurt of tribal shamanic people is considered a replica of the cosmos (equivalence of micro- and macrocosm). Consequently, during rituals, the pillar at the centre becomes 'cosmicised' and 'world pillars' or 'pillars of the sky' connecting earth to sky and heavenly realms. The shaman traverses the centre pole (*'axis mundi'*) to the heavens and underworlds. The smoke hole at the top is known to some groups as 'window of the world' or 'orifice of the sky', and the shaman's soul passes through it on flights to the celestial regions (Eliade 1964).
>
> (Peters 1989: 121)

He makes the point that there are some very interesting connections to be drawn out between shamanism and practices in some established religions: we have already seen some connections being made between the archetypes of Jung and the Christian mysticism of St Teresa:

> Another parallel between shamanic practice and yoga is the so-called 'Deity Yoga' of Tibetan Buddhism. Here the yogin first visualises the

Buddha, then becomes one with him, embodying the values of compassion and wisdom. After merging, the yogin (like the shaman) moves and acts like the embodied deity (Hopkins 1974). Yogin and shaman both experience and possess the qualities of the transpersonal.

(Peters 1989: 122)

So shamanism again values and works with imagery and ecstasy, and uses ritual to do so. Which brings us on to Tantra. Quite a few men now have been involved in Tantric workshops or other events. Tantra too has this character, as is well explained by Philip Rawson:

Each individual, by performing Tantrik yoga, can discover that the central column of the radiating world is identical with his own subtle spine. Performing intense inner work, he may then discover that the world which appears projected around him can be withdrawn into a flower-like mandala at the base of his spine. His own inner Creative Goddess, who seems to him like a luminous snake, Kundalini, coiled asleep within that mandala around a lingam, can be awoken by yoga, and will rise up the central channel of his subtle column, passing through a series of inner mandala-transformations as it goes. These, called chakras, culminate in the Thousand-petalled Flower at the crown of the head, where male and female principles unite in bliss; the transcendent, the human and the cosmic become one.

(Rawson 1973: 116)

It is worth making the point that imagery is very powerful in all these traditions, and image-work, which Dina Glouberman (1989) has argued is a better term than visualisation, is used a great deal. As Coomaraswamy says:

To have lost the art of thinking in images is precisely to have lost the proper linguistic of metaphysics and to have descended to the verbal logic of 'philosophy'. . . . This is primarily due to our own abysmal ignorance of metaphysics and of its technical terms.

(Coomaraswamy, quoted in Campbell 1988: 73)

He is clearly talking here of transpersonal, rather than prepersonal, imagery. Images and symbols have this extraordinary ability to communicate, because they span some of the lowest and some of the highest levels of development. They can be less than words: they can go beyond words. And again, they can be invoked in rituals where a group participates.

Ken Wilber is in general much better at describing the Centaur and the Causal, but he lays down quite a good paragraph about the Subtle:

I will simply say that this realm is universally and consistently said to be the realm of high religious intuition and literal inspiration; of bijamantra; of symbolic visions; of blue, gold and white light; of audible illuminations and brightness upon brightness; it is the realm of higher presences, guides, angelic beings, ishtadevas, and dhyani-buddhas; all of which – as we will soon explain – are simply high archetypal forms of one's own being (although they initially and necessarily appear 'other').

(Wilber 1980: 68)

This leaves out the importance of ritual at this stage, but otherwise it seems a good summary statement.

It is an area where symbols are pursued for the insight and growth they may bring. Words become of lesser value, because we are now moving out of consensus reality. The mental ego is desperately worried about this, because it thinks of words as being the only things which are really safe. Much of the taken-for-granted aspects of the world are now radically questioned: in particular, the boundaries which divide us from the world in general and other people in particular do not seem so important. Because of the dangers of self-inflation at this stage, a supportive community becomes very important, so that one can keep an eye on one's pretensions to spiritual exaltation. On the other hand, many people draw back from this level because it seems so scary and so open to misuse. But we shall see that this level is not only very important for the average client, but also very important for the practitioner to explore.

THE CAUSAL LEVEL: THE SPIRIT

Column four in Table 7.1 is put in, not so much because it is of great relevance to psychotherapy, but because it indicates that column three is not the end of the road. Again it is possible to hold back, the familiar contraction ensuring that one will stay at an earlier level rather than advancing to this, the deep water of spirituality. Here at the level of the causal self, the level of spirit, we have to give up all the symbols which were so useful and got us so far at the previous level. This is the realm of religion proper, and all the advanced forms of mysticism. This, then, is a third initiation.

So here are the four columns which show how the therapist has to develop himself or herself if the intention is really to be able to handle the whole person who is there in the consulting room. The therapist who does not develop, who gives in to the contraction which prevents progress along the scale, will be unable to help the client move to the next level. Thus the therapist can be a block in the way, rather than a facilitator, helper or guide.

What this chapter is saying is that each column describes and represents a very different position. The idea of the self is different, the aims are different, the values are different. This represents a limitation to the possible integration of psychotherapy.

PSYCHOTHERAPY INTEGRATION: THE DUCK-BILLED PLATYPUS AND THE SPHINX

Now what is the relevance of all this for what is possible and what is impossible in psychotherapy integration? The four columns in Table 7.1 summarise briefly much of what has just been outlined, and what I would like to say is that integration *within* a given column is always possible, though there may be all sorts of historical and other reasons for making it difficult. Integration *between* columns, however, is impossible, because the actual notion of the self is different in each case.

This may sound like rather a dogmatic statement, but it follows strictly from the arguments given up to this point. It would be helpful at this point if we could look at the psychotherapy research literature to see what it has to say about this problem. But a careful reading of texts such as Dryden and Norcross (1990), which is a compendium of all the research arguments about integration and eclecticism, shows that there is no research which directly bears on this question.

What this book does give, however, is a list of which combinations of therapies are most popular. The study of Norcross and Prochaska (1983) showed that cognitive and behavioural approaches were the most favoured team mates. This fits with column one. So does the third favourite, which is psychoanalytic and cognitive; there is a practical difficulty here about the unconscious, but it seems that this can be overcome. This again fits with Table 7.1. But what about the second favourite, which is humanistic and cognitive? According to the argument above, this would be impossible.

What I would suggest here is that when the attempt is made to integrate the humanistic and the cognitive, one of two things will happen. Either the cognitive will be transformed into a mere adjunct to the humanistic, or the humanistic will be transformed into a mere adjunct to the cognitive. In other words one will be assimilated into the other, rather than staying with the assumptions of its own heartland in one column or the other. For example, take the Erskine and Moursund (1988) book. In it they put together the theory of transactional analysis with the techniques of Gestalt therapy. But in doing so they force TA to remain within column one, and the same with Gestalt. None of the outcomes in the case histories so fully given in the book is a discovery of the real self. The outcomes are all triumphs of adjustment, whereby the person is rendered able to take up customary roles with greater success. There is no ecstasy in this book.

I think it is possible for TA to be used in a humanistic way (P. Clarkson 1993), but this is not what Erskine and Moursund actually did. Nor does it seem to me that the work of Iris Fodor (1987) is any better in this respect.

Some of the implications of what I am saying are quite surprising. For example, I am saying that it should be possible to combine classical psychoanalysis and behaviour therapy, the Kleinian and the cognitive, because they are both in column one. This means, of course, that the development of cognitive analytical therapy was to be expected, and has now arrived on the bookstalls. And the Brussels programme of an integrative model in psychotherapy training (Roose 1991) also fits well with this analysis, combining as it does the psychodynamic, the behavioural and the systemic approaches.

Now there is a difficulty which appears here which may seem insurmountable: that is, that paying attention to the unconscious is different from, and may sometimes be incompatible with, paying attention to conscious wishes and choices. This is true, but once we understand that there is more than one way into the unconscious, it is essentially a practical difficulty rather than a theoretical problem, and I am sure it will be overcome in the next few years.

It is very revealing that both psychoanalysis and cognitive-behaviour therapy relate very well to the National Health Service and to medicine generally. This is because they share with medicine the basic model of restoring people to health, by one means or another.

On the other hand, it also explains why people in column two find it so difficult to relate to medicine, unless it is complementary or holistic medicine. They do not hold to the basic medical model, and indeed criticise it regularly. I myself have been known to say things like 'Anyone who wants to cure a client is deeply into countertransference!' (Rowan 1994).

It also explains why psychoanalysts of the classical school in column one often say that everything that happens in therapy is transference or counter-transference, while psychoanalysts of a more liberal kind in column two want to make clear distinctions between different relationships which are going on in therapy, of which transference and countertransference are only two. For example, it is crucial for people in column two to have a notion of authenticity, and if everything is transference or countertransference, there is no room for authenticity.

It is of course always possible to alternate methods, but that is not the same thing at all. Some of the attempts at integration which have been made, as for example Anne Douglas (1989) and Fonagy (1989), seem to me to fall into this trap, and to believe that they are integrating when they are only alternating. By alternating I mean that the same therapist uses one approach with one client, and another with another, or with the first on another occasion.

It may also be possible to devise some very subtle forms of integration, where the attempt is made to see different approaches as complementary rather than unified, or where bridges are built between disparate schools of psychotherapy. There is a very full discussion of all these matters in the magisterial book by Mahrer (1989a) on this topic. Of course I am not saying that there are not all sorts of interesting questions as to how, when and why a therapist would want to move from one column into another. All I am trying to say is that there are certain approaches which cannot be melded, moulded or fused into one, and that there are others which can.

To sum up, then, what I have been saying is that if two forms of therapy in a single column want to come together, they may construct something which may look as unlikely as a duck-billed platypus, but which may well be viable and productive. From such a union a new school of integrative psychotherapy may spring up. But if two forms of therapy in two different columns try to come together, the result will be more like a sphinx, with parts which never quite fit, and do not lead to any successful school or training. The only apparent exception to this would be a training which assimilated something in one column to something in another, changing its nature in the process.

Some objections have been made to this view by Michael Wilson (1994). He says that someone working at the highest level can operate eclectically at any other level.

> My conviction is that there is no 'falsification' of systems or approaches but an inclusion, or grafting on, of techniques to facilitate further growth. Theoretical frameworks are not written in tablets of stone. And eclecticism is the incorporation from different systems (regardless of columns) of what might be of use in the counselling relationship.
>
> (Wilson 1994: 25)

I agree with him. My case is precisely that because each level is nested inside the next, it is easy for someone to move back to any level which has been fully explored at an earlier stage. But I think Wilson underestimates the way in which we usually feel we have to give up, to abandon, our previous adjustment in order to go on to the next stage. This happens each time we move to a new level. It is only later, with a mature appreciation of the stage we are now in, that we can recognise that the previous stage was not actually abandoned, only superseded and contained.

All I am contending for is that the therapist should not get confused, but should be able to help the client at whatever level the client may be working at the moment. My own experience is that it is very useful for a therapist to know where a client is in the process of psychospiritual growth, so that he or she can be encouraged to move on to the next step. But if the therapist loses the sense of where the client is, he or she may do something which the client finds quite mysterious or offputting.

Wilson's second point is that too many things are mixed up together in my column four, so that it looks as if I am lumping together types of pure spirituality which are really rather different from each other, such as Christianity and Taoism. Again I think that Wilson is right. I have lumped several unlike things in column four. The reason for this is that I wanted mainly to talk about columns one, two and three, which I believe are the main ones which therapists actually use: mostly column one, in fact, column two to a lesser extent, and column three only occasionally. I do not think many counsellors use column four much in their actual work, though they may find such a spiritual discipline very useful for their own development. If we wanted to talk more about column four as such, as I believe Wilson is trying to do, we should have to distinguish, as Ken Wilber (1980) does, between the Lower Causal, the Higher Causal and the Nondual. But for that the headings I have used would be more or less irrelevant. So a different approach would have to be used, and a different chapter written, which would be very interesting to those embarked upon a spiritual quest, but not so interesting to the everyday therapist I am trying to address.

All in all, then, there is much to agree with in what Michael Wilson has said, and in fact I find his views quite compatible with my own. It seems to me that we have here more a difference of emphasis than a real difference of opinion.

IMPLICATIONS

Now because of the phenomenon of nesting which I mentioned earlier, the movement from right to left is always easy. For example, if a good deal of our work is in column two, there is no difficulty in suggesting small pieces of work which belong to column one. This is because everyone who has a centaur self has a mental-ego self as well, nested within it, so to speak.

But a therapist has to have entered column two before being able to help a client to enter column two. The client may not be able to enter column two unless and until sufficient work has been done in column one. You cannot start a serious process of questioning all your roles if you are still busy becoming adequate as a role-player. Demaris Wehr (1988) has suggested that women may need more work in column one than men, because a male-oriented society has wounded them so badly in the area of personal agency and empowerment.

A lot of the work in column two is the dissolution of structures which have become too rigid. There is disintegration to be done before any new integration can take place. This is why the process is so confusing at the best of times.

But a lot of the work in column one is just the opposite. It is about building up the ego to be more capable, more mature, more able of handling the everyday shocks of ordinary existence. If column two is often about providing solvent, column one is often about providing glue. This is why I am doubtful about putting together Kohut and Rogers in the way that Tobin (1991) and others have suggested. It seems to me that Kohut is mostly about glue, and Rogers is mostly about solvent. And of course a good therapist has to know when to use the solvent and when to use the glue. The implication of this is that therapists, in their own training, need to have moved at least into column two before doing much work there, and preferably need to have moved into column three as well, if they are not going to be thrown by some spiritual emergency.

There is now a considerable literature about spiritual emergence, and the spiritual emergencies which may result from moving too suddenly from column two into column three (Bragdon 1990, S. Grof and C. Grof 1989, C. Grof and S. Grof 1990). It is possible, through therapy or through meditation or various other studies, to have an experience belonging to column three which can be disconcerting both to the person having the experience and those around at the time. Is what is happening a breakdown or a breakthrough? This is a very important question, because if it is answered wrongly the person can suffer much more than is necessary.

For example, David Lukoff has described the case of a man whom he calls 'Howard C. Everest', who suffered from manic-depression, but including genuine mystical features. An episode of psychosis is treated as initiation and rebirth. At one point Howard was admitted to a mental hospital, which failed to understand what he was going through. But he left after a time and gave up his psychiatric medication, and led quite a successful life.

> In another era, in another place, perhaps the myth-making capacities which were awakened in Howard during his psychotic episode would have led to his being selected by his elders for training as a shaman. At the very least, Howard has provided us with a modern Hero's Journey myth.
>
> (Lukoff and Everest 1985: 151)

Here Lukoff was operating from a column-three understanding and appreciation of what was going on.

Again, someone who is capable of working in column three is automatically capable of working in column two or column one, due to the nesting which was mentioned before. But if we never work at the level of column three, we may be denying an important part of the client who comes to us. This happens in many forms of therapy, for example in the work of Erskine and Moursound already mentioned, where there is no recognition at all of the need to integrate this kind of material. People like this, who work all the time in column one, may not recognise the existence of column three at all, and may even denounce it as nonsense, as has Albert Ellis (Ellis and Yeager 1990) in a book which seems to me quite undiscriminating in its blanket denunciation of all that is not in column one.

Here it may be that we have the same phenomenon which Kohlberg (1984) noticed in his studies of moral development. He found that in terms of his six levels of development, someone mainly located at one level could often appreciate and even admire the next level above, but could not understand at all the level two above, and was forced to misperceive it and misdescribe it. Something like this may have happened with Albert Ellis.

I do not want to talk about column four, because it has little to do with psychotherapy. It may of course be very useful to have some experience of column four, just to get some distance and some perspective, and not to get caught up in the assumptions of any of the previous levels, as if they were the whole truth. I just wanted to make it clear that column three was not the end of the road. It is not even particularly important or desirable, and certainly not better than any of the other columns. I have said more about this elsewhere (Rowan 1993a). Most of the work in psychotherapy is done, and will always be done, at the level of column one. Certainly this is true of brief therapy and crisis work, and as we know, short-term therapy is becoming more popular rather than less.

All I am contending for is that we be clear about what we are doing, and do not confuse ourselves or our clients. It is now time to look at the process of therapy in detail, step by step, to see at each point how the alchemical analysis helps us.

8

WHAT HAPPENS IN THERAPY?

In outlining the process of dealing with men in psychotherapy or counselling, I find it useful to follow the framework given by Jocelyn Chaplin (1988). This suggests that there are seven typical phases of a therapeutic cycle. She makes it clear that not all clients move through all seven phases with one therapist on one occasion:

> It may take them many years to go through the cycle, or it may take just a few weeks. They may use several different counsellors, workshops or 'spiritual' guides during their growth cycle. And most people seem to go through many cycles during their lifetime.
>
> (Chaplin 1988: 1)

However, I have found that another valid framework for therapy is offered by the work of the medieval alchemists, which we have already met briefly in the Introduction. Alchemy has of course been studied, in relation to psychotherapy, particularly by Jung and his colleagues. Jung's basic statement about it is:

> The process is in both cases an irrigation of the conscious mind by the unconscious, and it is related so closely to the world of alchemical ideas that we are probably justified in assuming that alchemy deals with the same, or very similar, processes as those involved in active imagination and in dreams, i.e., ultimately with the process of individuation.
>
> (Jung 1968: 346)

Jung was very interested in the idea of opposites, as too is Chaplin, seeing opposition as one of the driving forces in the process. One or two others have also tried to make sense of alchemy as a sequence of operations in relation to the sequences which may happen in therapy, and I have felt free to plunder what I found useful from all of them. As I worked with the material, it seemed to take on a life of its own. I found myself taking a sentence here, an idea there, to form something new which seemed to want to come into being. So important did it come to seem to me that I have ordered this whole book in the same way.

There are, as anyone who has come into contact with the alchemical writings will know, a number of different versions of the alchemical process, which affect

105

the order in which the various operations are applied, and even their names and how many of them there may be. Edward Edinger, who has been into all this more thoroughly than most, has this to say about alchemy:

> The sequence of operations (with one or two exceptions) does not seem to be psychologically significant. Any operation may be the initiating one, and the others may follow in any order.
>
> (Edinger 1985: 17)

I have made my own choice, without I hope being unduly arbitrary, in line with the experience of psychotherapy, both for me and for my clients. There are now eleven phases or stages. The reason why this fits well with the Chaplin work is that, as Chaplin herself says, some of her phases can be repeated on a different level later in the therapy. With this understood, let us embark on our journey. The eleven phases are:

1 Getting started and building trust (*Materia Prima* and *Nigredo*)
2 Identifying themes: separating out the opposites (*Fermentatio*)
3 Exploring the past: understanding the opposites and inner hierarchies (*Separatio*)
4 Dissolving the inner hierarchies and facing ambivalence: accepting the opposites (*Calcinatio*)
5 Making changes: living with the opposites (*Albedo*)
6 Connectedness: expressing the opposites (*Conjunctio*)
7 Endings and new beginnings (*Mortificatio* and second *Nigredo*)
8 Deeper explorations: rites of passage (*Solutio* and third *Nigredo*)
9 Struggles: deeper oppositions (*Coagulatio*)
10 Breakthrough (*Sublimatio*)
11 Integration (*Rubedo*)

GETTING STARTED AND BUILDING TRUST

Materia Prima and *Nigredo*

We start with the *Materia Prima*. This is what needs to be worked on, and is the most important and mysterious substance of all. We have to have enormous respect for the *Materia Prima* if we are to do any good with it. In alchemy it is the 'black lead' – the most despised material of all. It is also 'under your nose' – something which was always there, but rejected. It is often associated with images of flooding: a natural crisis which requires responsive action, as we saw earlier. In therapy this is the basic character of the person, as seen through that person's eyes, what Feinstein and Krippner (1988) call 'the old myth'. The old myth tells us why we are as we are. It is the basic story we tell to a new therapist. Eric Berne calls it the 'script'; it is what we go by in the most important aspects of our lives (P. Clarkson 1992). It is the story we tell ourselves about the way things are with us, and with the world. All these things are compulsive – they are fixed ways of seeing the world which are held on to defensively.

The *Materia Prima* seems to represent our natural unreflective state of being. But the image of flooding returns: there is probably some kind of crisis which takes the client into therapy. Whenever we are beset by affects, compulsions, irrational eruptions of any kind, there is the *Materia Prima*. As Edinger (1978) once suggested, it is the set of symptoms which drives the client into therapy. As Liz Greene (1988) put it, it is the life wound, the life conflict. Fabricius (1994) believes that 'psychologically the event means the eruption of the unconscious into the sphere of consciousness'.

Both to the client and to the therapist, this phase may involve frustration, bewilderment and disintegration. This chaos may precede any understanding. It is the therapist's skill to contain this chaos without denying it.

What we then have to do is to join with it in the alchemical process, so to begin with there is a *Conjunctio* (a joining, connection or close meeting), and the first form this takes is a joining of all these materials – that is, the basic character of the person, the natural unreflective state of being, the current affects, compulsions and irrational eruptions, the symptoms being presented, the eruption of the unconscious and the whole life wound. This can be done because attraction, love and hope are also present.

The idea of the *Conjunctio* is deeply mysterious, and it comes back again in many different forms throughout the process, as we meet with other forms of joining and connecting. It is both the beginning and the end of the process.

The second form it takes is the meeting of the therapist with the client. At the beginning it takes a motherly, womblike form (Chaplin's first phase). The actual process takes place within the vas (the alchemical vessel, like a chemical retort), and it is important that this vessel (the vas) be closed tight. The therapist is responsible for this containment, for this motherly boundary-holding and protection. The therapist will observe confidentiality about the client, and the client is asked not to talk about the therapy with anyone else, particularly if they are involved. (This may not be universal, but it is true of the kind of therapy which I practise and advocate in supervision.) However, many of the alchemical accounts speak of a permeable membrane which closes the vessel, and expands and contracts. In therapy, this would allow for discussion of the case in supervision, for example.

The first thing that happens in therapy is the formation of a working relationship. Unless this can be done, nothing further is possible. So of course there has to be a process of acceptance or rejection for any potentially new client. If we feel that a would-be client is not suitable for us as therapists, we should not accept them. But a particular problem arises in connection with men, which creates a negative block, which we call the *Nigredo*. This is well described by Aaron Kipnis:

Initiation into therapy is humiliating for many men. When women approach therapy, they're acting congruently with their gender identity. Women are supposed to be in touch with their feelings and seek help. . . . Men, however, often consider psychotherapy as dissonant with their traditional gender identity of being competent in the world.

(Kipnis 1991: 267)

This means that one of the issues which may arise in this early stage is male competitiveness. This comes so naturally through socialisation, as we saw earlier, that it is likely to arise in therapy too. When the client is looking for faults and weaknesses in the therapist, it is important to pick up this theme early on, as otherwise it can get in the way of the therapy itself. One way of defusing it is to admit to any mistakes which have been made and which are obvious to the client.

It is therefore doubly important to establish good rapport with the client if he is a man. This has been called the mothering phase of therapy, because it is to do with acceptance and receptiveness. There is one technique which is very useful in setting up the right kind of relationship here, and that is mirroring the client. This means copying the client's body posture, way of talking, rate of breathing, gestures, and so forth. If this is done too obviously the client may feel offended, as if there were some kind of aping or mockery going on. So it has to be done tactfully and not too obviously. If it is done well, two things happen: one is that the client feels more relaxed, as if he is in good hands; the other is that the therapist begins to pick up the client's *weight* – that is, the way the client's body feels, from the inside. This body feeling is valuable in picking up the subliminal messages which the client is giving off.

There is a film of Ronnie Laing meeting a client for the first time, and in it we can see him sitting in just the same posture as that of the client. I asked him if this was accidental or deliberate, and he replied that it was quite deliberate and intentional. So this is something which many therapists have discovered for themselves. In this way we make it possible to meet the first problem we often encounter in dealing with men:

Some men want to get right down to business and be done with therapy as soon as possible. . . . The therapy tends to be problem-oriented, and the man wants to end the therapy as soon as the crisis abates.

(Kupers 1993: 110)

That is why it is important with men to make a contract at the beginning, so that both parties know where they stand. I myself hand out a written text at the end of the first interview, laying out my terms and conditions, and this seems to be a growing trend. It does seem to help, in any case of dispute (about fees for broken appointments, for example), to have something in black and white to refer back to. So there are other advantages, too.

There is a general rule-of-thumb, which can be mentioned to clients, that the longer the problem has been in existence, the longer it will take to deal with. Most clients can see that a recent bereavement is likely to take a shorter time to handle than a deep depression which goes back into childhood. It may happen, of course, that a short-term problem ties back into much deeper problems, so that the person is triggered into replaying old memories which intensify the current difficulty. In psychoanalysis this is called transference, in co-counselling it is called restimulation, in Gestalt therapy it is called unfinished business, in social psychology it is called reintegration, and it is a well-established source of extra stress and strain. It can not only affect the presenting problem itself, but also affect the relationship with the therapist. If a man competes with the therapist just like he competed with his father, or tries to seduce the therapist just like he tried to seduce his mother, this can bring up very valuable material; it can also be hard to cope with.

But it is important, in this early phase with a man, not to give in too much to the desire for instant results. As we saw in the case history in Chapter 3, this can be a continual grumble as much as a real request. It stems from the way in which men tend to treat themselves, as well as other people, as things, as objects, as machines. But men are not things, they are people with a rich psychology. They are much more complex than they think. It has been said that the human mind is infinite, and I believe this is true. To the extent that we pretend that we are machines with limited capacity, this becomes true for us to that extent. Of course we are limited in all sorts of ways, but much of the limitation is self-set and self-maintained. And it is in therapy that we can discover where our limits really lie.

So in this first phase of the therapy we are in the *Nigredo* – the blackening. This is a phase where uncertainty reigns, and where things may get worse before they get better. This is the real engagement with the therapy, which may, as Samuels (1989) suggests, involve an important dream which signals change, or the onset of depression that often precedes change. Or it can represent the end of the honeymoon period of the relationship. It is the point at which there is an uncertainty about engagement: has the process really started or not? There is a chaotic feel about this, as if nothing were settled or certain. Everything is dark or black. Different forms of the *Nigredo* may return at later times when the process seems to go into a state of uncertainty again. Again it is a rich and mysterious category, which must not be reduced to any one of its particular forms. One form of the *Putrefactio* comes in here, the breakdown of the material. The *Putrefactio* in alchemy is the breaking down of material, and it becomes quite disgusting in many of the accounts. Yet it is healthy in the end – a necessary part of the process as a whole.

In the first stage, the crucible must be heated very slowly. If too much heat is applied too soon, the glass may crack and the material be lost. So gentle heat is applied, and then the material does not sweat or bubble, but gradually comes to a temperature at which it becomes malleable and workable. In terms of psychotherapy, this is the stage of gaining rapport, and the client gradually gaining confidence in the situation and being able to identify the problematic themes which are emerging.

One area where this is particularly likely to come up is over the expression of emotion. Usually in the early stages, the client is trying to control emotions, and the therapist is trying to encourage the client to express emotions. This can turn into quite a battle if the therapist is unaware of what is happening. Men have been socialised to believe that showing feelings is weakness and leads to being taken advantage of, and losing something. In some cases men do not have a vocabulary for emotions at all, and cannot identify or express them in part because of this. In such cases it may be a good idea to show them a list of emotions and to ask them which one they are experiencing at the moment. Here is a typical list, taken from Beth Erickson:

HAPPY

Excited Elated Exuberant Ecstatic Terrific Jubilant Energized
Enthusiastic Loved Thrilled Marvellous Justified Resolved
Valued Gratified Encouraged Optimistic Joyful Proud Cheerful
Assured Determined Grateful Appreciated Confident Respected
Admired Delighted Alive Fulfilled Tranquil Content Relaxed
Glad Satisfied Peaceful Hopeful Fortunate Pleased Flattered

SAD

Devastated Hopeless Sorrowful Depressed Wounded Drained
Defeated Exhausted Helpless Crushed Worthless Uncared for
Dejected Rejected Humbled Empty Miserable Distraught
Deserted Grievous Demoralized Condemned Terrible Unwanted
Unloved Mournful Pitiful Discarded Disgraced Disheartened
Despised Upset Inadequate Dismal Unappreciated Discouraged
Ashamed Distressed Distant Disillusioned Lonely Neglected
Isolated Alienated Regretful Islanded Resigned Slighted
Degraded Deprived Disturbed Wasted Abandoned Lost
Disenchanted Deflated Apathetic

ANGRY

Strangled Furious Seething Enraged Hostile Vengeful Incensed
Abused Hateful Humiliated Sabotaged Betrayed Repulsed
Rebellious Pissed off Outraged Exploited Throttled Mad
Spiteful Patronized Vindictive Used Repulsed Ridiculed
Resentful Disgusted Smothered Frustrated Stifled Offended
Displeased Controlled Peeved Annoyed Agitated Irritated
Exasperated Harassed Anguished Deceived Aggravated Perturbed
Provoked Dominated Coerced Cheated Uptight Dismayed
Tolerant Displeased

SCARED

Fearful Panicky Afraid Shocked Overwhelmed Desperate
Frantic Terrified Vulnerable Horrified Petrified Appalled
Full of dread Tormented Tense Uneasy Defensive Insecure
Sceptical Apprehensive Suspicious Alarmed Shaken Swamped

Startled Guarded Stunned Awed Reluctant Anxious Impatient
Shy Nervous Unsure Timid Concerned Perplexed Doubtful

CONFUSED

Bewildered Trapped Immobilized Directionless Stagnant
Flustered Baffled Constricted Troubled Ambivalent Awkward
Puzzled Disorganized Foggy Hesitant Misunderstood Doubtful
Bothered Undecided Uncomfortable Uncertain Surprised
Unsettled Unloved Unsure Distracted Perplexed

(B.M. Erickson 1993: 454–455)

It is not suggested that this list is a solution to the problem of male unacquaintance with feeling words, because most of it is willed and motivated – merely that it can come in useful when some of these other obstacles have been surmounted, and there is still a problem of vocabulary.

But this early phase of the work is not a time to indulge in too many *beginning* techniques of any kind. It is a time for the client to feel that he is being contained and held. One of the things which can help very much in this is the set of boundaries which are set up. A regular place, time and fee give a structure and a sense of stability which is very reassuring to the client. Conversely, any failure of the therapist to keep these simple boundaries will be picked up by the client as breaches of trust and sources of insecurity.

IDENTIFYING THEMES: SEPARATING OUT THE OPPOSITES

Fermentatio

The first stage is all about containment of the original conflicts which may arise between client and therapist, so that they can give way to examination of the issues. But now we have to get down to the issues themselves.

Now the therapy gets more complex, and *Fermentatio* is an apt term, as Samuels (1989) has suggested, for the mingling of personalities that takes place in the transference and countertransference, in the therapy relationship generally, and within the unconscious of both therapist and client. Again there is a *Conjunctio* involved here. This third *Conjunctio* represents the meeting of the client's conscious and unconscious minds. This is the stage where dreams are being produced, or memories are coming back. Trust is still building. One key point here is that the client starts to show signs of carrying on the process between sessions. We get remarks like 'I thought more about what we said last week', or 'I suddenly woke up knowing the answer to that question'. The therapeutic process has 'taken', so to speak, and we are sure that something has started to happen. Andrew Samuels calls this stage a brewing, a mingling of elements that will produce a new substance. All the elements of it will return within the later stage of the *Citrinitas*.

This is the part of the therapy where techniques and different approaches become important. Different forms and schools of therapy will proceed in different ways, though I believe they all have two things in common:

- They have some way of bringing relevant material into the present.
- They all have some way of moving the therapy forward.

But rather than try to describe all these different modes of action, I want to argue that there are basically three legs on which all psychotherapy stands: the regressive, the existential and the transpersonal. If we ignore any one of these, we do so at our peril.

By *regressive* I mean the whole business of delving back into the past, and into the personal unconscious, to find out what went wrong there, and how it can be put right. Certain approaches specialise in this, as for example classical psychoanalysis, Kleinian analysis, the body therapies such as bioenergetics and postural integration, and directly regressive approaches such as primal integration and Primal Therapy. It seems to me that no therapy can really ignore this area. Even approaches which appear at first to ignore it do actually have to cover it, as we can see from any reasonably extended case history (e.g. Dryden 1987, Kutash and Wolf 1986).

Laing (1983) makes the point that we must also talk about recession, by which he means a move from the outer to the inner world. Going back is no use unless at the same time we are going deeper into our own experience. Regression without recession is of little use or interest.

This represents what Petruska Clarkson (1993) calls the reparative or developmentally needed relationship in psychotherapy. It often involves attention being paid to what she calls the transference and countertransference relationship, but this is a matter of degree. A psychoanalytically trained therapist would use it as a major technique, while a humanistic therapist would merely pay attention to it and deal with it as necessary. A cognitive-behavioural approach might not recognise it at all, and indeed might try to avoid any regression.

By *existential* I mean any approach which emphasises the here-and-now at the expense of the past and the future, although of course all approaches have to deal perforce with past, present and future-oriented material. Also of course virtually all therapies work their most effective magic by bringing the past into the present in some way. But I am speaking here mainly of an approach which says that the most important thing to pay attention to is whatever is going on right now, either inside the client or between the present participants. Approaches which specialise in this aspect include group analysis, personal construct therapy, cognitive-behavioural therapy, NLP (neurolinguistic programming), existential analysis, person-centred therapy and Gestalt therapy. Again all therapists do very often enter this area in one way or another. A particularly strong argument for paying attention only to this aspect of therapy is given by Spinelli (1994) in his version of the phenomenological-existential approach.

This represents what Clarkson (1993) calls the working alliance, and also includes what she calls the I–You relationship. It is of just as much interest to a cognitive-behavioural therapist as to anyone else.

By *transpersonal* I mean the way in which some approaches emphasise the spiritual centre in people: the direction of the person, the higher potentials of the person, the deeper perspective given by a sense of the divine. There are several levels within it, but for the purposes of psychotherapy, in the terms which Assagioli (Ferrucci 1982) introduced many years ago, it has to do with the higher unconscious as distinct from the lower unconscious. As well as a depth psychology, he urged, we also need a height psychology. These approaches emphasise the intuition and creativity of both therapist and client, and the way in which the boundary separating therapist from client can sometimes disappear, with advantage. Such approaches include Jungian analysis (Zurich and archetypal versions), psychosynthesis and transpersonal psychotherapy. Since 1980 there has been some very good work published in this area (e.g. Vaughan 1985, Wilber *et al.* 1986, Grof 1988). Some forms of psychotherapy contrive to ignore this area, but at their peril.

This represents what Clarkson (1993) calls the transpersonal relationship. It can be seen that there is substantial agreement with the Clarkson approach, which is also intended to be integrative.

A truly integrative approach, in my opinion, would deal with all three of these areas, and in this way be able to cope with the whole person who comes into the consulting room or the group space. But even an approach which stands only on one leg can still do a good job. Let us look at each of them in turn.

Regression

Obviously the main technique is taking the person back to the trauma on which the neurosis is based. Laing (1983) has argued that we should also talk about recession – the move from the outer to the inner world. Mahrer (1986) makes a similar point. Going back is no use unless at the same time we are going deeper in to our own experience. In practice, it seems that recession and regression go very well together. One of the clearest statements of the case for doing this comes from Grof (1979) when he talks about the COEX system. A COEX is a syndrome of experiences which hang together emotionally for a particular person. It is a pattern of feelings, meanings and other mental and physical experiences which keeps on reappearing in the person's life.

This gives us one clear way of working with a client. I might take an experience in the present and say something like:

Get in touch with that whole experience. What does it feel like? How does it affect your body and your breathing? What are the thoughts and meanings tied up with it? [Pause] Now see if you can allow a memory to come up of another time when you had that same sort of experience. Don't search for it, just focus on the feelings and let them float you back down your time track to an earlier time when you had those same feelings.

When a memory comes up, I encourage the person to go into it and concretise it as much as possible – relive it in some detail, getting right inside it, express whatever needs to be expressed there, deal with any unfinished business from that time. Then we go back further, in the same way, and do the same thing with an earlier memory. Then again, and again, as often as necessary. In this way we descend, as it were, the rungs of the COEX ladder which leads us into deeper and deeper feelings, further down on the affect tree.

As we do this, we can go into the experience with the client, much in the way which Mahrer (1986) calls 'carrying forward experience' – that is, entering into the experience and co-feeling it with the client. In this way we can say things which make the experience fuller and richer for the client, and which take the client closer to the heart of that experience.

Often it also helps if the client breathes more deeply and more quickly than usual. There is a very good discussion of the whole question of hyperventilation in Albery (1985), where he examines the medical evidence in some detail. It does seem to all of us who work in this area that deep breathing is very helpful in allowing access to deep emotional layers, going deeper both in regression and recession.

Now it is obvious that a procedure like this takes time, and it is really best to go all the way with a particular COEX in one session, rather than trying to take up the tail of one session at the head of the next, which usually does not work. This means that the therapist who uses regression tends to prefer long sessions, which also enable the client to take a break or breather if need be during the session. I personally conduct some one-hour sessions, but I also have some one-and-a-half-hour, two-hour and three-hour sessions; some people working in this area have used up to ten-hour sessions.

In this process people open themselves up to deeper feelings, and thus become more vulnerable, so a high degree of trust has to be built up between client and therapist. But trust is not a feeling, it is a decision. Nobody can ever prove, in any decisive way, that they are worthy of trust, so the client just has to take the decision at some time, and it may as well be sooner as later.

Existential

We are not here talking about existentialism as a philosophy, though that is quite relevant, as is phenomenology, which is not a million miles away from it. We are talking about any approach which lays a great deal of stress on interaction in the here and now. Of these, the person-centred approach of Carl Rogers, psychodrama and Gestalt are quite prominent in the humanistic camp. A useful approach is simply to get the client to talk to a person, rather than talking about them. For example:

114

CLIENT: My father never paid any attention to me. He always –
THERAPIST: Try putting your father on this cushion and talking to him.
CLIENT: That's ridiculous. He's dead.
THERAPIST: He may be dead out there, but the father inside is still just as much alive as ever. Just imagine him sitting there on the cushion, and say whatever comes. It may be telling him something, asking him a question, making some demand on him, anything at all.
CLIENT: That won't do any good: he never listened anyway. He always ignored me by –
THERAPIST: That's the point: he won't listen to you. Just see him sitting there and tell him that.
CLIENT: Daddy, daddy, please pay attention to me. Please put down the newspaper and talk to me. Daddy, please look at me.

Doing it this way triggers far more feelings than talking *about* the father or hearing interpretations *about* the therapist being the father. And because the therapist is outside the action and facilitating it, it can be pushed further and further into deep unconscious material. Humanistic therapists, like psychoanalysts, are very interested in working with the fantasies and primary process thinking of the unconscious, but prefer to work directly with them rather than refracting them through the transference. The theory of this is laid out in Grof (1985) and Mahrer (1986).

> To support the emerging feelings and to work through the defences I encourage the person to repeat the key words and phrases which contain the feeling.
>
> (Freundlich 1974: 5)

This repetition of key phrases is a favourite move in most cathartic forms of therapy, for example psychodrama, co-counselling and Gestalt therapy, and as Mahrer (1986) points out, it is one way of amplifying bodily sensations. The repetition of the key words in a louder voice helps to intensify the feeling as the defence recedes. The person's throat opens up, the voice comes out more clearly, and the person is able to say the words which need to be uttered. The hurt and need are finally felt and experienced. The person is then freer to make current needs known.

Bill Swartley suggested the principle of opposites: if something doesn't work, try the exact opposite. When a person won't express the feeling, perhaps it is more possible to express the defence against it. Many times, when people have said that they seem to have a block against doing something, I have asked them to draw a picture of the block, or put the block on a cushion and talk to it, or to speak for the block. This often results in a strong and effective piece of work, where the block is perhaps a parental voice, or some other important subpersonality or deeper potential.

In my own work, I have found the notion of subpersonalities extremely useful.

Very often a person's defences have got into such a convoluted tangle that they are very hard to sort out by following any one single line. But by eliciting the subpersonalities we can then see exactly how the internal games are constructed and played out (Rowan 1990). It is also possible for clients to understand the notion of subpersonalities very well, and there is now a book which can be recommended to them (Rowan 1993b).

Transpersonal

Material in this area tends to emerge in the form of images and symbols, rather than in the form of straightforward memories or factual narratives. It can come out in guided fantasies, in drawing or painting, or in dreams. I like working with dreams, as they can always be interpreted, understood or simply appreciated on so many different levels (Wilber *et al.* 1986). If we want to do justice to the whole person, we have to be prepared to deal with the superconscious as well as the lower unconscious. This seems to me part of the general listening process (Rowan 1992a) which is basic to all forms of therapy and counselling.

It is impossible to handle this area well, of course, unless one has experienced it oneself. It is an unfortunate fact that most of those therapists now practising did not have this taught as part of their training, and did not have it recognised, appreciated or encouraged during their own therapy. However, it does seem as though many therapists, on their own path and in their own way, have made independent discoveries in this area. For their benefit I have tried to put together a good deal of the relevant material in my book (Rowan 1993a) on the transpersonal.

The essence of it is to assume that the person has a spiritual nature as well as a body, and feelings, and an intellect. It is to be aware that as well as it being possible to fall short of the ego and the personal, it is also possible to go beyond the ego and the personal, as we saw in Chapter 7.

Integration

As stated earlier, it is possible to work with regression on its own, or with the existential on its own, or with the transpersonal on its own, but I believe the best work is done when therapy can rest on all three legs in a stable way.

A pioneering piece of research (Marina 1982) has brought out a number of interesting points about the change process in one form of integrative therapy. What we are essentially talking about, it suggests, is a very fundamental cognitive-affective restructuring or personality change.

This can happen because the personality is a system such that each part depends on each other part. A change in one part of the system affects the whole of the rest of the system.

For example, one woman in the research study had four main issues which all reinforced one another: *Feeling suicidal*; *Feeling worthless*; *Being jealous and full of rage*; and *Feeling like an intruder*. During therapy, a new element came in on the scene: *Feeling myself more loving*. This started to affect the whole balance of the other elements. After a time, *Feeling like an intruder* was replaced by *Feeling that I've got the right to be here*, and other similar changes later took place in the other elements.

We do not know the details of the events which led to the incoming construct *Feeling myself more loving*. Since the person was in primal integration therapy, this may have been responsible. On the other hand, it may have been due to other life events, and the therapy perhaps merely made it easier for the change to work its way through the system. One of the things which most plagues any kind of a decent outcome study is that the client has a life outside the therapy sessions, and that most of the things which happen to the client happen there.

EXPLORING THE PAST: UNDERSTANDING THE OPPOSITES AND INNER HIERARCHIES

Separatio

So having opened up the presenting problems in all the relevant ways, we come now to the third of the seven points on the Chaplin cycle. Here we meet one of the most interesting aspects of the work with men. All the therapists who work with men seem to be agreed that the family of origin has to be looked at. So many of the current hangups come from there that it has to be examined.

But men are often very resistant to this work, questioning its validity and its necessity. They see their childhood as boring or idyllic. Often they say they can remember nothing, or very little, about it. But they can be helped to see that their present problems have their roots in the past.

> Men can also learn about the unresolved emotional issues from the past that trigger automatic behavioural responses in the present. Of great importance for many men is that they come to an acceptance of their need for connectedness, long buried with a deep sense of grief and often masked by feelings of anger and/or indifference.
>
> (Allen and Gordon 1990: 144)

Anger and indifference – what important themes these are for men; and how often they have to do with unresolved issues still remaining from their families of origin. Just as women often cover up anger with hurt, men often cover up hurt with anger.

Because men are often suspicious of feelings, they would rather settle for an intellectual insight rather than feel the pain of really knowing at a gut level what happened to them in their family of origin.

> Even though intellectual assent to an idea may be possible early on, it can take months, sometimes even years, for clients to come to acknowledge at

117

an emotional level the connection between an event that happened so far in the past and their rigidified present.

(B.M. Erickson 1993: 128)

Beth Erickson has a good example of how this works, when one of her clients remembered that his father had left home, and he had had to be the man of the family when he was 11 years old. He did not want to be like his father had been, but he did not know how to be anything else, so he used distancing to survive. He pushed his mother away and he pushed his sisters away. He saw his mother as needy, and as having to protect himself from her neediness. Now his partner aroused the same sort of feelings. He felt her care for him as like his mother's care, and felt he had to push her away, to protect himself. This is the sort of discovery which makes such a difference when it is made at an emotional level. Until we resolve our source relationships, we are never really present in another relationship.

The other reason why it may be important to deal with the past is that many men suffer from alcoholism, with all the accompanying problems associated with the dysfunctional family, codependence and so forth. There is a tremendous literature on this (e.g. Diamond 1987) dealing with the recovery movement and all its ramifications. But whether or not alcoholism is the problem, shame often has to be dealt with, and shame almost always comes most strongly from experiences in the family of origin (Krugman 1995). It is important to see the difference between shame and guilt:

> Guilt says I've *done* something wrong; shame says there *is* something wrong with me. Guilt says I've *made* a mistake; shame says I *am* a mistake. Guilt says what I *did* was not good; shame says I *am* no good.
>
> (Bradshaw 1988a: 2)

Bradshaw makes an important distinction between ordinary shame, which comes and goes, and toxic shame, which stays with one all the time. Shame in itself is an ordinary human emotion, as variable and healthy as any other, but it can be transformed, in the family of origin, into a fixed state of being.

> As a state of being, shame takes over one's whole identity. To have shame as an identity is to believe that one's being is flawed, that one is defective as a human being. Once shame is transformed into an identity, it becomes toxic and dehumanizing. Since one feels his true self is defective and flawed, one needs a false self which is not defective and flawed.
>
> (Bradshaw 1988b: vii)

We saw earlier how the false self can arise as a result of trauma; now Bradshaw is saying that it can also arise from other conditions in the family of origin, and he spells these out in some detail.

All through this book we are seeing how men are subjected to an intense barrage of expectations to be masculine in a particular way. If shame says that

118

one is not measuring up to these expectations, and never will, immediately defences have to be raised against that: the false self is one such defence, addiction is another. In fact the two are connected:

> The cycle begins with the false belief system that all addicts have, that no one could want them or love them as they are. In fact, addicts can't love themselves. They are an object of scorn to themselves. The deep internalized shame gives rise to distorted thinking. The distorted thinking can be reduced to the belief that I'll be okay if I drink, eat, have sex, get more money, work harder, etc. The shame turns one into what Kellogg has termed a 'human doing', rather than a human being.
>
> (Bradshaw 1988b: 15)

This is a good description of what many men have turned into. We shall see later how this affects the world of work, for example. So often men indulge in endless activities, all of which seem very important, in order to avoid their real feelings – or even the very idea that they might have any feelings, as we saw earlier.

This is the stage where the internal conflicts can emerge and be heard. In order to do justice to such conflicts, the therapist needs to tease out and distinguish the warring parties. No longer can we assume that the person is a unity. Instead we speak of the *Separatio* as an important part of the process at this stage. Internal conflicts arise and have to be dealt with. The former belief in a single self becomes a conviction that one is radically flawed: one part may be opposed to another. The persona may oppose the shadow, the topdog may oppose the underdog, the critical parent may oppose the natural child, the person may oppose the automatic thoughts, and so on. The healing of the splits is important, but the splits, painful though they may be, have to be acknowledged before this is possible. As Metzner (1986) says, the destructuring of the old personality must precede the restructuring of transformation. The therapeutic alliance may go through strains at this stage, because the unconscious is separating from the conscious, and becoming more of an issue. Even those who do not believe in the unconscious may find this problem arising. It may be very important to emphasise the question of boundaries just now. But also here there is a sense of finding clues, and making sense.

One thing which may happen during this phase is that the man may get in touch with his inner child. It is a mistake, of course, to think that there is just one inner child. In a recent book (Rowan 1993b) I identified nine versions of the inner child which had been discovered by various people. And of course the 3 year old is different from the 5 year old, who in turn is different from the 7 year old, the 10 year old and so forth. John Bradshaw (1991) has devoted a whole book to the question of how best to work with the inner child, and he gives a number of exercises offering ways of working in this area.

Another book (Abrams 1991) has a number of exercises which could be done to get in touch with the inner child: Linda Capacchione on 'The power of your other hand'; Joyce Mills and Richard Crowley on 'Contacting the child within';

John Bradshaw on 'Liberating your lost inner child'; Nathaniel Branden on 'Integrating the younger self'; Jean Houston on 'Recalling the child'; Adelaide Bry on 'Replaying the movies of your childhood'; all these are useful and suggestive.

DISSOLVING THE INNER HIERARCHIES AND FACING AMBIVALENCE: ACCEPTING THE OPPOSITES

Calcinatio

Let us move on now to the fourth of Chaplin's phases, which has to do with accepting and dealing with the opposites within us. It is well known in psychology that it is the relatively undeveloped and immature mind which sees everything as either black or white, either good or evil, and the more mature mind which can see more of the inner splits and deviations and exceptions within each thing.

In our culture, as we have seen earlier, everything tends to be seen in an hierarchical fashion. Most men who come into therapy start with the unspoken view that there is always a superior and an inferior: they have to avoid being inferior, even if they have no aspirations to be superior. Often there is a corresponding assumption that the intellect is better than the emotions, and should always dominate over the emotions. The more sensible idea, that intellect and emotions are just two players in the cosmic game, neither with any special claim, is far away from their thoughts. Yet the current phase of therapy is the one where such assumptions come to be questioned.

Often this affects the whole relationship between the therapist and the client. Once the initial jostling for position is over, the therapist is usually seen as perfect, or as more advanced generally, or as ideal in some way. This lasts through the honeymoon period of the therapy, when everything seems to be going right. But now, at this midstage in the cycle, there begin to be questions raised. Is the therapist really ideal? Is the therapist even very good? Is the therapist even any good at all? Just as in the previous stage the parents were questioned and re-evaluated, in this stage the therapist may be questioned and re-evaluated.

It is very important at this stage to be nondefensive. It is never nice to be attacked or questioned, but it is quite bearable so long as the client does not press any of the therapist's emotional buttons. If the buttons are pressed, supervision may be particularly valuable, and the therapist's own therapist may also be very useful. That is why I believe that supervision is necessary throughout one's career as a therapist, though it may take different forms with different levels of experience. Similarly, it is very valuable to have one's own therapist, either in an ongoing way or simply to be called in when issues arise which seem to be personal and close to home.

One of the standard challenges which often comes up at this stage is the question 'Do you really care about me, or is this just a job for you?' This is quite a dilemma, because if we choose the first horn we risk becoming involved with a much closer type of relationship with quite different boundaries, which might make the therapy more difficult; while if we choose the second horn, we risk seeming distant, aloof, inhuman, which again in a different way might make the therapy more difficult. What I usually say now is something like this: 'I am deeply committed to our work together, and it is very important to me.' This is true; and it seems to be all that is really being asked for.

At this stage there can be real discomfort for the client in these conflicting feelings. But they are compensated for by the sense of progress in having them at all. I remember in my early days crying for forty-five minutes at the sadness of never having cried for so many years! But it took me much longer to get in touch with my fear, because it had been buried much more deeply and there had been more layers piled on top of it. But all these things vary from person to person.

This phase also has to do with the discovery of mixed feelings and inner conflicts within the client, which the client is now prepared to work on. This is very simply done if we allow the method of talking to chairs or cushions. We can put the 'topdog' on one chair and the 'underdog' on the other, for example, and let them talk to each other. The old way of doing this was to get the client to sit on each chair alternately, but this is not always necessary. The two chairs can in themselves form perfectly good anchors for the different points of view, and the actual client does not necessarily have to move about at all. It can be a question of what the client prefers and feels more appropriate.

Many men have a Pusher subpersonality who is always demanding more work, more production, more speed. Harris (1995) has done research on how these images become internalised. Often there is a Sybarite subpersonality, who wants to take things easy, wants everything to be handed over on a plate, wants to be a lotus-eater. Working out the conflict between these two may make for much more integration within the personality. Similarly with other splits, such as Body vs Mind, Left vs Right, Masculine vs Feminine, Intellect vs Feelings, and so on. There can be three-way splits, such as Body, Feelings and Intellect, or four-way splits, such as Body, Feelings, Intellect and Soul.

Calcinatio is the stage where some of the first symptoms disappear or change their appearance. There is a definite sense that something has been achieved. Something noticeable has happened. There is a relaxation, a sense of losing some of the anxiety as to whether anything will really change. Some of the *Materia Prima* has been consumed in the flames. Samuels (1989) says that the original elements have ceased to exist in their initial form. The primitive passions contain the potential for the very highest or deepest experiences, but they must be burned first, so that they are transmuted. As Liz Greene (1988) says, fire burns and frustrates, but also purifies and enlightens. What is left is a fine ash, ready for the *Albedo* which comes now. Signs are definitely there. There is a deposit, as it were. Fabricius (1994: 120) tells us to 'Cook till it whitens.'

MAKING CHANGES: LIVING WITH THE OPPOSITES

Albedo

So we come to the fifth of our points on the cycle, where the work we have been doing in therapy starts to have effects in the outside world. This is a phase of realisation, of beginning to understand that some real change has taken place. This may feel very good, but it may also feel quite scary. Losing one's nasty symptoms may be an advantage, but it is still a loss. It still brings a feeling of unfamiliarity, of strangeness. There may also be a sense of unreality – is it really true? Is it permanent? Is the struggle over?

It is very common at this stage to have made real advances at work or in one's relationships or in one's daily life, but then to visit one's mother or father, or both. Back in the family home, one may get a sense of having lost it all. Out there one was making changes and forging ahead, but in here nothing has changed – one is still a child, subject to all sorts of unwanted feelings. It is important not to get discouraged at this stage. Setbacks of all kinds are quite normal and to be expected. Both therapist and client need to remember the underlying trend, not the latest set of figures.

It may be that real support is needed. In facing the boss, perhaps taking a friend along will make it easier not to backslide. In facing a parent, perhaps taking a brother or sister along will make it easier. The phrase is still valuable – 'You alone can do it, but you don't have to do it alone.' Men have this almost pathological need to be independent, and it is good to contradict this, and to act as if one were a real member of the human race.

Almost invariably at this stage the man experiences a greater sense of freedom, and a greater ability to take responsibility for his own actions and his own experience. Almost equally invariably the man experiences setbacks and disappointments which make him doubt himself. The therapist needs to remember that life is a rhythm, not a set series of steps.

In the *Albedo*, the colour has changed from black to white. The client may get here through a lot of tears, which release pent-up feelings. This is associated with the colour blue, which as Hillman (1993) tells us, is the colour of sadness but also the way from blackness to whiteness. In alchemy this is called the *Ablutio* – the washing – and it is stated that this is often accompanied by 'the rending of the books'. In other words, this is a stage which cannot be reached by intellectual effort. After this, the client may feel good or even ecstatic. The world now looks very different from how it appeared at the start. This is the end of the first phase of therapy, and both client and therapist may make the mistake of thinking it is the end of the process. The client can now engage in new actions, and appreciate a fresh approach to life.

It is possible to finish here. Most short-term therapy ends with the *Albedo*. Symptoms have been dealt with, the client feels better, the therapist feels that good work has been done, and honour has been satisfied all round. To continue in therapy at this point is to make a conscious decision to go on to a second phase, where much of the taken-for-granted process of the first phase is put in doubt, and may have to change.

CONNECTEDNESS: EXPRESSING THE OPPOSITES

Conjunctio

It is only now that a man can really move on to the sixth stage, where experiences of connectedness are possible. This is the phase of 'joining the human race'. This usually comes first through the man's primary relationship with a woman. Sometimes it needs some actual couple counselling (see Chapter 11 on relationships) before this can really get moving, but it is now in principle possible.

The man has questioned all his taken-for-granted assumptions, and found that he is not the sum of his conditioning. Because he has come to terms with his own inner constructions and contradictions, he can afford to reach out to others from a secure base. Because he now knows how to listen to himself, he knows how to listen to someone else, and really hear what they are saying. Not what he thinks they are saying, and not what he wants them to be saying, but what they are actually saying. This clarity is new and refreshing.

The relationship with the therapist becomes more like consulting a colleague than negotiating with a father-figure. The therapist becomes more of a person and less of a symbol.

The man can now move in the direction of more complex communication. Instead of just thinking of the next thing he wants to say, he can think ahead to what response his statement will provoke, and what his reply to that will be. His whole thinking can become more strategic, less limited to the next reaction. He can afford to connect with other people in a more whole-hearted fashion.

And he can now decide more how to use his time. Instead of just going from one thing to the next, he can pause when necessary, and take stock. If someone asks a question, he is not compelled to give an answer: he can say instead – 'I don't have the answer at the moment, but I can find it if you give me the necessary time.' If someone offers him a task, he can decide about in a noncompulsive way, genuinely thinking about it – is it something he really wants to do or not?

The therapist's job at this stage is to encourage, and sometimes even to coach, more adequate modes of interacting with people. Empty chairs can once again come in, this time as props for rehearsals. I sometimes use a tape recorder for the purpose, recording the first version, playing it back, then recording the second version, and sometimes a third or fourth. Often lack of practice in using more open types of interaction makes them quite problematic at first, but practice makes perfect.

Elementary rules of communication can be quite useful, too. I often use a simple division of methods of criticising someone else, assuming that he has done something you consider wrong:

1 *Silence* This is the least adequate, since the other person may not realise he has offended you, or how.
2 *Labelling* You call him a name or describe him in derogatory terms – this is inadequate, because it makes him defensive and competitive.
3 *Blaming* You have been affected and it is all his fault – this is a little better than labelling, because you have admitted that you are affected in some way, but it still leaves him with little choice but to be defensive and perhaps to fight back.
4 *Real communication* You admit that you have been affected, and simply tell him how you have been affected, in detail. Because this uses 'I' messages rather than 'you' messages, this does not make him defensive, necessarily, and it may open up the possibility of dialogue and negotiation around the issue. At least it gives him the information, the feedback, to which he is entitled.

The *Conjunctio* is crucially important in the alchemical process, and as we have seen it recurs more than once. Here it is an essential part of the initiation process. Unless men can learn how to relate to people in a full and adequate way, the therapy has not done its work.

ENDINGS AND NEW BEGINNINGS

Mortificatio and second *Nigredo*

This is the final stage in Chaplin's account, and it deserves great attention. Many therapeutic relationships end badly, and they can end very well. The essence of it is that a kind of loss is involved. Of course loss is one of the great human problems – none of us finds it an easy one to deal with. If we have been through all the stages mentioned above, something real will have developed between therapist and client – and it is this which is now being lost. Even if only a fraction of the course has been covered, there will still be issues to be resolved before a good parting can be achieved. So termination is well worth taking seriously.

It is important for the therapist to realise that changes will go on happening after the sessions have ceased. Therapy is a long-term process with its own laws and its own rhythm. Never assume that because the therapy with a particular client is unfinished, they are not ready to leave. They may well carry on making changes after the relationship is severed, and end up a year or two later further on again.

An interesting phenomenon is where clients want to leave, but where they have agreed with the therapist, right at the start, that say four sessions will be devoted to termination. They may be quite surprised, even offended, when this is brought to their attention, because they wanted to leave instantly. But if they come to these four sessions, they will in many cases decide to carry on. When this happens, the therapy usually wakes up and takes on another lease of life, progressing much better than it did before. Somehow the close examination of the issues, with termination looming, brings a freshness and clarity which was missing before.

It is quite proper to offer to be available for the client after the sessions are over. It must be made clear that this is not a continuation of the therapy – it might have to be at a different time on a different day – but a new contract, possibly with a different fee. The ending is really an ending, not an indeterminate pause.

But let us look now at the other option, that of carrying on with the therapy. If we do so, we meet something which in alchemy is called the *Mortificatio*. It is in this phase that we have the task of processing and digesting the material which has emerged. The *Mortificatio* is a painful stage, where there is a sense of being plunged into darkness again. The struggle to keep the old stuff has still not finished, so there is resistance and fear. Relationships may come under examination here, and painful realisations about the way one has held on to someone for the wrong reasons. Transference and countertransference may emerge much more powerfully than before. Frustration and rage are common at this stage, and it is important to let them be subjected to the process of *Mortificatio*.

> Mortificatio is the most negative operation in alchemy. It has to do with darkness, defeat, torture, mutilation, death, and rotting. However, these dark images often lead over to highly positive ones – growth, resurrection, rebirth – but the hallmark of Mortificatio is the colour black.
>
> (Edinger 1985: 148)

This is something which must not be avoided or set on one side, because it is an essential stage in the alchemical process.

DEEPER EXPLORATIONS: RITES OF PASSAGE

Solutio and third *Nigredo*

We are now well into phase two – the long haul where the deeper difficulties have to be dealt with. Whiteness is not enough, by itself, say the alchemists, it is dead. These deeper difficulties may have come to the surface only during the first phase, and may have been hidden from the client up to that point. Opening up to the obvious questions may have resulted in the uncovering of more long-standing problems. The *Solutio* is a stage where the new boundaries of the soul have once again been questioned, and where all is put into the melting pot once again. This is a genuinely new stage of the therapeutic process. All the previous results are now put into the crucible, the vas, the alembic, and subjected to more heat – in other words, a deeper level of consciousness now has to be approached. This may feel at first like another *Nigredo*. We are back at Chaplin's second phase, and will have to work through all the phases over again in modified form. One is suddenly very vulnerable, and feelings come up which threaten to swamp the rational ego. There may be feelings of drowning. Dreams start to come up with watery themes, as Greene (1988) has suggested. One may merge with a partner, and experience quite new feelings in a relationship. Peak experiences, too, may come at this stage. Sheldon Kopp says that at this point we have entered phase two of the therapy:

> Should the patient continue into this second or middle phase of therapy, we are likely to spend one to three years of deepening intimacy.
>
> (Kopp 1977: 141)

He adds that silence, which has been an increasing tool used in the work, becomes even more useful at this stage. The therapist needs to be able to resist the client's demands for more interventions and more action. The interpretations or other interventions used at this stage will be designed to deepen the client's understanding of unconscious fantasies and feelings. It is a slow process.

This whole movement beyond the *Albedo* is called the *Citrinitas* – the yellowing of the work. It is hard because it seems to spoil the whiteness which had been achieved. As James Hillman wisely puts it:

> White resists this . . . for it feels like a regression to the vulgar drivenness of earlier elements in the work – *Materia Prima* and *Nigredo* – which the arduous hours of analytic reflection have finally sophisticated and pacified.
>
> (Hillman 1991: 84)

He goes on to say that the yellowing is much more than a spoiling of the white – it is also a brighter illumination, clarifying vision. He argues that the apparently negative nature of the yellowing is quite necessary to the full completion of the work – another of the twists and turns we have come to expect.

STRUGGLES: DEEPER OPPOSITIONS

Coagulatio

The stage called *Coagulatio* is where all this questioning starts to firm up and become more solid again. Realism returns. This is where we realise that we are in a difficult stage, the *Citrinitas* (Hillman 1991), the yellowing, where the white is seen as not the final stage after all. More work has to be done, and unusually demanding work at that. The negative transference may arise in new and more acute forms, so that the skills and self-knowledge of the therapist are most put to the test. Countertransference also can become more acute, and can be a benefit or a problem. It may seem that the therapy is going wrong, has lost its way, is put in doubt. Earlier symptoms may return. Commitment is one of the key concepts at this stage, as Alvin Mahrer points out:

The ordinary person may be said to be engaged in a perpetual agonizing struggle to preserve the self, whereas, in stark and utter contrast, the integrating person [the person we are following here] is willingly engaged in suicidal self-destruction. These two persons are proceeding in opposite directions. The integrating person knows that the way to liberation, to integration, to metamorphosis, is through the eye of the nameless horror which the ordinary person desperately tries to avoid.

(Mahrer 1989a: 482)

More pain may be experienced, both by therapist and client. Again a new kind of the *Putrefactio* returns, the breakdown of existing material. But it reforms in new patterns. Things take shape. New insights make new connections.

This is a stage where previously warded-off material can more easily emerge, because there is more pressure to connect up earlier and later experiences. It may take this long for sexual abuse, for example, to work its way through the layers of repression or dissociation or amnesia. These are things one needs to know in order to heal, but does not want to know, because they are so painful. On the whole, the acceptance of this new material brings with it the strength which is needed to deal with the pain. This tends to be a heavy stage of the therapy. Liz Greene says:

Earthing anything involves both positive and negative emotional experiences. On the one hand the coagulatio brings things into concrete manifestation, so it is concerned with integrating unconscious images and movements into the ego and into actual life. But the act of bringing potentials to birth in this way also implies limitation and even imprisonment, because the moment you concretise something, you have cut short its potentiality. It is no longer full of limitless possibilities, but has become an actuality, and has crystallised. Because the form is now definite, there is a sense of depression around the coagulatio.

(Greene 1988: 307)

Therapy is full of ups and downs. This is rather a down phase, even though there are important ups within it.

BREAKTHROUGH

Sublimatio

If the task of facing one's very worst fears, one's most intolerable pain, can be carried out, a fifth form of the *Conjunctio* can come about. One may actually dare to join with and become that which one most hates and fears. The existing sense of self can then die and be reborn. This is the final *Putrefactio*. There is a transformation from a negative image of one's insides into a positive image which can be a new self-centre. This is the final stage, the *Sublimatio*, the final purification. Liz Greene says:

The sublimatio can only come when there has been a death, a relinquishing
of the fantasy of merging.

(Greene 1988: 316)

Fabricius (1994) speaks here of 'the ultimate unity of death and primal birth'.
Alvin Mahrer is one of the best people to describe this phase of the work:

As I surrender into death, and as a dilated self always emerges as a
consequence, there is a newfound paradoxical permanence to 'I', a strange
kind of continuity. I gain a sense of substantiality and permanence in being
able to die and emerge dilated. My own self acquires a strength, a
wholeness, an intact organisation to the extent that I can surrender it into
death and emerge from the death still there – different perhaps, altered in
many ways, but still there is something continuous.

(Mahrer 1989a: 499)

It becomes clearer now why we have been emphasising the notion of initiation
so much. What we are going through in therapy is a real initiation, a way of
losing our old unnecessary assumptions and compulsions. We are letting the
therapy eat our falsities.

INTEGRATION

Rubedo

At this point emerges the final colour: we get the *Rubedo*, the reddening, a more
human colour with warmth and heart. Not the silver of the *Albedo*, but the true
gold we were seeking. This is a stage of spiritual fulfilment, the achievement of
something genuinely new. There is a movement from frustrated desire for an
external object to the transformation of that desire into an internalised image
which contains meaning, purpose, and regenerative capacities for one's own life,
as Greene (1988) has urged. Alchemy speaks here of the chymical wedding or
hieros gamos, where a genuine resolution takes place, and the refined soul
emerges. This refers to a final movement within the client, the emergence of a
new person, the Self.

This is not a lonely place to be, as Alvin Mahrer again points out, because the
person who has been through this initiation into integration and actualisation is
warmer, more open, more expressive and more capable of being genuinely there
in a relationship:

The highest levels of interpersonal relationships are those characterized by
integration *and actualization*. This kind of relationship exceeds one of
integrative love, mutual integrative oneness, and mutual integrative being-
one-with. Because of the nature of actualization, these highest levels of
interpersonal relationships are *also* characterized by mutual contexts
enabling each participant toward increasing depth and breadth of

experiencing. When relationships are of this order, they define the highest and most valued interpersonal relations available to human beings.

(Mahrer 1989a: 579)

Far from being an isolated self, the man who has been through this process can genuinely connect with others. All the barriers to doing this have been torn down. There may still be misunderstandings, as we shall see in Chapter 11, but there are now no obstacles to putting them right.

So far we have looked at the therapy process in a very general way, but it is now time to look at some more specific issues.

Part IV

CALCINATIO

At the end of the calcinatio everything that can burn is burnt away and only ashes are left. And ashes belong to the symbolism of bitterness: defeat, failure and the sackcloth and ashes of mourning all belong to that experience of bitterness. But in alchemy the other side of the ash symbolism is that ashes were also associated with the 'vitreous body' – the glassy body left behind at the end of the calcinatio process. It corresponds to the 'glorified body' which is immortal – the indestructible residue that's left over from the calcinatio. So it's an image of the immortal Self that is refined and can endure the fire.

(Edinger 1995: 139)

9

INDIVIDUAL THERAPY WITH MEN

There are pressures on men to be masculine. It has often been pointed out that we should speak of many masculinities rather than just one masculinity, because there are many ways of being a man, not just one. However, it may still be true that there is one dominant masculinity, and many subordinate masculinities. The hegemonic pattern which we met earlier requires clarity and simplification to be effective. What this means in practice is that men are pressured into being masculine in just one way. To be a proper man, a man who is successfully masculine, is to be constrained into quite a narrow band of expectations. We looked at some of these, including the four themes of Brannon (1976), in Chapter 2.

As we saw there, what men want when they take up these images is a woman who will complement them. This woman will have what Connell (1987) has called 'emphasized femininity' – a corresponding pattern with the complementary values. Such a woman will want a manly man who exhibits as many as possible of Brannon's qualities, and will support him for displaying them.

So in this kind of system, there will be pressure on men to conform to this pattern of masculinity, and on women to conform to this pattern of femininity.

RESISTANCE TO THERAPY

This means that there is very often a strong resistance to any suggestion that a man might need therapy. As Ian Harris says, 'Most men respond to crises by being stoical' (Harris 1995: 193) Sometimes this is just a question of admitting to weakness or vulnerability, which is anathema. Sometimes, in such cases as the man who has still not dealt with his father or mother, the therapist seems to them like a parent or other authority figure, and they are in the process of trying to become more independent of such figures in their lives.

This is why this phase is a *Calcinatio* process. It means burning away the falsities and mistakes of the past in a kind of fire. This fire is painful and may arouse feelings of wanting to escape from it.

In men generally there is a reluctance to enter therapy. As we have seen, the main message of the culture to men is that they should be in control at all times.

How can one be in control and at the same time explore the unknown corners of one's inner world?

But men are wounded. They need to recognise this if anything is going to change. Each man thinks he can hide his wound, and the trouble is that this can be so successful that he can kid himself there is no wound. Michael Meade puts it well:

> If a man doesn't know he is wounded, he can deny the facts for ever. One fact about a man who doesn't know he is wounded is that he can't see that others are wounded. More than that, he'll put his wound into others because of his vague sense that there's a wound somewhere. He'll only see it when he puts it into someone else and will feel strangely better when he sees it there. Then he'll lose touch with it and have to stick it on someone again.
>
> (Meade 1993: 50)

It is essential to own up to our wounds if we are to be healed, and to stop wounding others.

However, men can be quite fascinated to discover that as well as having painful things, perhaps shameful things, to explore in the lower unconscious, they may also have exciting things, wonderful things, even perhaps ecstatic things, to discover in the higher unconscious. And they may be able to enter into much better relationships with women. So anything which gives men permission to explore their higher self, their soul, will be welcome. This is of course very much the case in initiation, which as we have seen can be a major theme.

Fred Hanna and his colleagues (1995) have researched the way in which transcendence is crucial in the big breakthroughs in therapy. There has to be a moment of going beyond the existing perceived limitations of the man involved. From a new perspective, the whole problem looks different. This then affects the person at every level, which as we have seen is one of the key characteristics of initiation.

Something which often gets in the way of this is an intense suspicion of organised religion. This can often be overcome by pointing out that what is being suggested is not a belief system imposed from outside which has to be accepted as it stands, but a personal experience which the man has for himself.

One exercise I often do is to suggest that the client lays out four cushions (could be chairs) to provide locations for his body, his heart, his head and his soul. He takes up each position in turn, and says how things look from there – perhaps addressing a current problem or a problematic person. It is a curious fact that even men who have never mentioned such a thing before find it quite possible to take up a position on the soul cushion, and generally to produce some extremely wise comments.

Men tend to have a rather cavalier attitude to their bodies: they are there to be used as instruments, but instruments which are not really cared for or treated properly. It is almost regarded as unmasculine to think about one's body as something to be treated well. But Kenny Klein (1993) has reminded us that the body is not only masculine but also sacred.

MALE CYCLES

Terry Kupers has coined the term 'pathological arrhythmicity' as a kind of spoof diagnostic category, which points to an important characteristic of men: too little response to natural cycles. Men so often pay no attention to their internal clocks, to their internal responses, to their internal feelings. Men work long hours without letting up, turn up to work even when not feeling well, hide natural responses and true feelings. There is a sort of unspoken pressure to keep alert and vigilant in case of attack. He says:

> A degree of arrhythmicity that is functional at the work place can be constricting in the personal realm. For instance, it can interfere with the capacity to be intimate or to be fully relaxed and playful.
>
> (Kupers 1993: 31)

But it is not only in the personal realm. This ignoring of the natural rhythms of life can be hazardous at work, too. One particular area where this shows up is in the area of sleep. Men seem to drive themselves very hard in this area, or to allow themselves to be driven hard by others.

At Three Mile Island, where 80 per cent of the workers were men, sleep loss and exhaustion led to a failure to recognise the loss of coolant water (Mitler *et al.* 1988). It was this that caused the near meltdown of the reactor. Here is a concrete example of how sleep deprivation can go too far.

Workers' sleep loss was also found to be the common feature for the explosion of the space shuttle *Challenger* and the catastrophe at Chernobyl. When the *Exxon Valdez* spilled oil, although the captain was blamed, investigators later conceded that the underlying culprit was the decision to send the exhausted crew back to sea after skipping their scheduled day's rest (Katcharian *et al.* 1990)

This is just one expression of a problem which goes even wider: the whole question of safety at work. All the most hazardous jobs are largely carried out by men, and the number of deaths and injuries incurred as a result is huge. Yet although unions have pressed for better safety standards, the standards which have been obtained and set in place have often not been enforced. The number of inspectors is even in theory not very high, and in practice the establishment is often incomplete. Even when standards are enforced, the penalties are often laughably small, and when deaths are concerned it would often make sense to bring manslaughter charges: yet this is very rarely done. Consequently the male desire to override natural rhythms and appropriate limits may often result in death and injury, not just inconvenience or stress.

Men have a complex relationship with their own bodies, often regarding parts of the body as having an independent existence. It is quite common, for example, for the penis to be given a name – Henry Miller called his John Thursday, or in French Jean Jeudi, which sounds better.

The point of drawing atttention to this is that men pay little heed to their own bodies, and male therapists very often ignore the many cues and clues which are

135

offered by body language. When men do pay attention to their bodies, it is most often in an instrumental way, to discipline it for some purpose or other. What is being attempted here is some encouragement for men to really consider the basic movements of their bodies, and the basic information which their bodies are trying to give them. Loving our own bodies and understanding them better go hand in hand.

SEXUALITY

One of the most important areas where body, mind and spirit come into contact is in the field of sexuality. It is a puzzling field for many men, because of the pressures we have already mentioned. There is a stereotype of male sexuality which weighs heavily on men: 'hard as steel, twelve inches long, and goes all night', as someone put it. And it is indiscriminate: 'a woman, a man or a dog – throw them on a bed' is another quotation. There is supposed to be no fear, no hesitation, just a continous randiness which never gives up.

This is of course very far from the experience of most men. To start with, there is the question of whether we are men at all. Many men have considerable doubts about this, at one time or another. The study of gender shows that these doubts are quite valid. 'Being a man' is not a simple question, or an open-and-shut case. Nor can it be established through an assertive sexuality, as some men seem to think.

As Lorber (1994) has shown through her extensive scholarship, gender is wholly constructed, symbolically loaded and ideologically enforced. She questions all the usual conventional assumptions about gender, and quotes a bewildering array of different physiological and psychological factors which can vary right across the board. There are all sorts of intermediate genders.

> There is no core or bedrock human nature below these endlessly looping processes of the social production of sex and gender, self and other, identity and psyche. . . . *For humans, the social is the natural.*
>
> (Lorber 1994: 36)

We have seen in an earlier section in this chapter that the body itself is constructed out of our experience and the defences we have erected. This paves the way for a very strong statement of the ways in which gender is enforced. There is no such thing as a fixed and simple boundary of gender, and yet these boundaries are made firm and fixed by our culture, patriarchal as it is. The patriarchy finds it very convenient to have just two sexes, so two sexes it is, whether it makes sense or not. For men to focus on sexuality, then, in order to confirm their identity as men, is to work themselves further into the very mire from which they were trying to escape.

We saw earlier how masculine hegemony is constructed in this way, and we are now seeing exactly how gender works. In society we are not just gendered, we do gender at every moment. And when we do gender, men are doing dominance and women are doing deference. This is a terrible simplification to find ourselves in.

Yet this is extremely uncomfortable for men, because they do not feel powerful in the way which this theory might suggest they should. In the field of sexuality men often feel extremely inadequate, and unable to get what they need or want. They may not want the 'one good fuck a day' which the stereotype tells them to want, but they feel very much at the mercy of women to get anything at all.

Of course this operates differently in gay relationships, but in a way gay relationships are even more problematic than heterosexual ones. James Harrison (1995) has a good discussion of some of the issues here.

NORMALITY AS PATHOLOGY

When we come to sex itself, men are caught in a terrible bind. They know they are supposed to be in control, but they do not feel in control. They know they are supposed to satisfy the female, but they often do not. And so we get performance anxiety – a set of worries about getting it right, extending from the first exchange of words to the post-orgasmic ending.

Let us look closely at the 'normal picture'. Here is an account of an ideal sexual encounter: *He feels an increasing closeness to an attractive woman, leading to sexual intercourse, leading to mutual simultaneous orgasm, followed by expressions of satisfaction all round.* Show that account to men, and the vast majority of them will say that this sounds ideal. What could be better? What could be pathological about it?

First of all, there is nothing much about the other person. She is 'attractive', that is all we are told. There is nothing about knowing her as a person. So far as we are told, he does not really know her. But how would anyone want to do something so intimate and personal with someone he did not know? There is something wrong about this.

Secondly, the operation is described as 'sexual intercourse'. Again there are assumptions hidden here. It sounds as if just one act were involved, and as if that one act entailed penetration. 'If you don't get it in it doesn't count.' Yet if it were a real act with a real person, it might involve a lot of different activities of a sexual nature, possibly including penetration, possibly not. And if there were to be penetration, why should it not be repeated? In this way we can run the whole gamut of sexuality, not just a one-pointed pursuit of a single ejaculation.

Thirdly, the idea of 'simultaneous orgasm' is a programmed instruction rather than a naturally emerging possibility. Many men distance themselves sexually from their partner by 'thinking of other things' during intercourse, in order not to come too soon. But in reality, no one can be responsible for another person's orgasm. So if the man comes 'too soon', there are several answers to this. One is to wait and then have a second attempt: invariably the second ejaculation is slower than the first. Or a third, or a fourth. Another possibility is to stimulate the partner's clitoris – or whatever else the partner likes – by fingers or tongue until an orgasm appears. The anatomical facts are such that research tells us that only a minority of acts of intercourse can lead to female orgasm, because of the position of the clitoris. There is no such thing as a vaginal orgasm (Kitzinger 1985).

Another mistake is to confuse the orgasm with ejaculation. The orgasm is a response of the whole body, which includes muscle groups of many different areas (Boadella 1987). To restrict it just to ejaculation is to confuse intercourse with masturbation. Yet the two things are very different. It is common after an orgasm with a lover to experience satisfaction and a prolonged mutual period of coming down together. Masturbation ends with the ejaculation, and a minute later things are 'back to normal'.

So if this is pathological sex, what is normal sex? In order to answer this question, we need to take a detour around the prime source of misunderstanding in the field of sexuality: the question of sexiness.

SEXINESS

For a man there seems nothing more natural than to respond to the sexiness of a woman. It seems instinctive. A woman looks sexy; she just does. How can anyone deny this, or how basic it is? Yet we as men are often, even now, not wise to what is going on when we look at a *Playboy* centrefold or a sexy calendar or a copy of *Penthouse* or a real woman.

The difference between a penis and a phallus is that the phallus stands up. A penis may or may not stand up, but a phallus has to stand up or it is not a phallus any more. There is a strong link between the phallus and what is seen as sexy. Not for nothing are strip joints called SEXY BAR and other such titles. These places are designed to make the phallus sit up and take notice, just as pornography is so designed. So there is a strong link in this way between sexiness and pornography.

We are all familiar with the feminist critique of pornography – how it reduces women to a figment of the male imagination, such that they are fit only to relate to a phallus – and phallus as power rather than sexuality (e.g. Lederer 1980). We can do what we like to a picture, and the picture cannot resist. The woman in the picture is welcoming; she is designed to be welcoming; she cannot be other than welcoming; she is there for any man who watches. Perhaps sexiness is really about power too, rather than sexuality. Perhaps seeing a woman as sexy is seeing her as a flattering illusion rather than reality. Perhaps it is seeing her as there to be used. Perhaps sexiness is closer to pornography than it is comfortable for us to realise. And perhaps pornography is closer to rape than it is comfortable for us to realise. Perhaps there is a cloak of illusion hiding all of this, because it is uncomfortable to bring it all out into the open. The word 'glamour' originally meant 'illusion'. So, if all this were true, sexiness would be hiding something really quite nasty, as has been spelt out rather convincingly by Susanne Kappeler (1986).

Since 1990 some men have been stirred up enough to put on workshops where we can come face to face with some of our own attitudes and behaviour. An experiential exercise offered by one men's workshop was to get the participants to put themselves into the same poses as those adopted by the models in a popular pornographic magazine. The men reported that these poses made them feel both vulnerable and absurd, and artificial in the extreme. They felt ready to be put down, exploited, rather than ready for sex. There was a strong feel of illusion about the whole thing.

The woman in a pornographic calendar at first sight looks all right to many of us: how can we criticise on a calendar what we would look at with interest on a beach or in a bedroom? But the woman has been placed there for us, usually by some male publisher who is making more money out of it than she is. She is standing, sitting or lying there to serve us. Not doing any activity of her own choice, having to do with her own life and her own meanings, but doing whatever will entice or impress or please the phallus. She is being put down and reduced to a fragment of a person. It is as if she lives only for the phallus, has the right to exist only if she pleases the phallus. The male watcher seems to have the control. But any real sexuality is about freedom, not about control. The illusion comes back again.

Women can put on sexiness just as we as men can put on the right face or the right suit, or have the right car. They often understand very well what they need to do in order to appear sexy. In one workshop I attended, the women knew what would attract the men much better than the men knew what would attract the women. Certain clothes are sexy, certain poses are sexy, certain expressions are sexy. Drag artists study this, often to brilliant effect. Male prostitutes who look like women study sexiness and can don it like a garment. If it can be put on and taken off in this way, how real can it be?

But it is not just the illusion that is offensive. The example is given of a garage where stuck up all over the workshop were pornographic pictures, mainly taken from magazines. There seemed nothing very remarkable about them except their quantity, until one was observed at eye level which looked like a Polaroid snap. It was of a naked women bending over with her back to the camera, and right where her legs joined, a nail had been hammered in. It was a picture of a woman with a nail splitting her most secret and sensitive sexual part.

The use and the putting down of women represents in a small way the hatred of women (Jukes 1993). When men say 'I love women, and just wish I could make love to more of them, ha ha', they are not really talking about love, but about power and control. The desire is *on condition that*. On condition that they serve stereotyped male fantasies.

All the women in pornography are there only *on condition that*. They represent the power which we as men rarely have – the power to make a woman say Yes. And this fantasy of *making* a woman say Yes is at the root of rape.

In adolescence I wanted to fuck. But all the girls I knew always said No. I was going around with this erection all day sometimes, and knowing what it was for, and not being able to do anything about it. What was so precious about their bodies, I thought, that they would not even try it? They would enjoy it too, I knew, I just knew. How could they be so negative and frustrating? Dressing themselves up to make me come on and then saying No. Maybe laughing at my frustration. It was enough to make anyone angry. If only I could get my own back on all those girls who said No when I was 15. If only I could teach them a lesson. Maybe rape would teach them a lesson – make them laugh on the other side of their faces.

It was in a therapy group that I discovered that this was the way my mind had worked. There on the floor I 'raped' the youngest and sassiest woman in the group, and when I had done a lot more work on this, I was able to leave my fantasy behind. (Perhaps I should add that she volunteered for this, and got something out of it for herself, and later became a very good therapist.)

The women who have been used to create pornography feed this fantasy. Pornography is all about women who say Yes instead of No. It feeds the male fantasy that women really want to say Yes all the time, but are held back by inhibitions and fears, which need only a few drinks, or a good meal, or a bit of force, or a sum of money, to overcome. The women in the pictures have taken money to show themselves sexually, to allow themselves to be used in male fantasies of masturbation. Maybe for a little more, they would go all the way. Maybe they should be taken in any case, just to show them what's what.

But the very same fantasies extend into real life. They are not restricted to the pages of pornographic magazines hived away in the recesses of sex shops. Some time ago I was in a filling station, and a woman came in to buy something in the shop. She got out of her car and flashed her long legs as she did so. She was in a very short pink dress, and looked young, blonde and attractive; she wasn't wearing a bra. As she walked, her breasts bounced under the dress. I couldn't take my eyes off her. I waited with interest for her to come out again a few minutes later. It was an exciting bit of my day.

But what I had been seeing was my own fantasy. I knew nothing about this woman in reality. I was projecting upon her a sexiness which may or may not have been there, and in any case was not there for me. *It was as if I was not interested in any part of her life except that part which had to do with being sexy.* I had turned a real live woman into a near-pornographic image in one second flat.

It reminded me of a time when I had first become aware of the way in which I looked at women in the street. My basic thought had been, I discovered, 'I could certainly use that!' It was basically about exploitation, as if I were saying to her 'Let's start off with me exploiting you, and see where we go from there.' It was the same sort of thing as the famous explorer Captain Cook in the South Pacific: he might see this island, might even love the island, cherish the island, and look after the island, but basically what he was about was exploiting the island.

So maybe men hate women, and maybe men love women, but love or hate, sexiness is about exploitation. It is about women meeting the conditions of men. It is about men winning and women being reduced to something less than a human being.

In a group which I co-led with a woman, this one man kept on paying the women in the group compliments which they did not really appreciate, such as 'I really like your breasts!' They told him they did not like it, but he could not see the point. He was being honest, genuine and sincere, what more did they want? So I asked him, if people were paying him a compliment, what would he like them to say? He said after some thought: 'I really like your moustache!' So I got him to stand on one spot, and everyone in the group went in front of him and told him: 'I really like your moustache!' They went round and round, saying it over and over again, in an endless chain. He looked pleased at first, but after several minutes had gone by, he said 'Stop! Stop!' I asked him what was the matter. He said 'After a while it was as if I was nothing but a moustache – as if all anyone were interested in about me was my moustache.' He had finally got the point.

This is exactly the experience which many women have talked about – of being reduced to some small aspect of themselves which is appreciated or noticed, because it serves male interests. It is as if men were not interested in them, but in that part of them. It is still common to talk about 'a leg man', 'a tit man', and so forth.

Sexiness is a sort of fantasy which men put on women, and then fall for the fantasy they have themselves created. It is like Pygmalion falling in love with his own creation. Except that sexiness is only a part of a person at best. Perhaps it is easier to cope with part of a person than it is with a whole person. It is certainly easier to hurt and ill-treat someone who is less than a full human being. So sexiness is an attempt to reduce a woman to something which can be controlled and used more easily. Sexiness is like a collar and lead, like a bridle and bit, like a yoke and harness, like a ring in the nose. It is all about power and control, not about sexuality or sensuality, and certainly not about intimacy with another person, and that is offensive: it makes me angry.

In fact, it may well be that sexiness is actually all about avoiding intimacy. (We shall see more about this in Chapter 11.) By seeing a woman as sexy we can actually avoid being close to her or open with her – it can be like a sort of code by which we use roles and rules to keep our distance. It is as if we can relate below the neck and avoid relating above the neck. It is safer that way – we cannot get drawn in – we cannot swim out beyond our depth. But how frustrating this is to anyone who wants to meet a real person.

Being sexy is something that men may often require as a condition of their being interested. But this kind of interest is a basically exploitative interest; the best a woman could get out of it would be some kind of horse-trading exercise – you give me this and I'll give you that. That is not love, or anything like it, more of an insult.

GOOD SEXUALITY

So coming back now to our question as to what would be OK in the realm of sexuality, what do we do now? We simply respond to the whole person who is there, rather than as some figment of our male imagination. We do not automatically keep women at arm's length mentally and also emotionally. We do not do anything automatically.

If we want to have any kind of human relationship with women, we have to give up pornography, and sexiness, and rape. We have to insist on being fully human, and not settling for part of a person. We do not like being reduced to a fragment ourselves – how come it is OK to do it to someone else?

A woman read this, and asked, only half-jokingly, 'What are you men allowed to have a guilt-free hard-on about?' I feel this question deserves a reply, because it raises a genuine issue for men who have some consciousness of the feminist challenge and feel quite uneasy about it. I think there are three answers which are quite direct:

- something genuine
- something whole
- something satisfying

Something genuine

There is a real difference between relating to a fantasy and relating to a person. To the extent that the hard-on is really only about our wishes and fantasies and illusions it is suspect. To the extent that these fantasies are about exploitation and using women it could well induce guilt, which would be quite appropriate and actionable. If we want to give up the exploitation and use of women, giving up our fantasies about that seems part of the deal.

There are two kinds of guilt: ordinary guilt, where some reparation can be made to the injured party, or where some action can be taken to correct the matter; and neurotic guilt, where we agonise about things which cannot be changed and where there is no hope of reparation. There is nothing wrong with ordinary guilt, so long as it leads to action. Some men have taken to calling this grief (Bly 1990), and this is fine if it works.

Something whole

There is a difference between relating to a whole person and relating to a cut-off part of a person. To the extent that our hard-on is just about some part of a person, and the interest in the person is limited to that, it reduces the person to that part. This kind of reduction is insulting, and it is OK in my book to feel guilty about insulting someone, particularly if you are supposed to be approaching them in a positive way.

On the other hand, if the hard-on is there in response to the presence of a whole person, and applies to the whole of that person, there is no reason for guilt at all. There may be other kinds of guilt, if the person happens to be in a close relationship with someone else, or if we ourselves are in a committed relationship with someone else, depending on our conscience in these matters, but this is separate and distinct from the basic question being asked here.

Something satisfying

There is a difference between having a hard-on in relation to some situation which promises satisfaction, and one which relates to a situation which does not. Yet many men continually put themselves into situations where their hard-on leads them into unsatisfying experiences. This can go so far that you get the condition which is now known as sex and love addiction. This is where the man is continually feeling the need for sex, continually getting hard-ons, but continually choosing badly and having brief relationships which get nowhere and do not lead to the expected satisfaction.

The reason why this should lead to guilt is that such relationships are basically exploitative, whether they are paid for or not. They are merely to satisfy an itch, and the itch does not even go away. This is sad, and might well lead to grief, or guilt.

But if a hard-on leads to an experience which is satisfying, which makes you feel good afterwards, this is usually because it is satisfying to both parties. There is something inescapably mutual about sex, and really it works well only when both partners are getting something out of it. This is the true freedom which mutual sex always promised. One-sided sex is just not as satisfying, and of course it may well be exploitative.

Obviously I have been talking here about heterosexual relations, because the original statement above was specifically about that, but the principles just outlined seem to apply just as well to gay relationships. As Martin Humphries has said:

> This could lead to a redefinition that opens up the image, lays bare the emotions, so that we have an eroticised reality of men who are both gentle and strong, who give full expression to their feelings, listen to their hearts and allow their warmth to be taken, used and reciprocated.
>
> (Humphries 1985: 85)

He is talking about gay relationships, but the language is familiar.

WHAT ARE WE AIMING AT?

One lesson of all this is that it is important to give up any notion of correct masculinity, as if there were just one right way of being a man. Good sexuality, as we have seen, emphasises mutuality and responsiveness to the other person, in a way that is genuine rather than role-playing. But of course this is just the opposite from the usual textbook message to therapists. What we are usually told is that men are too uncertain about their gender identity, perhaps because of an absent father, and that they need to be encouraged in the achievement of gender certainty.

This is perhaps a particular danger for those Jungians who lay a good deal of stress on the animus and anima. It is all too easy to lay down an order of gender which is certain and sure, and to believe that this is the truth. We saw some discussion of this in Chapter 4.

Many writers now know that traditional views on gender are being questioned, and therefore avoid the issue completely. I was surprised to find how many books on the family, for example, avoid all questions of gender.

The general view of humanistic psychology is that all roles constrict and prevent self-actualisation. This is as true of gender roles as of any others. And gender certainty is certainty about gender roles. We can now see more clearly how what we are being certain or confused about are social stereotypes which serve one particular version of society – the patriarchal version.

Joe Pleck (1981) has devoted a whole book to exploding the myths around the masculine sex-role. Men often feel desperately unhappy when the masculine role is questioned, and try to shore up their position with a whole set of myths: the myth that families need fathers; that there is such a thing as sexual energy, which builds up and builds up until it has to be let out; the myth that harsh punishment builds up men; and so on. So if we are going to demolish falsehoods, what are we to put in their place? What are we aiming at?

PENIS AND POWER

Around 1978 I was really very occupied with the whole issue of sexuality and male violence. It was this coercive violence which ultimately underlay all the less obvious ways in which women were put down by men. A brilliant article by Kokopeli and Lacey (1982) has the memorable sentence which really came home to me – 'Rape is the end logic of masculine sexuality.' Rape, they said, is not so much a sexual act as an act of violence expressed in a sexual way.

Some of the feminists (Brownmiller 1976) were seeing rape as the key to patriarchy, and at the same time the ultimate insult to women. As such, it deserved the ultimate punishment – castration. There seemed to be something in the thought of castrating rapists which made the feminist spirit rise: there was a badge which showed an axe with blood dripping from it and the words 'DISARM RAPISTS'. But it also made more thought-out sense. Mary Daly said:

> The method of liberation, then, involves a *castrating* of language and images that reflect and perpetuate the structure of a sexist world. It castrates precisely in the sense of cutting away the phallocentric value system imposed by patriarchy [which] . . . has amounted to a kind of gang rape of minds as well as bodies. . . . Now [we] are rising up to castrate not people but *the system* that castrates – that great 'God-Father' of us all which indulges senselessly and universally in the politics of rape.
>
> (Daly 1973: 9–10)

These are strong words, which make a strong appeal to some women who I see

144

as being very central to feminism and what it stands for. But they make me scared, because the feeling that comes through is that, if this talk of castration goes on long enough, it is *my* penis which is going for the chop. Castration strictly means removal of the testes, but at an unconscious level it also means removal of the whole penis. It seems to me that this image of castration cannot be accepted by men. It is too close, too personal, too threatening.

But if that is the case, what can men see as their hope, their function, their role in a feminist world, or a post-patriarchal world? I got a clue from something very personal which happened to me.

In my therapy I had started to criticise my father's attitude to sex and to women. I became convinced that he really hated women and wanted to punish them with his penis. I was angry that all his attitudes to sex and to women were power-oriented, patriarchal. I acted out a scene where I tore his penis (his bad, exploitative, aggressive penis) right off and stuffed it down his throat.

Later I started to see that it was part of myself that I was trying to get rid of – my own bad penis, hostile attitudes, power orientation. But what was I going to have instead? The prospect of not having a penis at all seemed unacceptable and in any case unrealistic and inappropriate. One answer seemed to be the idea of having a nicey-nicey penis, which would never do anyone any harm. But the nicey-nicey penis seemed too sweet, too totally determined by being the very opposite of the bad penis, like two ends of a line (Figure 9.1).

BAD PENIS ——————————————— NICEY-NICEY PENIS

Figure 9.1 Bad penis – nicey-nicey penis

Was the answer to move to the middle of the line, and be a bit of each, a compromise between the two?

The answer which came up was No to this. There was another possibility, which emerged in a later session. I could have a good penis. This I saw as being strong and powerful, but non-oppressive. If the bad penis was like a bayonet, a pistol or a club, and the nicey-nicey penis was like a passive tassel or a glass tumbler, the good penis was like a bridge, a crane or a communication tower. It could genuinely reach out to people, connect with people and cooperate with people. And this seemed to be on another dimension to the first line, including both the assertiveness of the bad penis and the receptivity of the nicey-nicey penis, but not reducing to the one-sidedness of either of them. The line now turned into a triangle (Figure 9.2).

Putting this in formal terms, the bad penis was the thesis, the nicey-nicey penis was the antithesis, and the good penis the synthesis of the two. What this meant to me in practice was that there was a good way of being a man, an OK way of having genuine male power that could be non-oppressive to women. I think I have to add here that I couldn't have arrived at this without having

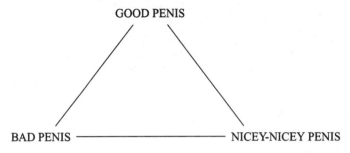

Figure 9.2 Bad penis – nicey-nicey penis – good penis

already worked through my very complicated feelings about loving and hating my mother, which I have described in an article elsewhere (Rowan 1992). I was already a lot clearer on my feelings about women when I began this.

So far this is all about me, and my experience in my own process of development. But then I came across another piece of work, very similar, but much more fully worked out. Aaron Kipnis (1991) produced a table (see Table 9.1).

What it means, as I see it, is that we now have a theory of power which is specifically relevant to men. Instead of shuffling along a line where the only choice is to be harmful or harmless, we can go on to a positively good place, where we can define our own real strength in a non-patriarchal way.

From the power-over position in the first column of Table 9.1 we can relate to women only as oppressors; from the powerlessness position of the second column, we can relate to women only as superior to us – we are underlings; but from the power-with position in the third column we can relate in cooperative ways with any women or men who have got to a similar position in their own terms.

It is a curious fact this same theory is also to be found in management theory. For example, Fordyce and Weil (1971) have a theory of power which contrasts power-over and powerlessness, and shows that power-with can reconcile the two without falling into the excesses of either alone. The same idea is to be found in the excellent book on group dynamics by Starhawk (1990). But perhaps the most eloquent expression of these ideas comes from Joanna Macy:

> How does power as process – 'power with' rather than 'power over' – operate in our lives? We don't own it. We don't use it like a gun. We can't measure its quantity or size. We can't increase it at our neighbour's expense. Power is like a verb; it happens through us.
>
> We experience it when we engage in interactions that produce value. We have such interactions with loved ones and fellow citizens; with God; with music, art and literature; with seeds we plant; or with materials we shape.

Table 9.1 What are we aiming at?

ena	Uninitiated		Initiated
	Heroic *(hyper-masculinity)* Old male ((power-over))	*Feminised* *(hypo-masculinity)* *Transitional male* *(powerlessness)*	*Authentic* *(integrated masculinity)* *Ancient/new male* *(power-with)*
hysical	hard dominating tough soldier killer coercive controlling lord and master	soft submissive gentle pacifist gatherer pliant controlled immobile	flexible capable strong warrior hunter firm vigilant generative
Emotional	closed numb codependent demanding aggressive cynical sex partner defensive repressed bastard over-responsible	unprotected flooded dependent smothering passive naive pleaser wounded contained nice guy irresponsible	receptive feeling interdependent nurturing assertive fresh/humorous lover vulnerable wild/playful direct responsible
Mental	compartmentalised penetrating analytical splitting linear hierarchy exploitative rules and laws doctor	merged diffused synthetic joining circular anarchy conservative procedures magical thinker	choosing insightful discriminating holds paradox holonomic community resourceful personal ethics healer
Spiritual	patriarchal absolute uninitiated immobile single self divided dogma exclusive priest	matrifocal vague seeker in flight selfless dissociated belief inclusive cult minded	polytheistic paradoxical initiated grounded braided self embodied direct experience selective mentor/elder

Source: Kipnis 1991 (slightly amended by John Rowan)

Such synergistic exchanges generate something that was not there before and that enhances the capacities and well-being of all who are involved. 'Power with' involves attentive openness to the surrounding physical or mental environment and alertness to our own and others' responses. It is the capacity to act in ways that increase the sum total of one's conscious participation in life.

This kind of power may be most familiar in relationship to a partner, spouse, or child. As you help them develop their strengths and skills, your own sense of well-being increases. This power, which enhances the power of others, does not originate in you, but you have been party to its unfolding. You are its channel, its midwife, its gardener.

(Macy 1995: 258)

What I believe is that the inner and the outer, the personal and the political, are basically one and the same. My own personal changes and the changes in other people and in the wider scene are not widely distant. This is why I feel my own personal history may be highly relevant to what other people are going through. We all have to make changes, if the patriarchal world is going to change, at the personal level and the institutional level too. I like what Terry Kupers says about this:

The challenge that confronts men is to find ways to be powerful without oppressing anyone, and in the process to redefine power, heroism and masculinity. This is an immense challenge. And men will never meet it in isolation. We need new kinds of bonds among men and between men and women, straight and gay, if we are to construct, collectively, new forms of masculinity and new and better gender relations.

(Kupers 1993: 183)

None of this is easy to do – we all have our various hangups which get in the way. But if the theory is of any use, it can help us to see what directions to look in.

CASE EXAMPLE

One man came to me with an interesting problem. His work was being interfered with, to the point where he found it difficult to carry on at all, by sexual fantasies. He would be talking to his boss, for example, and the sexual fantasy would come on, and he would become tongue-tied and have to leave the room. Or he would be tackling a problem, and the sexual fantasy would arrive, and he would have to leave it. So this was something quite disabling. It had to do with a girlfriend he had left behind in another city, and whom he could see very seldom because of her family's opposition, and was virtually a re-enactment of his last meeting with her.

Some time was spent in getting all the details and the background, but then it seemed to me quite a straightforward thing to deal with. So I asked him to tell me the fantasy, in detail, exactly as it came to him. He did so. I asked him to tell me again. He did so. Then I carried on doing this, for the whole session. By the end, he had been through the fantasy ten or eleven times.

When he came back, he reported that he had not had the fantasy in the previous week, and we went on to other aspects of his life.

148

This approach, which Adler and Frankl called paradoxical intention (Clifford 1990) and which is also used in hypnotherapy (Karle and Boys 1987), is very useful in those cases where something has become automatic. To de-automatise anything seems to make it much more amenable to treatment, and may even be enough on its own. Of course there is an old argument about symptom substitution, but in this case there was no such problem, because the therapy went on from there.

GRIEF WORK WITH MEN

Some problems are relatively simple, others are much more complex. Having looked at a relatively simple one in the last section, it is time to look at something more complex. One of the most difficult for men is the problem of grief. It may be remembered that in the case example of Chapter 3, it was grief that brought about the breakthrough in the therapy.

This is an important area, because it is often a man's first adult acquaintance with deep emotions. They may shock him by their intensity, and there may be a crisis as a result. As we have seen many times already, the image of the male in our culture is a tough one, and any sign of weakness is suspect. Yet here is something where the man does feel weak. One client said:

> I felt as if I were being turned inside out. It just felt all wrong. I wasn't myself. I thought – 'This can't be me'. It was just like nothing I had ever felt before. I didn't like it. I just wanted it to be over. But it wouldn't go away.

Grief very often lasts much longer than the man expects. Surprisingly often, it leads to illness, particularly in the case where it is the partner who has died. Sometimes in such cases it leads to suicide – ten times more often for men than for women whose partner has died (J.C. Smith *et al.* 1988). Warren Farrell (1993) speculates that it is the loss of love that devastates men; another possibility is that it is the loss of emotional support that is the key thing; either way it seems that this kind of loss is felt very keenly by men. Yet it may be denied:

> I have learned never to underestimate a man's ability to deny his feelings following a death.
>
> (Roberts 1994: 220)

A therapist would do well to take it seriously and encourage the male client to unburden himself, even if he does not much want to do so. Lister (1991) has a good account of the research in this field.

Robert Bly has extended the word 'grief' to mean more than the emotions connected with mourning. For example, he says:

> Some Turkish Sufi groups begin their night-work with a repeated word reminding them of the grief of what they have not done the past year. The

emotion is not around sin, guilt or shame: but around what one has not done.

(Bly 1990: 76)

Today, grief for men includes not only the loss of parents, but also the loss of the certainty that there is a caring, appreciative woman for them, who will be there when they return. It includes feelings not only about the absent father, but also about the absent job. And Robert Bly has said that grief, rather than anger, is the doorway to a man's feelings.

To accomplish this, therapy can explore men's past losses or examine present ones to unearth man's sense of abandonment.

Once identified, therapy can help men sort through their feelings to resolve old problems and understand the basis of their present ones.

(Pasick *et al.* 1990: 163)

Let us go on to see how this can be so.

DEEP EMOTIONS

Grief may be the man's first introduction to deep emotions, as we have said, and as such it is a way in to the inner life. It is an opportunity for a therapist to reach a male client on a deep level. It is very important, therefore, for a therapist to stay with such deep feelings and not allow the client to skip over them as fast as possible. Some men, of course, do not want to do this:

I am articulate, that is one of my greatest assets. But I confide my personal feelings less and less, as I find my life easier and easier to handle by myself. In fact, I've always kept my emotions to myself, and been raised to believe that feelings are to be mastered and controlled, and I can do it. That is the area where I have contempt for people who can't do as I do.

(Hite 1981: 94)

Here the non-expression of feelings is a positive value, and we shall come back to this issue in Chapter 11.

Tears are often important in therapy, most of all when they are rare. Many men have not cried for years, and this is sad in itself. It was in 1968 that a headline in *Time* magazine said 'It's OK to cry in the office', but it was not true then and it is still not true now. When men feel bad, they cry – and then they feel bad about crying. It is giving way to weakness. A representative quotation in this area:

I have been raised not to show my feelings. Once when I wasn't getting along with my lover my whole body got sick because I was so miserable. My stomach felt like it got hit by a train. But I didn't tell my friends why I felt so shitty, even though they asked. Sometimes I behave like a robot but I don't feel like one.

(Hite 1981: 55)

A therapist can challenge this pattern and give a male client permission to show feelings. Often with men anger covers up for hurt, and a good therapist can usually get behind the anger to the hurt, making it possible for the client to show some deep emotions. When this happens, it makes the whole therapy easier, because more of the client's resources have been brought into play.

FATHER HUNGER

One of the areas of bereavement which may be most effective is the loss of a father. It is often not until a father dies that the son realises how much the old man meant to him. There are often great regrets that more communication did not take place before it was too late. As Malinak *et al.* (1979) found, there is often a lot of unfinished business in relation to the death of a father, made worse by the fact that feelings are never discussed between father and son.

As with all bereavement, a good therapist will allow the client to explore not only feelings of sadness, but also any other feelings (such as for example anger) which may be present. This is an important bit of permission-giving which must not be underestimated. But there is a kind of bereavement which has often occurred before the father dies at all. Robert Bly says:

> As I've participated in men's gatherings since the early 1980s I've heard one statement over and over from American males, which has been phrased in a hundred different ways: 'There is not enough father'. The sentence implies that father is a substance like salt, which in earlier times was occasionally in short supply, or like groundwater, which in some areas has simply disappeared.
>
> (Bly 1990: 92)

He goes on to say that the father is often absent in fact, and still more often absent in mind. The son becomes suspicious of what the father is up to. He does not look for a mentor, because he mistrusts older men generally. The fathers often mistrust themselves, do not consider themselves good role models, do not want the sons to follow in their footsteps. Frank Pittman takes up this theme:

> So we grew up constantly faking our masculinity, and never knowing quite how much masculinity would be enough. We've all been, to varying degrees, male impersonators – awed by the splendour of the masculine mystique and ashamed of the meagre masculinity we found in ourselves.
>
> (Pittman 1993: xvii)

But Bly's point is that there was once a positive image of the older man – the king – who was looked up to and respected. John Lee describes what happens now:

If I ask men to fill in the blank after the phrase: 'Dad will always . . . ', the same eight out of ten men will reply, 'Dad will always criticise me, leave me, hurt me, abandon me, or yell at me.'

(Lee 1991: 31)

The positive figure has gone – all the images are broken and all we have left is a hunger for the father which cannot be satisfied. Instead, young men try to outdistance the father, to fly above him.

Society without the father produces these birdlike men, so intense, so charming, so open to addiction, so sincere, as those great bays in the Hellespont produced the cranes Homer noticed that flew in millions toward the sun.

(Bly 1990: 102)

Many men want to avoid the father. They would rather talk about their mothers. Fathers are to be left behind. But they are not left behind, they are right there. Samuel Osherson (1986) speaks movingly of 'healing the wounded father'.

A therapist must walk carefully in this area, because it is such a sensitive one. But it is a very central area for male identity, and cannot be ignored.

GAY AND BISEXUAL MEN

There are a number of specific issues here which need to be handled well if the client is not to feel got at. Here we shall examine the issues and how they are handled.

First of all, it is essential to understand how homosexuality is normal to men. All men have in them the potential to be gay, because all men have an absorbing interest in themselves and other men.

The people whom they admire, respect, adore, revere, honour, whom they imitate, idolize, and form profound attachments to, whom they are willing to teach and from whom they are willing to learn, and whose respect, admiration, recognition, honour, reverence and love they desire . . . those are overwhelmingly, other men.

(Frye 1983: 135)

A lot of men's lives is gender-segregated. Men historically have preferred to work with other men, and to mix with other men in their leisure hours. Many jobs are almost completely owned by one gender (Lorber 1994: Chapter 9). Who is a man standing next to, and talking to, as we look around us? Mostly it is other men. So for a therapist to deal with a gay man is not to encounter something strange and new, but rather something with which he is very familiar. Admitting this may be the hard thing.

The second point to make straight away is that to the extent that the gay man comes from an unfamiliar culture, everyone really comes from an unfamiliar culture. All therapy is intercultural therapy. Each family is unique, each person is unique, each situation is unique, and every time we make the assumption, 'Oh, this case is just like this other case', or even worse, 'This person's background is just like my own', we make a mistake. So we as therapists always need to be open and questioning, rather than thinking we know. A good phrase is 'beginner's mind': if we can cultivate a beginner's mind, at all times in every session, that is the best we can do. The moment we think we know what is going on, at that moment we lose touch with the present and move into something more fixed and less alive. If a man mentions his mother, we might ask 'What is a mother?', rather than assuming we already know.

Somebody once said that it is good to know a lot of theory, but that it is also good to leave it outside the door when actually with a client. It certainly seems to me that theory is good for analysing later what went on, or for planning what to tackle next, or for discussions with a supervisor, and so on, but not for guidance during the session.

The third point I would make is that a good therapist needs to understand and appreciate the oppression that gay men have experienced. They are not acceptable in a heteropatriarchal society, and get a great deal of flak thrown at them. This ranges from odd remarks to physical punishment. They suffer in a million tiny ways, and in some big ways too.

In reality, however, there is very little difference between gay or bisexual men and straight men. There is, for example, no difference in mental health between gay and heterosexual men (Harrison 1987: 220).

Sexual orientation is established early in life and not readily subject to change. As we shall see in the next chapter, there is a great deal of homophobia and internalised homophobia about, but it does not change anything. It is simply a prejudice. As we shall see later, some people think it would be better termed heterosexism. Most therapists suffer from it, and it reveals itself in such questions as 'How do you know you are homosexual?', or 'Why do you think you became homosexual?' These are questions one would never ask a heterosexual man, no matter how confused he was about gender.

A therapist dealing with a gay man would do well to find out about resources available to gay men – they may not know about them. Be prepared to give out such information. This is particularly helpful in those cases where a gay man has not come out and is very secretive about his orientation. Because he does not go to gay clubs or read the gay press or want to be seen in gay bookshops he may be very ignorant about what is available by way of help and support and further information.

One very important distinction is between homosexuality and effeminacy. Many gay men are not effeminate at all, and resent the assumption that they are feminine in their ways. Gay men may or may not like women, and the statistics from several recent surveys show that they surprisingly often have sex with women. Bisexual men of course may have sex with either gender, and this is a genuine preference, not a case of 'any port in a storm', as some gay activists have suggested. They may be worried that their children will reject them. As therapists, we have to be aware of our own prejudices in this area, and work on them as we discover them. It is not enough to say to a client 'You are pushing at my limits', though this is at least honest: through supervision and our own therapy it is necessary to work at areas where we have discovered our own prejudices.

Another area of prejudice is the assumption, sometimes made, that gay men want to seduce young boys. Homosexuality and paedophilia are two different things, and should never be confused. A paedophile is interested in children as such, and often has no particular preference for boys as against girls. What he loves is their youth. Once a child passes a certain age, he or she loses the interest of the paedophile, which may in fact be deeply disappointing for the child. Much of the evidence on child sexual abuse has been well summarised by Kevin Browne (1994).

Gay men need to deal with their own ageism. There is a tendency, just as with straight men, to prefer younger people, and to exchange an older partner for a younger one at a certain stage.

Today there are a number of issues around AIDS. The latest thinking seems to be in favour of getting tested for HIV, because insurance companies are much more relaxed now, having had good experiences rather than bad about the incidence of health claims around AIDS. But in any case of doubt, it is good practice to ring the local AIDS hotline, because they will have the latest information.

Bisexual men are perhaps more complex than gay men. They tend to get married before they have explored their gay side (Matteson 1987). Confusion may be a sign of mental health for bisexuals. If with a partner of one sex, a bisexual man may have dreams and fantasies about the other sex.

AIDS is a special problem for bisexuals, because of the danger of passing it on to children. It is particularly important for them to practise safe sex. It is quite all right for a therapist to ask about this, and it should not be regarded as pushy or inappropriate.

Bisexuals should be encouraged to understand that their way of life is not just a station on the way to becoming gay. Marriage, for them, may be just as satisfying and stimulating as it is for any heterosexual. Homophobia is just as much of a problem for bisexuals as it is for gays. A therapist needs to help a bisexual to feel that he is OK as he is.

Couple counselling can be a minefield, particularly in a marriage where a bisexual man has not yet revealed his homosexual side to his partner. It may be good to have a team of gay male and heterosexual female counsellors. There is a good discussion of all this in Matteson (1987). Again be prepared to give information about gay resources. There can be grief work around the loss of a monogamous ideal. A bisexual man may use his wife as an escape from fear of intimacy with a man. There are all kinds of angles to this, but the thing for the therapist to remember is basically the same as for all other clients – respect.

AGEING MEN

There are certain issues about the second half of life which need to be addressed specifically, and therapists need to know what these are.

Butler and Lewis (1982) have pointed out that old age is the period in life with the greatest number of profound crises, often occurring in multiples and with high frequency. They also state that 'individual psychotherapy is *least* available to older persons and yet should be a part of any therapeutic relationship' (Butler and Lewis 1982: 320, italics in original). Availability is more than likely tied to money and earning power, which declines with age and retirement. The critical psychological events for older men concern their reactions to death and grief, decisions, and disabilities. Butler and Lewis (1982) contend that older persons often exhibit a strong desire to resolve problems, to put their lives in order, and to find satisfactions and a second chance – thus making them prime candidates for therapy, which Butler and Lewis have already said is less likely to be available to them.

The professional therapist may need to give special or extra help to the older men's caring networks for them to become more therapeutic – defined as open and supportive of critical life topics as well as accepting of the personal concerns of older men.

One of the most depressing facts which comes out of any examination of the psychological effects of ageing is that it is all a downward path. The following functions get steadily worse as we get older: conduction velocity of nerve fibre; basal metabolic rate; male strength of grip; cardiac output; vital capacity; reaction times to light or sound; stated frequency of sexual intercourse; brain weight; liver weight; intelligence tests; visual recognition; rote learning. And the sad thing is that these things do not start falling off at a late age, but early. From the age of 20 onwards there is a steady decline.

For many people, particularly in the upper income groups, this is disguised by success experiences of one kind or another, which give an illusion of unimpaired faculties. It may be only at a certain point where failure is experienced that 'it all comes home' and adds to feelings of depression and identity crisis. In order to stop this, Chown and Heron (1965) found that older people tend to clamp down on their emotions, but are strongly disturbed by unexpected disasters.

This connects up with a good deal of work on rigidity, which seems to show that older people tend to revert to concrete thinking. However, it is not true that older people necessarily become more conservative in a strictly political sense. The vast majority of people vote the same way all their lives.

Neugarten (1963) showed that adult men in their forties are preoccupied with the idea of virility and resistance to coercion, while those in their sixties emphasise friendliness, conformity and adaptation to what comes. Older men move into an area of wanting to be liked, and to be seen as warm and friendly. Birren (1970) found that older lawyers and doctors protect themselves from emotional overload by not becoming as involved with their clients as they used to do.

This suggests that men disengage from active social involvement of a kind which may involve conflict. Cumming and Henry (1961) put forward a theory of disengagement, which states that older people tend to cut themselves off from social interaction more and more. Bromley (1988) says that this theory is still popular, but has also been criticised as encouraging people to neglect the elderly.

Reichard *et al.* (1962) studied eighty-seven men aged between 55 and 84, half retired and half not. They found five different ways of coming to terms with age:

1 the mature (constructive)
2 the rocking chair (dependent)
3 the armoured (defensive)
4 the angry (hostile)
5 the self-haters

Of these, the first three were well adjusted, and the last two poorly adjusted. This research is interesting, but has never been followed up and checked out thoroughly.

There are some similarities between the 'mature' group in the Reichard *et al.* study and the self-actualising person described by Maslow (1987). It is important, therefore, for the therapist to see this kind of possibility, and not to assume that nothing much can be done with the older client. It is true that 'success rates' tend to be lower with older men, but the statistics are quite suspect, and it is wise to take each case on its merits.

Another way of looking at old age is to see it as a social role, surrounded by a great many social expectations. It is possible to see old age as a kind of ghetto, subjected to a lot of prejudice and disadvantages. This tends to be worse for working-class people, who according to Kerckhoff (1964) make fewer plans for old age, and have fewer resources for dealing with the changes which come with it.

Most people experience, with retirement, a drop in income, and in our culture that has many implications, particularly in terms of loss of power and effectiveness. Together with that goes, for men particularly, a process of role relinquishment which may bring back memories of all the other times in life when one has had to be separated from something familiar, perhaps going right back to the anxiety of being separated from one's parents and getting lost. Going from one central role to another always seems to involve some anxiety and some crisis of identity, and here there is more often than not a real sense of going down more than up.

Something which may help to make this transition less painful is part-time work, and many retired people find this solution quite acceptable. It must also be remembered that although income is lower, expenses are often lower too, and so the person is not necessarily suffering too much.

But it is not only the work roles which change. The parental role now virtually reverses. Children, once a liability and a responsibility, now become an asset – even though often a dubious and undependable one. Instead of the children being dependent on the parents, now it is quite often the case that the parents become more dependent on the children, and on the wider family generally. Those who do not have children, or who have become estranged from them, may feel particularly isolated. This is becoming more common today, because smaller and more scattered families are prevalent.

The relationship between the parents may change now too. If the husband spends more time at home, the line between living and working almost disappears. There is more dependency on what the home can offer, in the way of entertainment and work. Yet it may be at this very time that a change of dwelling becomes necessary. Maybe one wants to move out of a house which is now too big, and with repair bills which are too heavy. Or maybe one is sick, and cannot run a house properly. Maybe one is a widower, with even more crushing role changes to cope with.

All these drastic changes are taking place at a time when one finds change most hard to take. Older people are looking for and needing stability, rather than rapid change. It may well be, in situations like this, that one looks around for something permanent, which is not going to change, and which can be depended on absolutely. Religion often fills this bill, offering an unchangeable God or access to unchangeable spiritual truths. It can easily be seen that most of the people attending church services are older, as are those who attend spiritualist meetings and buy church magazines, etc. (Fukuyama 1961).

In spite of all this, studies show (Bromley 1988) that given reasonable physical health and financial resources, the average retired person soon adapts to the changed circumstances and shows an improvement in physical health and outlook. It is the transition which creates problems of adjustment. And so the man may come into therapy from this sort of angle.

Preparation for retirement is now catered for by many firms, voluntary organisations and centres for adult education, but many people enter retirement inadequately prepared. Of course this is made more difficult in a time of long-term unemployment and premature retirement, which may be much more unexpected than straightforward retirement.

Sexual problems may come to the fore. Visits to the doctor should be encouraged, because neglect may come from fears about health, and so real issues may be ignored or set aside. A man who has been healthy all his life may not want to know about psychological or physiological changes which are now coming to him.

Relationships with grandchildren may be satisfying. Relationships with his own children may be frustrating and may need a lot of work to put right.

Death can become an important issue. There is a good deal of good material out now about this (Osterweiss *et al.* 1984, Parkes and Weiss 1983, Rands 1984, Rinpoche 1992), but again the key thing is the therapist's own attitude to death. All therapists of whatever persuasion really need to pay attention to their own work on themselves in this field.

Part V

ALBEDO

It is the white ash of albedo, containing the opposites of despair, mourning, or repentance. . . . It symbolizes the purity of the glorified body. . . . Psychologically, spirit is now free to express itself through the personality level.

(R. Miller and I. Miller 1994: 98)

10

MEN AND WORK

This is classically an important area for men, and needs to be looked at specifically. There are central questions of identity and involvement which arise here, and a good deal to be said about them. It is in work that most men find their greatest satisfactions and their greatest miseries. But initiation is particularly important here, because without initiation, work can be just a meaningless ritual. Even though it may sound extreme to say this, I believe that it is only after their initiation that men can relate to work in a human fashion. We are now looking at this whole area from the point of view of having been initiated. Before initiation there is a strong tendency for men to treat work as too central, and to reduce themselves to some kind of robot in the service of the job and their responsibilities.

Like fish oblivious to the water that surrounds them, men are generally unconscious of their absorption with their jobs.

> Men's language is the language of work. When they are asked what they 'do' they describe the nature of their jobs. Even as young boys, when asked what they want to be when they grow up, they know the question means, 'what profession will you choose?'
>
> (Pasick 1990: 35)

It is not suggested, of course, that initiation is a one-off thing which happens on a Tuesday and never has to be repeated. It is, as everything in this book emphasises, a long process which nevertheless is punctuated by breakthroughs which may be more or less dramatic. When the phrase 'after initiation' is used, it should therefore be taken to mean 'after some important step in the initiation process has been taken'. The *Albedo* is one of these points: something has been achieved, something has been won. We can then go on with renewed faith in the process, renewed courage for the struggle.

Since the 1970s the area of work has been becoming more and more problematic, because of large-scale structural unemployment. But it is more general than that. If we accept Emery and Trist's (1965) distinction between four types of economic and social environments

161

- placid, randomised environments
- placid, clustered environments
- disturbed, reactive environments
- turbulent-field environments

and say, with them, that what we have now is a turbulent environment, this means that we are faced with a situation where there is not only uncertainty and conflict between identifiable component systems, but also uncertainty and conflict in the environmental field itself – in the whole setting within which the action takes place. In an era when Rolls-Royce goes bankrupt, the USA goes off the gold standard, the price of oil breaks all conceivable barriers, Chernobyl puts the whole nuclear programme in doubt, what certainties are left?

> Men are taught that they must achieve occupationally. In order to obtain power, prestige, money, and other indices of achievement, many men readily sacrifice emotional expressiveness, intimacy and interrelatedness. Because manliness, or one's sense of self as a man, is also tied to the 'good provider role' (Bernard 1981), men often become controlled by their occupational obligations and the economic structure. To be a real man, and a successful man, the male must be an effective breadwinner, whatever the physical and emotional costs involved. Finally, successful men are independent and do what is necessary to make their way in the world.
>
> (Gilbert 1987: 279)

This is recognisable now as the standard stereotype of hegemonic masculinity rearing its ugly head again.

So now instead of having one huge problem – finding work and working within an organisation – we have two: the other huge problem is doing without a job. Many older unemployed men are convinced that they will never work again, and many school leavers are convinced that they will never have a job at all. This latter problem is of course worse for people in disadvantaged groups.

If for men a job is the main source of identity, and if to be in control is so important for men, as we have seen it is, then to be deprived of a job is to be deprived of any real identity. And if a man should be married to a woman who does have a job there is a kind of role reversal which may or may not be easy for him, but in any case is problematic.

For an initiated man, these issues may start to look unreal. He may begin to think in terms of being self-employed, or changing careers, or having a portfolio of different tasks rather than 'a job'. For him, the whole distinction between work and leisure may get blurred. This often happens, for example, in the case of therapists themselves.

COMMUNICATION

In any case, however, what is very important for men is to understand communication. Whether it is working in a job, or whether it is a question of finding a job, or whether it is getting other people to interweave their tasks with yours, communication is essential. It is one of the areas where men are weakest. They tend to think that if they say something clearly, the other person will understand and act accordingly. They often do not appreciate that communication is a two-way thing. You cannot know whether you have communicated unless you get some feedback confirming it.

Communication is sometimes reduced to 'communication skills' which can be taught on a short course, but this is to turn it into something mechanical, which it cannot be. It is something human, and depends for its success on human qualities. The initiated man is very good at communication, because he is genuinely present. As Alvin Mahrer puts it rather convincingly:

> The intensely experiencing person is with you: he does not merely talk about being with you or tell you about it. He is irritated at you, rather than talking with you about his irritation. He shares with you – instead of telling you about sharing, or explaining how important sharing is, or lapsing romantic about the notion of sharing.

> (Mahrer 1989a: 591)

As we saw in Chapter 9, communication does not come easily to men, but in reality openness is a very important key to communication. It is a synergistic question: if I am open that makes it easier for you to be open, and if you are open that makes it easier for me to be open. And if we are open, communication flows easily instead of meeting with blocks and misunderstandings.

One of the discoveries of modern management theory (Fordyce and Weil 1971, Senge 1990) is that openness and trust are necessary to good communication. Schutz (1984) has spelt out in great detail the importance of telling the truth. This comes hard to the man who has been socialised into the hegemonic pattern. He wants control, and does not feel easy until he has it: yet the implication of all the work which has been done on communication is that the attempt to control people always reduces the extent and accuracy of any communication. People just do not like being treated as impersonal things, to be controlled like things. Communication is possible only between equals. If one person tries to control another, that necessary sense of equality is lost.

One of the joys of initiation is dropping the need to control, the need to defend one's ego, the need to be right.

INTERPERSONAL QUALITIES

However, openness is only one of the interpersonal skills – better called interpersonal qualities – that are needed, either at work or in getting work, or in negotiating about work. Men neglect interpersonal qualities at their peril. One of the less obvious things about counselling and psychotherapy is that they offer a demonstration, live, week by week, of good interpersonal qualities. The client gets angry at the therapist, the therapist responds in a nondefensive fashion: what an excellent example of the quality of openness. The client ignores and rejects the therapist, but the therapist refuses to be destroyed: what a good example of the quality of persistence. The client gets confused and goes off in all directions, but the therapist gently brings him back to the point at issue: what a good example of the quality of gentle leadership.

If, of course, the therapist does not have such human qualities no such examples can be given, but it is hoped that any decent training covers such matters. It is also to be hoped that a training in counselling or psychotherapy would include enough personal work to ensure that the graduate were initiated as part of the process. In my experience most of the people on a good training course do consider it a form of initiation, and act accordingly. Any training which omitted therapy for the therapist would be unlikely to cover all the areas necessary to achieve this.

CHANGING PATTERNS

All this depends, of course, on each man's attitude to work: this is by no means predictable. There are several different possibilities which have been found in practice: Appley and Winder give a table of attitudes and values (see Table 10.1).

It is easy to see that a man at level 1 will behave very differently from a man at level 6. But most men seem to operate at levels 2, 3 and 4, wanting to build up a career which is involving but not too involving. Today, of course, many men have two or three careers during their lives, because the field of work is changing so rapidly and radically. An initiated man, having been through levels 2, 3 and 4, will usually end up at level 5.

All this puts great strain on men, and stress is one of the great killers of our time. This is all the more so, because it is mostly men who populate the most

Table 10.1 Attitudes towards work and values fulfilled by work

Basic attitude towards work as	Basic additional value fulfilled by work
1 Interruption	Short-run income
2 Job	Long-term income; 'One works to live'
3 Occupation	Mastery of skills
4 Career	Participation in important programmes; satisfaction of work-oriented values
5 Vocation	Self-identification and self-fulfilment
6 Mission	Near fanatic; 'One lives to work'

Source: (Appley and Winder 1977)

potentially lethal occupations. Employers have generally resisted health and safety regulations, and the inspection of health and safety provisions has been grossly underfunded. It is no wonder than men continually feel treated unfairly. But this concept of fairness is by no means simple:

The concept of fairness, like the concept of justice, can be applied in a number of different ways. *All these are principles of fairness or justice*:

- *equality* all parties should receive equal value
- *needs* to all people according to their needs
- *seniority* those with longer service should get more
- *skill* those with higher skill, or more skills, get more
- *education* those with more training get more
- *responsibility* those entrusted with more get more
- *opportunities* those who can gain the greatest benefit should have their way
- *equal concessions* each party should yield equally, or split the difference
- *historical precedent* what did we get before, and what are others getting now?
- *effort* those who put in more effort should get more
- *productivity* who produces more for the work put in?
- *public utility* those should get more who benefit the public more
- *supply and demand* those who are wanted most should get most

It is obvious that some of these contradict others, and that appeals to fairness or justice therefore need careful forethought. There has been a great deal of research on perceived equity in pay, much of it using either Homans' (1961) formulation:

P's rewards less P's costs compared with   *O's rewards less O's costs*
P's investments   O's investments

or Adams' (1965) formulation, which comes to much the same thing:

P's outcomes compared with   *O's outcomes*
P's inputs   O's inputs

Unfortunately it is not at all clear whether, say, responsibility at work is an input or an outcome. As Delafield puts it:

The problem of definition of inputs and outcomes has led to equity theory's hypotheses being far too flexible. If results in the past have not supported a particular hypothesis then it has been the tendency to assume that what the experimenters originally thought was an imput was being demonstrated to be an outcome. Thus no real test of the hypothesis was made.

(Delafield 1979)

So far as our study here is concerned the point is that men are often going to come into therapy with complaints about being unfairly treated. It is important to accept these as genuine hurts, and not to enquire as to whether they are justified or not. The calculation of what is justified is so complex that it is not worth going into. The man's pain is real, and this is what needs to be addressed.

PREDICTABLE CRISES OF ADULT LIFE

Therapy is often initiated at a time of performance failure. But these are not just random. Particular problems seem to arise at particular stages in a man's development. A good account of this process is to be found in the research of Daniel Levinson (1978), who suggests that each man moves through alternating periods of transition and relative stability. During the stable periods we create a life structure that is made up of a network of roles and relationships, affecting both our work life and our personal life. During the transitions we become dissatisfied, for one reason or another (which may be our choice or may be forced on us), and re-examine that life structure and decide whether to try to change it to try to maintain it.

He puts forward a stage theory. As with all stage theories, it is important to look at the sequence which is described, not at the precise ages at which the transition is supposed to take place. Some men move through these stages much faster, others more slowly. Up to 17, he says, is childhood and adolescence. From 17 to 22 is the early adult transition, and it is at this point that a man starts to become aware of the four tasks which Levinson (1978) found so common:

1 developing a 'dream' of adult accomplishment
2 finding a mentor
3 developing a career
4 establishing intimacy

It is always important with these kinds of studies to realise that life is not always so neat and tidy. George Vaillant, who directed the Harvard study of men over many years, said once:

> Over and over throughout the study, the lesson was repeated: childhood does not end at 21. Even these men, selected in college for psychologic health, continued for the next two decades to wean themselves from their parents.
>
> (Vaillant 1978)

Levinson goes on to say that from 22 to 28 is the great period of entering the adult world, where the young man needs to build up his ego and his capacities, and make discoveries about what he can realistically do, what recognition he can demand. If a man comes into therapy at this stage, it is important for the therapist not to try to break him down, as it were, but rather to build him up. An experienced practitioner once said to me that it is important for a therapist to know when to use glue and when to use solvent. At this stage it is glue rather than solvent which is needed. Levinson says that at this stage a 'special woman' may be important, someone who encourages and believes in the potential of the man, and tolerates his dependent ways and other shortcomings.

It is exactly the opposite at the next stage, which is the transition extending from 28 to 33. This is the great classic age for entering therapy. The man has established himself, in most cases in a career. He has got so far with it – perhaps done very well – and then something has happened which gives him pause. It may be something as concrete as being made redundant, or that his partner has left him: it may be a much vaguer feeling that all is not well. Whatever it is, it means that he cannot go on as he has been doing. Something has to change. And here therapy needs the solvent rather than the glue. The therapist has to encourage him in his self-examination, and discourage escape from the dilemma which is now facing him. This is a good time to enter on the path of initiation.

Then comes another period of consolidation, from 33 to 40, where much more mature attitudes to work and to relationships can emerge. This is a period of settling down, where real stability may be experienced for the first time.

But then comes the transition from early adulthood to middle adulthood – the famous midlife crisis. From 40 to 45 the man may be engaged in an inner struggle, and this may affect both work and leisure. For heterosexuals, relationships with women and with children will be affected. All that has been built up and taken for granted is again put in question. Again this may be stimulated more from outside, such as losing a job or losing a partner, or having a severe illness. It may come from disillusionment – the situation has been overvalued in the past, and now needs to be re-evaluated. Or it may come more from being introduced to some new set of possibilities which had not been recognised before, and which now look much more attractive. This may be either in the field of work or in the field of relationships.

Here again is a prime time to come into therapy, and again it is a case of helping the man to break down his previous assumptions and look at life afresh. There used to be a saying in New York – 'One analysis, one divorce' – and this refers particularly to this transition, where everything is up for grabs. A change of career may also happen at this time. At this stage, Levinson (1978) says that there are three main tasks:

1 to reappraise the adult years and decide what has been worthwhile and what has been left out
2 to integrate the great polarities of young/old, destruction/creation, masculine/feminine and attachment/separateness
3 to create a new life structure which will serve for the next few years

All these can be done best, in my opinion, with the help of therapy. A therapist can play a key role in enabling this transition to take place in a constructive way. So this again can be a window of opportunity to get initiated.

From 45 to 50 is a consolidation period for entering middle-age. This is the time for middle adulthood to take over from early adulthood. Again, as with the previous periods of consolidation, it is a time for building up structures rather than breaking them down.

From 50 to 55 comes another transition period. This is often precipitated by illness, by grandparenthood, by problems with ageing parents, by early retirement – a whole series of events which bring it home to a man that he is getting older. We have seen that the self-images created by hegemonic masculinity all have to do with strength, power and independence. Now all these elements of the self-image may be threatened. So here the work, if the man should come into therapy, is mainly about acceptance. Do not pretend that what is happening is not happening. On the other hand of course, do not exaggerate it either. It may come crashing home to the man at this stage that he has not achieved what he set out to achieve, that his dreams have not been fulfilled, that his relationship with his wife (be it the first, second or third), now that all the children have left home, is quite problematic. He may never have paid much attention to her in any real sense, and now there is no one else to pay attention to. But at this stage there is sufficient awareness of his dependence on his wife for him to look to the relationship with a new kind of acceptance, rather than another search for the ideal alternative. So a therapist can do a good job here, in helping the man to achieve this new level of self-acceptance as an older man.

From 55 to 60 is the culmination of middle adulthood, another period of structuring and consolidation. Then at 60 comes the transition to late adulthood. But Levinson has little to say about this.

In spite of the fact that Levinson's research can be criticised on many grounds, I have found this general schema very usable in practice. In particular, it seems to help the therapist in getting hold of the right end of the stick, and not trying to work against the grain.

PRESENTING PROBLEMS

Reuben Fine has suggested that there are six psychoeconomic disorders, which come particularly from work experience. These are:

1 *Work inability* The total inability to work usually indicates some deep disturbance, probably psychotic.
2 *Work incapacity* The man cannot handle the work which is assigned to him, even though it is apparently within his competence. This may be to do with attitudes to authority, or excessive daydreaming, or negative feelings about other colleagues, or panics or phobias about some aspect of the work.
3 *Work instability* The man goes from job to job, being unable to settle at anything. There may be many different reasons for this.
4 *Work dissatisfaction* This is pretty closely aligned with position in the organisation: the higher the position, the greater the satisfaction. But there is some dissatisfaction in virtually all work, and often it is a symptom of some deeper problem, such as unresolved feelings about the father.
5 *Underachievement* Many men come into therapy with complaints about not getting the level of achievement they had originally dreamed of. In the case of gifted men this may well be quite true: in order to do one thing they have had to give up doing other things they might have done, and might have done even better. One of these things might be to become a therapist. 'As I noted earlier, it is not only not uncommon, it is virtually the rule that anyone who enters

analysis for the resolution of personal problems will at some time or other want to become an analyst' (Fine 1988: 258).

6 *Overachievement* Men tend to push themselves hard, as we have seen all the way through. This may lead them into areas of work for which they are not really suited. Yet it is hard to draw back. Here the task of therapy is to encourage a realistic assessment of what is possible and desired.

Whether we find these labels useful or not, they do point to the fact that work-related problems are many and various, and may present many different problems to the therapist.

Robert Pasick has also suggested that there are some specifically work-related problems presented by men.

1 *Workaholism* A workaholic has been defined as someone who has a compulsive need to work, because it provides a tangible reinforcement of self-worth not found elsewhere. When workaholics are not working, they do not know what to do with themselves and are consequently restless and unhappy. The difficulty with workaholism is that it is often a more important problem for the wife and children of the man than it is for himself. Men who come into therapy because of the insistence of their wives are typical of this group. Unless they can discover their own motivation for therapy they may not persevere with it.

2 *Success addiction* This is similar to workaholism except that the craving is specifically for success rather than just increased time at work. 'Though this syndrome is most common in men during their peak career years (25–55), it is becoming more prevalent among college-aged men and women, and even some high school students' (Pasick 1990: 48). Again this often seems no problem for the man, until it results in some disaster or other.

3 *Stress-related disorders* The best known of these is Type A disorder, which defines the behaviour of a competitive, multiphasic (doing more than one thing at a time), achievement-oriented person who possesses a sense of time urgency and impatience, and who is both easily aroused and hostile. Such a man tends to stay active for most of the day, every day. Numerous studies have found a correlation between Type A conduct and coronary heart disease. But yet again the man may not see this as a problem: it may be the side-effects of this disorder which cause much of the motivation for coming into therapy, such as getting the sack or resigning from a job. (But see section on Burnout, pp. 170–171.)

4 *Work dissatisfaction and underemployment* These are particular forms of work-related stress. They have already been mentioned (p. 168). Here the man himself may see the problem as a problem, and be prepared to work on it productively.

It seems clear that work can be the source of many problems, and also that some of them are seen as problems by wives, partners, children and others, more than they are so perceived by the man himself. This makes some of these problems impossible to work on until there is a real crisis, and then it may be much harder to deal with than if it had been recognised earlier. It is a sad fact that many men pass up the opportunity for initiation because of the resistances to therapy which we have noted earlier.

A development of the 1980s has been the coming of EAPs – Employee Assistance Programmes. These were originally set up to deal with the problems of alcoholism, and this is still their main area of strength, but they now cover many other problems as well. They are often provided by a specialised organisation, who sells time and skills to the employer, who then uses the facilities offered to handle personal problems encountered by the workforce.

BURNOUT

One of the classic syndromes which has been studied is burnout. Cary Cherniss (1980) has suggested that there are three steps to burnout. Step one is an imbalance between a person's resources and the demands being made on them. Step two is an immediate reaction to this imbalance, where the person experiences anxiety, tension, strain, fatigue and exhaustion. Step three consists of a number of changes in attitude and action, such as a tendency to treat people in a mechanical fashion, or a preoccupation with one's own needs.

> Burnout thus refers to a transactional process, a process consisting of job stress, worker strain and psychological accommodation. Specifically, burnout can now be defined as a process in which a previously committed professional disengages from his or her work in response to stress and strain experienced in the job.
>
> (Cherniss 1980: 17)

There are now numerous burnout programmes for disaffected workers, and these can be very useful to the individual. But if the pressures continue and the situation does not change, the individual may be back at square one before long. So Cherniss makes the point that part of the answer has to lie with the organisation. It is not only in the hands of the individual man and his psychology, but also a question for the organisation to look at very carefully, particularly if many of the employees suffer from burnout. The organisation may be laying unrealistic burdens upon people, and may need to change structures and/or methods in order to achieve a high level of performance without burnout.

> In the final analysis, burnout will never be significantly reduced by focusing on only one level of intervention. Too often, stress research and clinical practice have tended to 'blame the victim' by concentrating only on the individual dimensions of the problem. There are hopeful signs that our current interest in job stress and burnout has expanded to include the contributions of the work setting. This organization level of analysis must

be included if we are to adequately understand and deal with the problem. However, this, too, is a limited focus for analysis. Ultimately, the cultural and societal dimensions also must be included.

(Cherniss 1980: 190)

This is of course the view we are taking all through this book. It is the cultural and societal level which carries the masculine stereotypes which we have seen can be so harmful, and so difficult to handle. There is a hideous collusion between the worst demands of the system and the worst compulsions of men.

Of course, a therapist cannot also be working at the organisational level, except in rare instances, and so we often have to do what we can with the individual as we find him, strengthening his sense of autonomy so that he can complain or organise or combine with others to press for organisational change – or perhaps leave the organisation and work somewhere else. An eloquent and helpful book in this area comes from Edelwich and Brodsky (1980) which is a well-written and sensitive account of what the individual problems feel like from the inside. A useful set of exercises can be found in Jaffe and Scott (1984), who distinguish between a creative path of response to pressures, and a defensive path. It is of course the creative path which could lead to initiation. This is also a book which could be lent to clients. It deals with peak performance, creativity and intuition as well as with the more obvious things.

MEN AND FRIENDSHIP

Male–male friendship is often a difficult area for men, and something needs to be said about it. Men often feel that they do not have the time to cultivate friends. This issue needs to be addressed, because of the emotional impoverishment suffered by many men. It is a common finding that men have fewer friends than do women, and spend less time with them. Ask a man who is his best friend, and if he mentions a man at all, it may well be one he has not seen for a year or more.

Stuart Miller, in a fascinating discussion of male friendship, came up with four questions which for him defined what a deep friendship was:

1 If your male friend called you at two in the morning and said, 'I'm out here by the highway and I need you to come at once and help me bury a body, no questions asked,' would you go?
2 If your friend needed to move in with you for a year, would you receive him?
3 If your friend asked you to mortgage your house for him, would you do it?
4 If your friend went crazy, difficult-crazy, would you keep him out of the hands of the mental health authorities by taking care of him yourself, for as long as it took?

(S. Miller 1983: 103)

171

These are quite extreme questions, and not particularly realistic, but they do probe the essence of what friendship is all about. Miller found that there was very little friendship about. He gives the example of a man who everyone would say had many friends, whom he sees often; but one evening, at the office, he had an excruciating pain in his stomach. He did not phone any of his friends, and next day the pain had gone. But what are friends for, if not to rally round in case of need? He did not even think of it.

It seems to be a question of priorities. What are the priorities in a man's life? Work is high priority; one's partner, one's children, may be high priority. But friends are very seldom high priority. Everything else comes first. The main reason why men do not have or do not cultivate friends is because they put work first. Miller is often tempted to say that male friendship is dead.

Robert Pasick (1990) is not much more comforting. After a review of all the research literature, he finds it hard to detect anything redeeming about male friendships. But some interesting ideas came out of Sherrod's survey of the field:

> the meaning and content of male and female friendships are vastly different, on the whole: Men prefer activities over conversation, and men's conversations are far less intimate than women's conversations. According to the research, men seek not intimacy but companionship, not disclosure but commitment. Men's friendships involve unquestioned acceptance rather than unrestricted affirmation.
>
> (Sherrod 1987: 220)

This does agree with the emphasis which we saw that Miller placed on action – what would friends actually do for each other? This fits too with the finding that men's relationships tend to be 'competitive-accepting'. Competition is regarded as healthy and desirable by most men. They can affirm their masculinity at the same time as they build up their friendships.

It is important to do this, because men neglect their friendships at their peril. Joseph Jastrab quotes a poem by the Sufi poet Jallaludin Rumi:

> You know, the jackass doesn't have much sensibility,
> But even he gains spirit from the company of his own kind.
> But when the jackass crosses the desert alone,
> How many more blows it takes to get him there.
> Now, this is what this poem says to you:
> If you're not a jackass, don't cross the desert alone!
>
> (Jastrab 1994: 18)

It is normal for human beings to be gregarious, to want the company of their own kind. It is a gross distortion of our humanity to demand, as hegemonic masculinity does, total independence, total self-sufficiency, total autonomy at the expense of all else, and the pretence of autonomy if we do not really have it.

Pasick ends by quoting seven factors which interfere with men's friendships:

(1) Men's adherence to a narrow definition of 'masculinity'; (2) homophobia; (3) dependence on women for emotional support; (4) excessive devotion to work; (5) reluctance to face conflict; (6) unresolved relationships with fathers; and (7) the influence of advertising and the media.

(Pasick 1990: 117)

We have already seen some details on most of these items. On fathers, Pogrebin (1987) found that while four out of five college-age women counted their mothers as among their best friends, *none* of the young men so considered their fathers. Let us now take up just one of Pasick's seven factors and look at it in a little more detail, so that we can see how it works.

HOMOPHOBIA

Let us start at once by saying that the term 'homophobia' is not a good one. It suggests some kind of a medical disorder for which the person is not responsible. Any kind of phobia is something the individual did not create, and may be struggling with. But homophobia is not like this: it is simply a form of prejudice. The individual did create it, is often not struggling with it at all, and may even be quite outspoken about it. The better term, I believe, is heterosexism.

it may be more useful to ask how the concept of homophobia is used in practice. In this regard, it is quickly apparent that the name is used to describe oppressive phenomena in the dominant culture, rather than a form of mental illness. My own preference is to use the term 'heterosexism', a usage which more and more feminist therapists are adopting as a more accurate and politically descriptive terminology.

(Brown 1992: 244)

This makes it clear that we are talking about a self-chosen prejudice. It does incorporate a fear of being seen as homosexual, but this is just a part of the prejudicial pattern: we do not talk about negrophobia or femiphobia, even though it would make just as much sense to do so.

The curious thing about prejudice is that the prejudiced man reacts not to the other man as perceived, but to the label put on that other man. This is of course very hurtful to the man who is feeling the prejudice held against him. If a man comes out as gay at work he can be sure to be the butt of many jokes, asides, sidelong looks and hidden smiles, and to be avoided as a friend.

One of the other curious things about this is that the prejudiced man fears being penetrated by a penis up his rectum, and feels disgusted by the idea that he might do that to another man. These thoughts may be accompanied by images of violence, of something being done to him against his will. Yet this form of intercourse is quite rare among homosexual men, especially since the AIDS scare. Why should it be the dominant image?

173

In the straight male imagination, anal rape is the penalty for losing and being dominated. The imagined disgrace intensifies the drive to move upward in every hierarchy.

(Kupers 1993: 50)

So here is one link to hegemonic masculinity, which we can now see is based not only on a set of positive aims, but also on a set of fears and things to avoid. This, as we have seen, affects the world of work in numerous ways.

One of the things a straight (heterosexual) man can do, if his masculinity is threatened in any way, is to say to himself, or to others, 'At least I am not gay'. This is the guarantee, as it were, that he is a proper male with the correct impulses.

In a *Psychology Today* poll of readers' attitudes about masculinity – a group of respondents markedly more affluent and better educated than the average American – a surprising 70 per cent reported believing that 'homosexual men are not masculine', a decidedly damning view in a society that so admires masculinity.

(Garfinkel 1992: 119)

We saw some of the origins of this in Chapter 4.

If he has sex with a woman in the presence of other men, that again can confirm him in his self-image of being a proper male. This is something a gay man could not do, he believes.

It is very important, in working with gay men, to explore all the facets of their often complex feelings, and not to assume that one knows how they feel. It is also important in working with straight men not to pass over questions of homosexual feelings or avoidances. The psychoanalytic establishment's approach to homosexuality has been criticised for its heterosexist biases and lack of social and historical perspective (Kupers 1993). We must be careful, too, to use words like 'gay' and 'homosexual' in a sensitive and appropriate way:

The word *gay* should not be confused with *homosexual*, as by definition they mean quite different things. Gay implies a social identity and consciousness actively chosen, while homosexual refers to a specific form of sexuality. A person may be homosexual, but that does not necessarily imply that he or she would be gay.

(Thompson 1987: xi)

This distinction is not universally observed, but it should be noted as an interesting question, not to be taken for granted.

The workplace is a setting for much male–male interaction, and a good deal of it is quite competitive, but heterosexism brings with it some difficult extra problems – problems where the therapist can be of real help.

FUTURE TRENDS

What is interesting about the world of work is that management theory is moving in the direction of the sort of thinking and the sorts of aims we outlined in Chapter 9. Just as the consciousness of men is gradually moving in the direction of the chart in that chapter, so the consciousness of managers is also moving in that direction. It is very interesting to see in a new book, for example, that in addition to competition and cooperation – the two favourite bookends of the usual theorising – they are now talking about co-creation.

> Co-creation combines the best of competition and cooperation with a balance between goal and process orientation. In some sense, co-creation seems to be the necessary mode of relating in the emerging paradigm, and actually represents what it is, just as competition seems to be the fundamental assumption of the old paradigm.
>
> (Joba *et al.* 1993: 55)

What is this emerging paradigm? It means balancing the active with the receptive, the intellectual with the emotional, the body with the soul, the tough with the tender, and doing justice both to the male and the female. In other words, we are now talking about post-initiation.

One of the typical concepts is 'alignment'. A clear and timely vision catalyses alignment. Alignment is a condition in which people operate as if they were part of an integrated whole. It is exemplified in that level of teamwork which characterises exceptional sports teams, theatre ensembles and chamber orchestras. When a high degree of it develops among members of a team with a shared vision, the individuals' sense of relationship and even their concept of self may shift. It channels high energy and creates excitement and drive.

Another idea is 'attunement', defined as a resonance or harmony among the parts of the system, and between the parts and the whole. As the concept of alignment speaks to us of *will*, so that of attunement calls up the mysterious operations of *love* in organisations: the sense of empathy, understanding, caring, nurturance and mutual support. Attunement is quiet and soft, receptive to the subtle energies which bind us to one another and to nature. This is very new stuff for men.

Another concept is 'empowerment'. This word had been used before, mainly by humanistic people in the sense of self-actualisation – that is, self-empowerment. But the new twist here is the emphasis on mutual empowerment. This has implications for men who are trying to challenge the invisible commands that tell them to be competitive at all costs. With mutual empowerment people support each other rather than trying to put each other down. This again reflects back on what we said earlier about friendship.

This approach talks about 'intuitive leadership' and encourages the development of intuition quite consciously and deliberately. Such leaders give inspiration and not just good ideas. They are often able to sum up the

175

organisational vision in a memorable phrase. The structure of the organisation shifts in order to enable all these changes to take place, and to give them full scope. When this happens, excellence appears. We used to talk about 'female intuition', but we can now see that intuition is a human faculty, open to men just as much as women, once they have been initiated.

A final thought is summed up in the phrase 'planetary consciousness'. Everything done in the organisation is related to this higher (or deeper) purpose. If we find on reflection that there is no longer joy in the struggle, that we are burning ourselves out in the effort, that we are no longer energised by what we do, then that may be a signal that it is time to move on to a new vision of what we are doing. Perhaps we have lost touch with our purpose on this planet. And perhaps the organisation needs to change to reflect what is happening.

The prospect for men is very good, if they can take account of this new thinking. Work can then indeed be the *Albedo*, the whitening, the feeling of things going right.

Part VI

CONJUNCTIO

This union of opposites integrates the split-off parts of yourself so you become most truly your Self for the first time. Your unified personality gives equal consideration to all modes of perceiving reality: intuition, thinking, feeling and sensation. When your personality is total, you can withdraw your projections from the world and begin to see each other's soul for the beauty it is.

(R. Miller and I. Miller 1994: 136)

11

COUPLE RELATIONSHIPS

A good starting point for considering couple relationships is the idea put forward by John Gray (1992) that men and women are from different planets, which have completely different languages and customs. The problem is that they think they speak the same language, and should have the same customs.

DIFFERENT PLANETS

This radical standpoint, by emphasising and even exaggerating the differences, enables us to take problem relationships as the norm, and good relationships as very unusual and hard to achieve.

Gray uses the language of myth to good effect. For example, on Mars if someone has a problem, they go into their separate cave and place a dragon at the entrance. No one is allowed in until the problem is solved. Then the dragon is dismissed, and the person comes out with the problem dealt with. That is the Martian way. But on Venus things are different. On Venus, if someone has a problem, they talk to people about it, so as to get the problem seen from as many different angles as possible. In that process the problem gets transformed – sometimes solved, but sometimes seen differently and not needing a solution. This is fine, so long as the Martians stay on Mars and the Venusians on Venus. But when Martians and Venusians get together, the Martians try to get the Venusians to solve problems their way, and the Venusians try to get the Martians to solve problems their way. Trouble results. Frustration results. Arguments result, which may go on for a long time.

Gray goes on like this, with many other insights which seem to me very deep and very telling, in a patriarchal context. He offers us a phrase book for translating Martian phrases into their Venusian counterparts, and vice versa. He has lists of things which Martians should never say to Venusians, and which Venusians should never say to Martians. He has many wise things to say about blaming. He has unexpected things to say about the different ways in which Martians and Venusians count up the points in the relationships, to check whether they are winning or losing.

It has to be said that this work is not political in any way. This means that it is unawarely patriarchal in many of its assumptions. But just as people criticised Juliet Mitchell (1974) for the same thing in her book on Freud – her answer was to say that Freud is accurate even if not politically correct – so here the point is that the society we live in is accurately dissected, even though the findings may be uncomfortable.

If you want to improve your relationship with someone of the opposite sex, I think you will get a lot of help from this approach. So many things which we think are peculiar to our own troubles turn out to be absolutely par for the course, and quite treatable because of that, if we have the will.

What Gray does not do, however, is to explain why these patterns should be so different. Going back to the question of the cave and the dragon, for example, why do men retreat into their own private space to solve problems? The answer is obvious, once we ask the question. It is because they do not want to appear weak. It is a way of keeping control.

THE INEXPRESSIVE MALE

It is one specific expression of a much bigger pattern, which has been called the 'inexpressive male'. Jack Sattel, in an extensive discussion of this point says:

> Male inexpressiveness empirically emerges as an intentional manipulation of a situation when threats to the male position occur. . . . male inexpressiveness is instrumental in maintaining positions of power and privilege for men.
>
> (Sattel 1989: 379–382)

Once we see this, male inexpressiveness does not seem any longer a sad product of oversocialisation, of conditioning, as sex-role theory would have us believe, but more a question of policy. It is more politic to be inexpressive, because that is one way of defending oneself. But it is actually quite crippling and self-damaging, because it means that the man is cutting himself off from what could be helpful resources.

As we saw earlier, the stereotype of the hegemonic male is to be independent at all times. And this means not being dependent on anyone else. But other people are resources – part of a social system which supports us. To deny that is to deny part of our humanity.

Terry Kupers tells a moving story of the way he got involved in a building project – a house in the country where he, his wife and two women friends would live. As the project went along, he found he knew less about building than most of the other people, including some of the women.

> As a man I 'should' take charge and know what to do. . . . It turned out that I worked most on the roof, by myself, as if by nailing roofing tiles I was constructing a safety barrier between myself and the people and problems that remained down below.
>
> (Kupers 1993: 74)

The result of all this was a vicious argument between him and his wife, 'punctuated by screaming matches that went on for several days'. They eventually came to understand that he had felt hurt at not being able to perform his 'proper' role, and she had felt hurt at being excluded from contact with him at such a time.

This ability of men to withdraw when vulnerability approaches is exactly the cave which Gray is talking about. It can be seen how sad this all is, yet it is all based on the idea that a man should be in charge – a phony 'should' which is quite unrealistic and absurd.

It seems to me that the reason men are like this is because of the whole developmental story we have seen in earlier chapters. Most of all, it is because we have internalised the Patripsych. In the back of our minds, no matter how much we change and challenge our conscious ideas, the unconscious pattern of a male-dominated hierarchy lives and breathes. In this pattern dependency is weakness, and weakness is forbidden to men. As one client said:

> Sometimes my wife gets upset with me because I don't express myself or talk about my feelings. Sometimes I just don't feel like talking – usually I feel distant from her or angry at her at these times, but I hate to admit that, especially to her. I feel a loss of self-respect when I get emotional. I don't like to admit that she can make me angry. It feels as if she has some kind of power over me when I get aroused, excited, nervous, insecure, wonderful and confused, all at the same time. It's humiliating.

If being stirred up is humiliating, if needing someone is weakness, if weakness brings shame, if shame is something one should never feel, it is no wonder that so many men are inexpressive. It seems safer to be isolated than to be connected. In reality, of course, it is safer to be connected than to be isolated, because we then have more resources to deal with whatever has to be dealt with. And the initiated man knows this.

The relationship between humiliation and dependence comes out most clearly in a traditional marriage, where each party knows the rules about what they are and are not supposed to do and be. Mary Gomes and Alan Kanner make the point well:

> In [traditional marriage] a man relies on his wife to take care of his physical needs by cooking, performing household chores, and caring for the children. Rather than experiencing his dependence as a humiliating failure to be autonomous, he incorporates his wife into his ever-expanding self. Often, even her name disappears – a potent symbolic reminder that her identity has been merged into his. In other words, domination becomes a way to deny dependence, a dependence that has been culturally defined as a failure and a humiliation, rather than as a natural and inevitable part of life.
>
> (Gomes and Kanner 1995: 115)

Of course the suppression of feelings makes all this easier. But the easiness can

181

be bought at too high a cost. There is more to be said, however, on this question of the suppression of emotion.

Warren Farrell (1993) makes the point that suppressing feelings can be very good, as in an emergency when action needs urgently to be taken, and when feelings might get in the way. But most of life is not emergencies of this kind: most of life proceeds at a pace where consultation and discussion are quite possible and much more efficient.

HAVING THE ANSWER

One of the most important ways in which relationships are ruined arises in the same sort of way. The female partner will raise an issue which has to do with two faces – facts and the feelings about them – and the male partner will attend only to the one face, the facts. The female then gets annoyed because he has not heard her statement about the feelings: she feels unheard. The male gets irritated by her statement that she does not feel listened to, and finds a good solution to the factual problem. She gets doubly angry that she is getting foisted off with a solution when what she wanted was to be heard on the issue of the feelings – and so it goes on. Take this example:

You didn't put your magazines away again – it really upsets me when you do that.

I didn't have time. I was in a rush to get down to the bank, and then I had a meeting to go to.

There's always some excuse, but I'm really fed up with it.

I'll do it when I have time.

You never do seem to have time.

I put them away on Tuesday, I remember that.

One day out of seven, yes, big deal.

All right, I'll put them away now. Does that satisfy you?

No, I want you to hear that it is important to me.

Well, it's not important. But I will do it now, just to please you.

But it doesn't please me, if you say that. I don't feel as if you have heard me at all.

Oh, you're so irrational. I don't know what is the matter with you.

No, you don't – I can certainly see that.

I'm off out – goodbye.

This is an oft-repeated scene in many relationships. It can be seen very clearly how the man reacted only to the factual information, and totally ignored the feelings. It was as if he were deaf to the language of feelings. The *magazines* were not important, but the *upset feelings* were important – and he bypassed them.

The reason for this, however, is important. Gray says that it is simply that men value objects and things rather than people and feelings. But we can go behind this and ask why. The answer seems to be that men believe that people and feelings are female. To be interested in them is to be feminine. From this come two lines of thought: first, if I am interested in feelings, I will be feminine, weak, vulnerable, easily taken advantage of; second, if I try to understand feelings, I am going to get it wrong – this is her territory, where she is at home and I am not. Either way, I shall lose. This is really quite a bad misunderstanding. Men have feelings, men can understand feelings, and men can understand women. Women are no harder to understand than men are – all it needs is to pay attention.

It is of course all right to be interested in feelings if that is your profession. Male counsellors and psychotherapists generally seem to be as good as females in the same professions. It is all so arbitrary. It is a matter of choice. And of course it is frustrating for a woman to realise that her man is quite capable of understanding her feelings, but will not do so.

Giving advice or suggesting solutions feels masculine, strong, capable. Listening to feelings may feel powerless, feeble. As a client said:

> If someone has a problem, they must want an answer to it. I'd just feel foolish standing around and sympathising. What is the use of sympathy if you can't do anything about the problem?

So if a woman innocently shares upset feelings or explores out loud the issues of her day, a man mistakenly assumes she is looking for some expert advice. If he can give it, he feels strong and useful. If it is rejected, he feels abused and useless. That is, unless he has been initiated.

THE MALE EGO

This brings us to one of the main issues, the male ego. It is a common belief among females that the male ego is a fragile thing, which desperately needs support. But it is worse than that. The male ego is actually sick. When I say 'the male ego' in this context I mean the ego which is founded on and formed from the assumptions of hegemonic masculinity, as described in Chapter 2, and from the pressures of the Patripsych, as described in Chapter 6. This ego cannot bear to be vulnerable. This kind of man will do anything rather than admit to being weak.

This is a sickness. It is harmful to the man himself. It cuts him off from any real intimacy with his partner. It cuts him off from human connection of all kinds.

An interesting recent development is that of men who have read all this stuff and now make a speciality of vulnerability. They are in touch with their feelings, and even outdo the female in the intensity of feeling. But it turns out that there is only one point to this vulnerability, and that is to be better looked after by the female. This is a relatively new game, and not widely reported, but some examples can be found.

This kind of man can be recognised by the emotions he cultivates. It is always hurt. He does not feel anger, he does not feel lust, he does not feel terror – these would be much too disturbing. He just feels hurt. The women around him start to get angry at him. And he gets hurt more.

There are in fact whole platoons of different ways in which the male ego can disguise itself and find ingenious ways of not getting caught in the trap of being recognised. Jenny James (1985) has noted twenty-eight of them, in her striking book on male sexuality. She describes them all with a wealth of detail.

In particular, however, there is one general way in which the male ego operates, which we glimpsed on pp. 183–184. Because it always assumes that it should be in charge, anything that goes wrong reflects on it and seems threatening to it. If a woman says to a man 'We never go out', the man hears it as a complaint. He reads into it that she feels neglected, that he is falling short of what he should be doing, that he is mean, that he should get it right. He may hear in it that he is lazy, unromantic and just boring. But it might mean:

> I feel like going out and doing something together. We always have such a fun time, and I love being with you. What do you think? Would you take me out to dinner? It has been a few days since we went out.
>
> (Gray 1992: 62)

The reason he does not hear it like this is because his sense of everything being all right has been challenged. The male ego has this incredible need to feel that everything is all right – that is, he is in charge. This is why men are so surprised when a partner leaves them. They had no idea that anything was wrong, because they had such a deep need to believe that everything was all right, and such a deep need to believe that they were truly in charge. Again, it is only some form of initiation which can enable men to escape from this trap.

NAGGING

This brings us to a much neglected topic which causes untold misery in relationships. When a man experiences a woman as nagging him, the very word itself makes it clear that so far as he is concerned it is her fault. It is something bad that she is doing to him. All the blame, so far as he is concerned, is hers. And so, he thinks, if the nagging is to stop, it is she who has to reform. It is she who has to change, to give up nagging.

This comes again from the need to control, to be in charge. Here it is in the area of conversation and discussion. The standard male pattern is to feel that he has the right to determine what is to be talked about, and when, and in what terms. 'Most men assume the right to determine the discourse and its frame of reference' (Jukes 1993: 276).

So nagging has been defined as what women do when the man has decided that the conversation is over. As soon as a man has decided that no more needs to be said on a topic, the attempt of the woman to get her needs met is regarded as illegitimate and punishing. What the woman says is regarded not as something about her, but as something about him. This is of course a misreading, but it is very common. Worse still, it is often a cause of violence in the home. The man who blames his wife for nagging, and gets more and more angry as she continues, is ripe to become a wife-beater.

> All the men we work with at the Men's Centre have this same problem. They describe it in many ways: women 'go on', they 'nag', 'never stop talking', 'give it that' – accompanied by a gesture of fingers opening and closing next to the mouth – and so on. What it always boils down to is that they do not want to listen to their partners' concerns.
>
> (Jukes 1993: 101)

Is there any way out of this? The crucial point is that it is only the naggee who can stop the nagging. Once the naggee takes responsibility for the nagging, it can stop. This step, of taking responsibility, is hard but quite achievable. Once the naggee gets the point that the solution is in his hands, he can move forwards; but until that happens, nothing will change.

The general solution is to give up the belief, which is absurd in any case, that the man should always determine what is to be talked about, and when, and in what terms. As soon as the woman is given some credence as having an agenda of her own, which is just as worthy of attention as anything the man may produce, things can move forward.

FOUR TYPES OF RELATIONSHIPS

As relationships grow and develop, they tend to fall into four great patterns.

1 *The stable-satisfactory relationship* is one in which both parties can explicitly reach agreement that one or the other is in control of the relationship at a given time, or in control of given areas of the relationship. There are two subcategories: the *Heavenly Twins*, where there seems to be an instinctive appreciation of the other's point of view, because there is so much sharing; and the *Collaborative Geniuses*, where in spite of differences negotiation is well used to arrive at decisions which are mutually satisfying.

2 *The unstable-satisfactory relationship* is one in which two people are in the process of working out their definition of a new or changed relationship. The two subcategories are: the *Spare-Time Battlers*, where there are cycles of up-and-down satisfaction; and the *Pawnbrokers*, who as it were lend to each other

and then get something back later, never being wholehearted about anything, never giving anything freely.

3 *The unstable-unsatisfactory relationship* is one where no implicit or explicit agreement is reached on the question of who is in control of which areas of the relationship, and any attempt at definition of the relationship by one member of the relationship is sabotaged by the other member. Neither can communicate directly with the other about what is going on in the relationship. Neither can explicitly take responsibility for defining or setting the limits to the relationship. Two types: the *Weary Wranglers*, who keep on repeating the same arguments and quoting the same examples over and over again; and the *Psychosomatic Avoiders*, who avoid overt conflict but instead go in for illnesses and other afflictions which keep them busy.

4 *The stable-unsatisfactory relationship* is one where conflicts are not recognised. Outsiders can see how awful they are, but the couple are not aware of their behaviour. Two types: the *Gruesome Twosome*, who pretend at a very high level that everything is basically all right, but indulge in using rigid roles to accuse the other of not living up to the original bargain; and the *Paranoid Predators*, who turn all the problems outwards into the external world, blaming everyone else but themselves, and setting tight boundaries around their own little world.

(Swenson 1973: 61–64)

It is better, of course, if we can avoid entering into any of these patterns, and can be flexible and creative. But many men would rather not have this, because of their fear of intimacy.

INTIMACY

Intimacy has been defined in an unpublished analysis of my own as a combination of openness, closeness and affection. Let us look at each of these in turn, because they are actually quite independent qualities.

Openness is first of all the ability to be in touch with our own feelings. We cannot be open about what we do not possess. But once we are in touch with our feelings we can share them with another person. Of course this makes us vulnerable to that other person. If someone knows our feelings, they then have the power to hurt our feelings. The initiated man realises that it is possible to be strong and vulnerable at the same time. Real strength is recognising one's own weakness. But this means being non-defensive. We cannot be defensive and open at the same time.

Closeness means being with another person, wanting to be with that other person, enjoying being with that other person. It means wanting to share things with them. It means missing them when they are not there.

Affection means loving the other person, feeling warm towards them, wanting good things for them. Affection means wanting to touch the other person, and if appropriate have sex with them. Affection means not wanting to see the other person injured or put down, but on the contrary wanting them to be happy and fulfilled.

So what is problematic about this? It seems that many men have no problem with affection or closeness, but many problems with openness.

> Men are uncomfortable with, and often inept at, intimate relating because they avoid it; then they avoid it because they are uncomfortable and inept at it.
>
> (Meth and Pasick 1990: 203)

This is the problem with control once again. The standard male pattern, as we have seen so many times, is to be in control, or to want to be in control, in any relationship. In a relationship with a woman they expect to be in control. But openness means giving up control – giving up the whole idea of being in control. This is hard unless one has been initiated. Control works well with objects and things (which as we have seen are the main focus for many men) but it does not work well with human beings. Human beings do not like being controlled. It may be remarked in passing that one of the reasons why men avoid homosexual relations is that they do not know which way the control will go.

As we saw in the case history in Chapter 3, men can be intensely suspicious of women. It may require some time in therapy before they can begin to trust a woman. And it may require some time with a woman before he begins to trust her enough to be intimate.

> Because of what men believe is at stake, many are slow to trust this way.
>
> (Meth and Pasick 1990: 203)

What is at stake? A great deal, in the minds of many men. Their whole picture of themselves may be based on the idea of being in charge, being totally in control. To lose this is a catastrophic expectation. But it is only one of many. Beth Erickson has this list:

> *Catastrophic fear of abandonment* (being left bereft) 'If I open myself to people and let myself love them and then they leave, I will feel abandoned and bereft as I did before. So I won't really let people in, because they inevitably will leave anyway. And then it won't hurt so much when they do.'
>
> *Catastrophic fear of merger* (being swallowed up) 'If I let people in, they will engulf me, swallow me up, and I won't have a life of my own ever again. So I'll just not ever let anybody close.'
>
> *Catastrophic fear of exposure* (sharing too much and then being rejected) 'If I show people who I really am and they don't like what they see, they will reject me and I will be devastated. So I will just keep all my feelings and most of my thoughts to myself.'
>
> *Catastrophic fear of one's own destructive impulses* (rage) 'If I let people close to me, eventually they will do something to get me angry. So since I

can't trust what I will do, I'll protect them from getting hurt and myself from the humiliation I would feel if I did hurt them by keeping everyone at arm's length.'

Catastrophic fear of attack (persecutory attack and annihilation) 'If I let people close enough to make them angry, I'll be destroyed by them. So I'll control every relationship by keeping everyone far away from me. Then I won't ever get hurt again.'

(B.M. Erickson 1993: 327)

This is a frightening litany. It works for both men and women, but men are particularly prone to the fear of merger. It is all too easy for a man to see an approach as invasive, and to take avoiding action. If the woman has a corresponding fear of abandonment, and wants to increase closeness to compensate for this, the results are only too predictable. We get the approach–withdrawal pattern which is so common in couple counselling.

One way of exploring this is to use an exercise. One that was developed by Sue Mickleburgh and me was this:

Take a piece of paper and a pencil or pen. Write down – 'If I let you in to the deepest place I know . . .' Now look at your partner, breathe, take your time, and when you are ready, write down the second part of that sentence. Complete the sentence in terms of your own feelings and your own reactions.

When you have done that, let me know and we can all share the results and explore what they mean.

What often comes out of this exercise is that men have never thought in these terms before, but actually find the exercise quite natural, easy and reassuring. Others find that their objections are much deeper than they had imagined at first. This very direct approach has the power to bring out any catastrophic expectations which may be lurking around.

To sum up on this, then, perhaps it will be well to look at the classic formulation:

Our job as therapists is threefold: (a) to help clients identify when their fears are being set off, (b) to help them learn what sets their partner's fears off, and (c) to help them find constructive alternatives for the shared management of these fears. Doing this will enhance the quality and the degree of intimacy between people.

(B.M. Erickson 1993: 238)

It can be seen from all this that intimacy is a big problem for men. Yet it is the only way in which they can get their real needs met in a relationship. Everything else is less than this. When two people can be genuinely intimate, there is a mutual support and a sharing of resources which makes both parties stronger and more resilient than either would be separately. It is what men really want and what they so rarely dare to ask for, or offer. Terrance O'Connor spells out the importance of this for the world:

> As we began to look at all our personal concerns from a global perspective, we could see that the patterns of control, denial and projection that sabotage intimate relationships are the very patterns that endanger the world. To change these patterns is to change not just our social lives but our relationship to the planet.
>
> (O'Connor 1995: 151)

One of the main outcomes of the initiation process is the ability to be intimate with a woman. This is the truth of the *Conjunctio*.

Part VII

MORTIFICATIO AND SECOND NIGREDO

As Jung points out, the alchemical mortificatio varies the archetypal motif of the slaying and dismemberment of the king for the purpose of renewing his power and increasing the fertility of the land.

(Fabricius 1994: 100)

12

INTEGRATIVE GROUP WORK

In group work particularly interesting work can be done towards initiation, because in a group all the phenomena of social life appear. We can test out the level of our initiation so far, and see how much it means in practice. Group work can give us another kind of initiation, as we shall see more fully in Chapter 13.

It seems worth while to pay some attention to group work, since so much of it is very bad. I am angry about this, and some have said that I am too vocal about it, but I cannot apologise for the strength of my views. Many clients and colleagues over the years have kept on telling me terrible stories of group work and how often it fails the participants. This is all the more important because more and more of it is being carried out with men, and with specific groups of men, such as violent men. Important considerations need to be addressed here, such as how much support and how much confrontation should be offered. If too much support is given, there may be actual collusion with abusive behaviour patterns; if too much confrontation is given, there may be a very high drop-out rate.

Much group work is of a poor standard, and this is mainly due to a bad tradition which says that one needs no training to be a group leader. In hospitals, for example, a nurse or a doctor may be told 'You will be leading the group tonight', with no preparation at all. Of course some highly trained and effective facilitators also work in hospitals, but they are few and far between.

Not only is it the practice which so often falls down, but even the theory is sometimes at fault. There is a theory, for example, which I consider quite crippling to any effective group work, which says that the leader must not interfere with the group, but must encourage it to take responsibility for itself. For example, Mullender and Ward (1991) seem to think that empowerment of the participants requires that they be totally self-directed. Some lip-service is paid to the notion that this approach 'does not mean falling over backwards to keep one's self and one's views invisible and unheard. It means playing an active role' (Mullender and Ward 1991: 40). But it soon becomes clear that this active role is quite minimal. We are told that the group itself needs to learn the skills of resolving interpersonal conflict (ibid.: 41), but nowhere is there any statement that the group leader can provide techniques to enable this to happen more fruitfully.

'Empowerment' is one of those terms which was first used by humanistic psychology, and later used even more in transpersonal psychology and its associated work with organisations. But you will look in vain for any mention of the humanistic, the transpersonal, or any such notions in Mullender and Ward. Even the work of John Southgate (1983), which one would have thought was highly relevant, is nowhere mentioned by them. Neither is Sue Holland (1990), whose work on a housing estate is well known. Nor is there any mention of co-counselling or any of its associated ideas.

There is a lot of talk about values, and broadly feminist and anti-racist values are recommended. But when we come to the question of what one actually does, what training is necessary to understand group process or group dynamics, what we get is nothing very much. There is really no difference between a group of six and a group of forty (Mullender and Ward 1991: 63). The authors tell us to go for open groups rather than closed or semi-closed ones.

A few exercises are suggested, most of them involving pencil and paper. But there is little appreciation of the emotional side of the group, still less of the imaginal side of the group. There is a lot of talk about consciousness-raising, but a lack of appreciation that this activity can only take the group so far, and that actual therapy in the group is needed at some point. No doubt the reason for this lack is the extreme emphasis on turning the action outwards all the time:

> So strong are wider social pressures towards 'blaming the victim', that to allow personal developments to have undue significance would be a dangerous step back towards patronising and pathologising orientations.
> (Mullender and Ward 1991: 137)

This misses the point which was put years ago in a cartoon in the Red Therapy pamphlet (see p. 208) which showed Fred Flintstone saying 'I ain't no bourgeois individualist, honest! I just ain't gonna be much help in smashing the system, because the system is doing a pretty good job of smashing me!'

All in all, this is a well-meaning book, but one which is working with one hand tied behind its back, because it is so resolutely cognitive and behavioural, without ever using those words. There is nothing here for working on the Patripsych.

In other words, these people engage in consciousness-raising, but totally ignore unconsciousness-raising. They cannot do justice to those underlying conflicts which get in the way of rational answers to problems. This is not palatable reading, I know, but these things need to be said by someone.

Equally uninteresting in another way is the work of Tom Douglas (1976). He seems to have more books out in this field than anyone else, but again is curiously lacking in any real appreciation of what a group can do. His discussions of group work never seem to say anything about the humanistic group methods which are so powerful and so useful, in dealing with the problems at all levels.

Let us not forget that it was within humanistic psychology that the word 'empowerment' first arose, as an outcome of self-actualisation. The whole idea of empowerment fits with the democratic character structure which emerges within humanistic group work. I want to examine this by a close look at one particular humanistic group method – encounter. The reason for this is that an encounter group includes methods derived from psychodrama, from Gestalt, from co-counselling and so forth, and so is more flexible than any of these.

It seems to me that encounter is by its very nature integrative; but it may be as well to spell this out in some detail, because there are several different versions of encounter, some more and some less integrative. For example, Rogers (1970) has talked about 'basic encounter', which is not very integrative; Schutz (1973) has talked about 'open encounter', which is fully integrative; Mintz (1972) has talked about 'marathon encounter', which is also fully integrative, and Yablonsky (1965) has talked about 'Synanon encounter', which is not fully integrative.

The great authoritative text on groups by Shaffer and Galinsky says that the encounter group proper is 'an outgrowth and compendium of all the group models that preceded it' (Shaffer and Galinsky 1989: 201).

This kind of group originated in the 1960s and reached its most classic development in the 1970s. It is now the most general type of group, and someone who has learned how to lead this type of group will find any other type of group relatively easy. But it does require a great deal of skill from the group leader.

It is of course a humanistic group, and shares with other humanistic approaches a belief that the person is basically OK. Consequently it refuses to call people 'patients', and calls them instead participants or group members.

It is also a holistic group, and shares with other holistic approaches the twin slogans 'Go where the energy is' and 'Move the moment to its crisis'. This energy can be expressed on the physical level, on the emotional level, on the intellectual level or on the spiritual level. The basic rule for the leader of an encounter group is to look for the signs of some kind of energy ready to come out. This can be positive or negative, but it is a fact that negative feelings can often take us further than positive feelings in this kind of work. This is why we call this the *Mortificatio* phase, and emphasise that it can mean another descent into the *Nigredo*, the blackness. The ego comes under fire, and in a sense has to be slain so that we can continue on to the next level of development.

My own belief is that the main line of development of ideas about encounter, as worked out in the 1960s and early 1970s, runs through the work of Will Schutz, Jim Elliott and Elizabeth Mintz, and it is their work which lies at the heart of this chapter.

THEORY AND PRACTICE

There are many definitions of what we mean by the term 'integrative', as Mahrer (1989b) has pointed out in his definitive book, and some are more adequate than others.

What I think is meant by the fullest and most appropriate use of this term is any approach which unifies the three basic legs on which psychotherapy stands: the regressive, the existential and the transpersonal. This is a wholehearted definition which implies a wholehearted approach, and this was all explained in Chapter 8.

Many of the humanistic groups manage to deal with all three of these areas, but the most coherent version is the encounter group, as developed by people like Will Schutz, Jim Elliott and Elizabeth Mintz. The encounter group manages it very naturally and with little difficulty. Let us look at each of these areas in turn.

Regression

Will Schutz has probably given the most adequate account of encounter in its full form. His book *Elements of encounter* (Schutz 1973) gives a succinct account of the history of the development of the encounter group, and also of the principles which emerged from that history. In his book *Joy: Twenty years later* he says:

> I still regard encounter as the queen of the human potential methods; the best method to experience before any other training, so that the person is clear, aware, self-determining, and ready to profit much more from any other training.
>
> (Schutz 1989: 161)

What happens in an encounter group is that the group produces an issue of some kind through one or more of its members, and the leader finds a way of dramatising that issue so that it can be worked through for the benefit of the individuals who raise the issue, and the group as a whole.

There is an assumption here that this may well lead into something to do with the past, and may also lead the person deeper into their inner world. This is because of the concept of the energy cycle. This is something which gets fairly close to the Gestalt notion of a cycle of awareness (P. Clarkson 1989). As a need begins to be felt, energy is mobilised to deal with it, and this rises to a peak when the challenge is met; after this there is a relaxation period, when the person winds down. If, on the other hand, the challenge is never met, then the tension of mobilised energy is held in the body, and chronic body structuring may be set up in the worst cases. So in his groups, Schutz looks for the signs of held tension, and seeks to enable the person to complete the energy cycle, by dealing with the real life events which need to be dealt with.

For example a tension between two men may lead to them both carrying out an exercise suggested by the leader, and this may lead to one of them getting in touch with feelings about his father (e.g. Shaffer and Galinsky 1989: 207).

Jim Elliott (1976) has given us what is perhaps the most thorough examination of what is actually done in an encounter group, and again made clear that this is a coherent and principled approach, not in any sense a ragbag of different techniques. Its emphases are on interpersonal communication in the here and now; contacting, exploring and expressing feelings; and moving towards self-directedness and self-actualisation.

Elliott says that growth is a three-stage process: first, destructuring; second, the emergence of noetic material (mental contents such as thoughts, feelings, desires and so forth); and third, integration of this material.

Elliott regards feelings as very important in this. Feelings, he says, are the royal road to the noetic world (the world of mental contents). Feelings are like icebergs, with the most socially acceptable aspects visible, and the more powerful, more primitive aspects submerged out of sight.

> Part of my strategy in working with feelings is to help people get deeper into the feeling iceberg. What I find when I start with a tiny 'insignificant' surface feeling is that it leads to other feelings, deeper down, that seem to occur in layers. The full expression of one layer leaves noetic space for the next layer to emerge. Growth, then, involves work on oneself in the form of uncovering layer after layer of feeling, until one gets to what have been called primal feelings, such as deep rage and pain. That's where the very earliest blocks are released and the most energy becomes liberated.
>
> (Elliott 1976: 95)

He goes on to say that it is important in such cases to elicit the complete configuration rather than have a dissociated feeling. This includes the somatic component, the imagery component and the belief component, as well as the feelings themselves. This enables the further processing to take place which leads to real integration with the rest of the person's life.

It can be seen here how regression and recession are very important, but they are not the end of the road. Work still needs to be done on integrating the insights into the person's ordinary everyday world.

A good example of this kind of work in action is to be found in Gerald Haigh's (1968) article, too long to quote here, where a woman goes into her feelings about her mother and resolves something very important once and for all. So again the regressive content can be very central.

Elizabeth Mintz (1972) has told us particularly about the marathon group, which is in a way most complete expression of what the encounter group has to offer. She makes the point that the power of the encounter group is related to its simultaneous functioning as a reality experience and as a symbolic experience. This is more implicit in the work of the other two people we have examined, but of course equally true of their work.

She is also clear that an encounter group is not only a growth group but also a therapy group. She denies that there is any real distinction between the two, as if the healthy were healthy and the sick were sick, and a neat line could be drawn between the two. In an encounter group we go down into the neurotic and even psychotic material which we all have within us. This often means regression into the past, and recession into the inner world.

In these ways the Mintz account is complementary to the two accounts already given.

It can be seen already how dynamic this all is, by comparison with the Mullender and Ward (1991) and the Douglas (1976) approaches already mentioned.

Existential

Let us come now on to how encounter deals with the here-and-now aspects of the matter. Schutz himself lays particular stress upon the existential issue of openness and honesty:

> Honesty and openness are the key to your evolutionary growth. Being honest allows your bodymind to become a clear channel for taking in all the energy of the universe, both inside and outside your body, and to use it profitably.
>
> (Schutz 1973: 16)

This is really the classic existential approach of the encounter group, but it is interesting to see that Schutz says that it only really happens once the other issues are out of the way. In this it is perhaps reminiscent of the point which psychoanalysts sometimes make, that when the client can really free-associate the therapy is over.

Mintz has some points to make about the way the group should be run. At the beginning of the group she lays down certain requirements:

> that the group must function as a group at all times, without one-to-one relationships or subgrouping; that social chatter and history taking are not useful; that after the ending of the group any personal data which have been revealed are to be treated confidentially; and that any reaction which one group member has to another is to be expressed openly and directly.
>
> (Mintz 1972: 17)

She goes into the question of what the norms actually are in an encounter group. Her list is so similar to those of Schutz and Elliott that I have taken the liberty of making up my own list which is based on all three (see Table 12.1).

I sometimes use this list as a handout to give to naive groups, especially if they are likely to be rather rigid and intellectual: I first used it with a group of engineering students, who found the whole idea of psychology very difficult, but found these rules quite understandable. It is excellent for groups of men, because it fits in with their typical desire to have things clearly described and laid out.

Will Schutz is particularly keen to emphasise the centrality of the body in all this. Nonverbal methods are used consistently, and body movements and postures are referred to constantly. Stuck feelings are usually held in the body in some quite noticeable way, and it often makes sense to exaggerate some physical action until it reveals what was behind it. Encounter agrees with the body

Table 12.1 Experiential groups: basic practice

1 *Awareness of the body* Your body is you. It expresses your feelings, if you will let it. You can learn how you feel by going into your own body and noticing what you find there. If you suppress your own body, you will probably be willing to suppress other people – and they may pick this up. In groups like this we often get rid of chairs and tables so that interaction may take place physically as well as verbally.

2 *The here and now* Talk about what you are aware of in this group at this moment. If you want to talk about the past, or about events outside the group, find ways of making them present to the group members. This can often be done by action or role-playing.

3 *Feelings* Let reality have an emotional impact on you, especially the reality of the other group members. Let yourself feel various emotions – but if they are blocked, be aware of that too. Feel what it is like to experience whatever is happening at an emotional level.

4 *Self-disclosure* Be open about your feelings or lack of them. Let people into your world. If you are anxious, let people know about it; if you are bored, it is OK to say so. Be as honest as you can bear to.

5 *Taking responsibility* Take responsibility for yourself – do what you want and need to do, not what you think the group wants you to do. If the leader suggests something, it is still your decision whether to go along with it. Be aware of what you are doing to other people by what you say and do, and take responsibility for that. Be aware of the 'I and thou' in each statement. You are not an impartial observer.

6 *Risk taking* If you are torn between expressing something and not expressing it, try taking a risk. Doing the thing you are most afraid of is usually a good idea in this group. You can reduce the danger of hostile statements by saying them non-evaluatively: instead of saying 'You are a cold person', say 'I feel frozen when you talk like that'. This is more likely to be true, and it makes you more real to the others.

7 *Listening* Listening to others lets us in to their worlds. But listening is not just about words – it means being aware of expressions, gestures, body positions, breathing. Allow intuition. Really be there with the other people in the group.

8 *Bridging distances* As relationships in the group become clearer, there may be one or two members you feel very distant from – or want to be distant from. By expressing this, a quite new kind of relationship may begin to appear. Opposition and distance are just as likely to lead to growth as closeness and support.

9 *Distress* When someone in the group is distressed, encourage the person to stay with that feeling until the distress is fully worked through, or turns into some other emotion. There is a 'Red Cross nurse' in all of us who wants to stop people feeling distressed, and usually jumps in too soon. A person learns most by staying with the feeling, and going with it to its natural end, which is often a very good place.

10 *Support and confrontation* It is good to support someone who is doing some self-disclosure, some risk taking, some bridging of distances. It is good to confront someone who is not being honest, who is avoiding all risk taking, who is diverting energy away from the group's real work. It is possible to do both these things with love and care.

11 *Avoidance* Don't ask questions – make the statement which lies behind the question. Address people directly, saying 'I' rather than 'it' or 'you'. Don't say 'I feel' when you mean 'I think'. Ask yourself – 'What am I avoiding at this moment?'

12 *The saver* Don't take any of these rules too seriously. Any set of rules can be used to put someone down – perhaps yourself.

therapies, and with Gestalt, that my body is a map of my experience and my being. Schutz says:

> You are a unified organism. You are at the same time physical, psychological and spiritual. These levels are all manifestations of the same essence. You function best when these aspects are integrated and when you are self-aware.
>
> (Schutz 1973: 16)

This is a good statement of one of the basic beliefs of the humanistic approach which is so fundamentally committed to integration.

Elliott emphasises more the existential interactions of the group members. He points out that the tangles they get into with each other represent here-and-now material for the leader to work with and untangle: the members then also learn how to deal with such tangles in their everyday lives.

> By using such a format, the encounter group leader can: 1) encourage interpersonal interactions among group members in the here-and-now; 2) elicit the feelings that accompany such interactions; 3) encourage the individual to get deeper into the feelings; 4) help the group deal with the norm-setting attempts that inevitably occur as a reaction to the expression of feelings; 5) help the group create an appropriate climate in which intensive work may be done; 6) train people in more effective ways of communicating and relating; and 7) help people grow by showing them how to disengage themselves from whatever they have become attached to and, from that new, freer position, become involved with whatever aspects of human existence they wish.
>
> (Elliott 1976: 32)

So Elliott is stressing here the value of members of the group working with each other, and we shall see later that this is a theme which has become more important as the years have gone by.

This area is of course well handled by Mullender and Ward (1991) and also by Douglas (1976). This is their area of strength: but even here it can be seen that they are much more restricted in what they have to offer. Of course there are differences between them, but as we have seen there are also differences, as well as great similarities between different exponents of encounter. Let us see how these work out when we come to the next category we are examining.

Transpersonal

This is a category of working where, as Stan Grof has said, we are involved with 'experiences involving an expansion or extension of consciousness beyond the usual ego boundaries and beyond the limitations of time and/or space' (Grof 1979: 155). It takes us into the region of spirituality. We feel we are getting information from we know not where. At first this sounds very unfamiliar and unusual, until we realise that virtually all therapists, counsellors and group leaders rely on their *intuition* a great deal.

Now according to the psychosynthesis school, which has done a lot of work in this area, intuition is one of the faculties of the higher unconscious. This higher unconscious, or superconscious, is a natural feature of the human mind, which does go beyond the usual ego boundaries. By giving it its proper name, we are able to work with it better and understand it more fully. Intuition, then, may take us into the realm of the transpersonal.

Let us move on to take up another, similar, point about imagination. Encounter group leaders use *imagery and fantasy*, and these too may take us into the transpersonal realm. When we ask a participant to bring to mind an image of his or her inner conflict, or suggest that they imagine what their opponent might turn into, or invite them to bring to mind a certain scene, we are invoking the imaginal world, which may open the way into the transpersonal.

So when Schutz tells the story of a British woman in one of his groups who was asked to become very small and go inside her own body (Shaffer and Galinsky 1989: 218), he was working in a way calculated to enable transpersonal energies to enter in. It is clear that imagery very often involves playing with the normal limitations of time and space. (In a later work, Schutz (1981) explicitly uses meditation, prayer, chanting and Arica spiritual exercises.)

Elliott does not say as much as Schutz about the spiritual aspects of his work, but he does say that human beings are not just physical objects but are best characterised by such words as freedom, choice, growth, autonomy and mystery. These are all characteristics of transpersonal work. He also refers to *creativity* and *liberation* (Elliott 1976: 58). Creativity, too, is one of the areas which may have to do with the superconscious as described by Assagioli (Ferrucci 1982). A good group leader will not only be creative himself, but also stimulate the creativity in other people.

Another phenomenon noted by Elliott is the Fusion Experience, which often happens after primals and similar cathartic experiences. The whole person is involved, and seems often taken outside their ordinary world. 'Looking back on the experience, [one has] the feeling that one was outside time and space. Typical comments are "The world fell away"' (Elliott 1976: 198). This is the kind of peak experience which is very characteristic of transpersonal work.

Mintz does not say much about spirituality in her 1972 book, but makes up for it by a later book which is all about it. Mintz (1983) gives an example where a young man's impotence was cured, not by the usual process of therapy, but by a group ritual in which he symbolically castrated each of the other men in the group. This arose quite spontaneously in the group, and she says of the event: 'It was an enactment of a mythic ritual, a primitive ceremony, which tapped the deep levels of the collective unconscious; it was a transpersonal experience' (Mintz 1983: 153–157). This is not to say that everything describable as mythic must be transpersonal, as Ken Wilber has pointed out at length in his essay on the pre-trans fallacy (Wilber 1983).

In the same book, Mintz talks of countertransference of such a kind that the group leader actually feels inside her own body the next thing which needs to happen for the participant. This links directly with the research on counter-transference mentioned by Samuels (1989), which again links this with the transpersonal, and with the Jungian idea of the imaginal world.

It is my strong impression that the climate has changed considerably since the early 1980s, in the direction of more open acknowledgement of the importance of the transpersonal. It was always important in encounter, but it is only more recently that people have said so very much. It is of course crucial to any complete initiation process.

In an encounter group it is possible to catch a glimpse of spiritual realities which go beyond ordinary consciousness. Richard Anthony *et al.* (1987) have suggested that these glimpses are extremely important in opening up a sense of spiritual possibilities. They can show briefly what is possible more permanently if spiritual development is continued. The gibe which is sometimes hurled at encounter groups that the sense of wonder which they engender is temporary and therefore false is seen to be a crass misunderstanding of the real meaning of the experience. The breakthrough and peak experiences which come through these means what Perls calls the mini-Satori are not illusory, even though they are temporary. They represent what I have argued at length elsewhere are mystical experiences (Rowan 1993a).

A good description of the encounter group is given by Shaffer and Galinsky (1989), who put it in the context of other approaches to group work and again make clear that it is a coherent and expressive form of group work, which can stand with any of its competitors in a sturdy and respectable way. They too see Schutz as central in the development of the encounter group model, and some of the comments made on him above are based on their account.

Mike Wibberley (1988) has given a stimulating outline of how encounter is progressing in Britain today. During the 1980s, the general tone of the encounter group became more equalitarian. Then it was not a question (as it was in the 1970s) of a few revolutionaries raising awkward issues, but rather of the ethos of the group as a whole. Leaders found they had to become more like members of the group, rather than keeping to the more formal and therapist-like role which they had formerly adopted. This is not a simple matter, however. As Wibberley points out:

> There is often ambivalence in the group, with some people wanting the leader to be 'one of us', and at the same time resenting him or her for not being the mythical, perfect authority who knows all the answers and is able to solve all their problems and lead them to Nirvana.
>
> (Wibberley 1988: 72)

But certainly my experience is that since about 1985 groups are much less likely to allow the leader to be very distinct and separate than they used to be.

I think this is a permanent change, and that the old group scene can never now return. I feel quite a pang about this, because the old methods, dominant though they often were, did work and did liberate a lot of people. The new ethos seems to me slower and less effective in the short run, though no doubt healthier in the long run.

Part VIII

SOLUTIO AND THIRD NIGREDO

But the solutio is not always pleasant, or it may be beautiful at first and then increasingly anxiety-ridden, because of the sense that the ground has dissolved under one's feet. One is being subjected to forces beyond one's control or rational understanding.

(Greene 1988: 290)

13

THE SEXUAL POLITICS
GROUP

There are many types of groups for men. Perhaps the most problematic of these
is the group which is devoted to sexual politics. This type of group is quite
difficult for men, and deserves some attention. What we are talking about here is
the way in which men can be oppressors, taking for granted male hegemony and
constructed femininity. To deal with this is the biggest test of our initiation.

TYPES OF GROUPS

Do we want to work on gender issues? If we accept the arguments given earlier
in this book, it seems obviously necessary. There are several types of groups
concerned with gender issues which have emerged over the years, and I have
personal experience of them all. The ones I have noticed are these:

- consciousness-raising group
- mutual therapy group
- experiential group
- therapy group
- ritual group

Consciousness-raising group

These were the first groups to emerge in Britain, around 1972, and they usually
consisted of heterosexual men who had been urged to work on themselves by
their partners. They tended to be uncomfortable places, where people criticised
each other for using the word 'girl' and similar minor matters. They tended to
change into discussion groups, action groups (leafletting, etc.), experiential
groups or therapy groups.

Sometimes they got into difficult areas. I remember one in the 1970s where a
group member always turned up in worn jeans and a grubby T-shirt, and told us
he lived in a squat. One day we got into going round saying how much we were
worth in terms of cash and property. It turned out that he had ten thousand
pounds in the bank. He never came back to the group after that day.

Mutual therapy group

Soon afterwards there followed on the self-help therapy group, usually based on humanistic group work, and involving a great deal of emotion. These always started off as mixed groups. Sometimes they got into the hands of people who wanted to concentrate on just one emotion – usually anger – and everyone in the group was expected to express this particular emotion.

I remember one time in Islington when such a group was working in a private house, and the neighbours complained to the police about the angry shouts that were coming forth. There was a knock at the door, and a burly policeman was standing there. He came into the room, looked round, and said 'Getting into our class anger, are we?', and cautioned us to be less noisy about it. He then clomped off again.

But some of these groups became very good, and one of them, called Red Therapy, wrote a large pamphlet in 1978 about their work. Later a book was written by Sheila Ernst and Lucy Goodison (1981) entitled *In our own hands* which came out of the Red Therapy experience, and which is still very useful to anyone wanting to set up a self-help group. Although it is ostensibly for women, it is equally usable by men's groups. In fact, a few of the 'women' whose work is described in the book were actually men in the Red Therapy group.

Sometimes in these groups one issue can dominate the group for weeks. I remember one group which included a couple, and the problems between the two of them occupied the group's time over and over again.

Sometimes some very dramatic things happened. I shall never forget one group where a woman was going into her feelings about supporting her partner financially while he worked on his PhD thesis. As soon as he got his PhD he left her. She spent about half an hour expressing her anger by taking a telephone directory, representing his thesis, and tearing it up. At the end of the time the whole room was covered in small pieces of paper.

After some years as a mixed group, this particular group split into two – a women's group and a men's group. It does seem that as soon as a mixed group gets into gender issues in any deep kind of a way, it splits up, mainly because the women find it too hard to take – too painful to bear (Long and Coghill 1977).

So we have to learn how to work in a men's group, even if we do not particularly want to at first.

Experiential group

This is similar to the mutual therapy group, but there is less emphasis on therapy and more on general self-discovery and the exploration of issues. There is often a paid leader or facilitator who provides the exercises for the group. Sometimes the job of providing and leading the exercises is rotated around the group members. Scattered through this chapter are details of some of these exercises. It has to be said that it is the responsibility of the leader to make sure that the feelings which are aroused by such exercises are worked through to a positive conclusion. Used ineptly, exercises like this can make people feel worse rather than better. So people using them must have enough experience of group work to make a good result possible.

One type of experiential group, coming from the co-counselling camp, often starts off very well, but degenerates into a self-congratulatory state characterised by words like 'celebration' and 'validation'. It is important to have a place for negative feelings as well as positive ones. Sexism is as much of a social problem as racism: we know it is no good just saying that it is great to be white, and equally it is no good just saying that it is great to be male. Some of the groups in the USA seem particularly prone to this error.

Therapy group

This group is led by a trained leader, which goes on for quite an extended period of time. The leader may have a psychoanalytic orientation, or may have a humanistic one. These groups generally go in for long silences if the leader is not active. They can go very deep, and at their best can work very well, but there is a persistent tendency for them to become less political over time.

Ritual group

These are much more recent, and were given a huge boost by the work of Robert Bly and his associates in the USA. The basic idea is to use myth and fairy tale and legend and tribal customs to set up ritual structures within which men can make discoveries and explore their experience on an imaginal level. Often there is much use of drums, and the energy level tends to be higher than in the other groups mentioned. The leaders here tend to be more dominant and more highly paid than those in the experiential group, or even in the therapy group. Story-telling may or may not form a part of such a group. Michael Meade (1993) has given us some very good examples of the sort of stories which can be used, and the benefits to the participants which can result.

The danger with the ritual group is that it can get so exciting and positive that gender issues get ignored altogether. There is so much interest in dealing with fathers and getting initiated into the men's group, and developing male bonding and mutual appreciation that it becomes more like a men's club or a men's support group than anything more political. This is not a critique, simply a sober statement of fact. Most of the people who run such groups would say that they are not attempting sexual politics. But I am, and in my book *The Horned God* (Rowan 1987) I have given details of alternative rituals: here is one of them, which has been used and revised several times since the book was written.

A RITUAL OF WOUNDING AND HEALING

James Horne has pointed out that in any really good ritual, there are always five steps: Pre-learning, Separation, Suggestion, Execution and Maintenance.

What we did in the first part [earlier in the day] was the Pre-learning part of this ritual. It put us all in possession of some ideas and some shared experience. Now we go on to the stage of separation. This is what is called in mysticism the stage of Purgation. It is the darkest part of the ritual. And in order to go into it, and get the most out of it, it has to be regarded as an initiation ceremony. Initiation is the process of going from one state to another state, and in this case from someone who is powerless to heal the wound of patriarchy to someone who is capable of healing that wound. If you allow yourself to experience all that is here to be experienced, it can be a deep experience. If you choose to make it into a shallow experience, easier to handle, that is possible too. It is entirely up to you what you make of it.

So what we are to go into now is the experience of being wounded. Specifically being wounded by women, and even more specifically by feminist women. Let us gather together all the questions and all the statements which have been addressed to us by women, which are critical or blaming. And let us particularly be sure to put up all those which seem to us to have some ring of truth in them, or to touch on some sore point.

[Questions like: How have you hurt women? How have you hurt children? How have you hurt other men? How have you been untrue to the best in you? Statements like: You don't let women in. You put women down. You should be more responsible. You exploit women. You should give up pornography. Stop raping your wife.]

These should all be self-oppressive accusations.

[Use a blackboard or flipchart to put up all the suggestions which are offered.]

Now find a space in the room where you can be alone with yourself. And use your imagination to take the worst of these accusations – the ones you think really do apply to you, or have applied to you in the past – and to feel what it is like to have someone who really matters to you addressing them to you personally. And instead of defending against it or answering it, really let it in as a wound. Really allow yourself to be wounded by these accusations. And see if you can allow yourself to feel those feelings and go to the very bottom with them. Let your imagination create the very worst situation in which this could happen. One man may have several accusers walking round and round. Another man may have just one accuser standing opposite him. Another may have a tribunal on a raised platform looking down at him. You may be standing, sitting, kneeling or whatever seems most relevant. And really let that situation and those accusations get through to you. Start now.

Silence

[Let the silence continue for five, ten or fifteen minutes, until one of the men starts to look a bit happier. Go to him and gently touch him. When he has opened his eyes, raise him to his feet and guide him to an open part of the room. When the next one comes to the surface, do the same thing and take him next to the first man, and encourage them to join hands. If the group is small, one circle will eventually form out of this process. If the group is large, form several circles of about eight men. Carry on like this until everyone has revived. This may take some time. At the last, it may be necessary to touch men who have apparently not revived. In most cases this will be all right, but in those cases where it is not, do not insist. If it means everybody waiting, it means everybody waiting.]

The healing

Stand in a circle, arms around each other. As each man says things like: 'The worst thing I did was . . .', 'The worst moment just now was . . .', 'I can't forget . . .', the other men make statements which feel true and justifiable, such as 'You don't have to be perfect', 'You are a good man', 'You don't have to control everything', 'I understand why you did what you did', 'Everybody makes mistakes', 'You did the best you could – could any of us say more?', 'No blame', 'You don't have to get it right all the time'. But each person must take responsibility only to say what they really believe and can say from the heart. No phony reassurance is required or useful.

Then a wordless chant begins. It gets louder and louder. Eventually clapping starts, and the circle breaks up and becomes a clapping and dancing group. The dancing gets more and more vigorous. Drums may be brought out. Something spontaneous may emerge at this point, expressing good feelings. This continues as long as it needs to.

Application

Now sit in your own space again. Eyes closed. Imagine going to one woman who has accused you of something, and telling her what you are going to do to make sure that that same accusation will not arise in the future. Wait for her answer, and if necessary change what you originally said. Continue with this imaginary dialogue until you feel that a mutually satisfying outcome has been reached. If that happens quickly, go on to another one – another accusation, or another woman, or both. [Wait five or ten minutes.]

Maintenance

Now find one other man, and sit together. Share what you have done, how that came out, what the result was; see if you can convince the other man that you have genuinely got somewhere. You have twelve minutes for that, six minutes each way. I will hit the gong after the first six minutes, and again at the end.

And now, with the same partner, ask about maintenance. Questions like: How will you keep this up? How could you ruin it all again? What would help you to remember? Name three ways of sabotaging your solutions. How can you get others to help you in retaining this change? What resources do you need to keep this up, and how are you going to get them? [Again two periods of six minutes, making twelve minutes in all.]

The ritual ends with a closing circle, when the men look round the circle and register all that they have been through. If any words or sounds emerge, fine.

What have we learned from all this group work? The main thing I have learned is how explosive the gender issues potentially are, especially when one tries to work on them in a mixed group.

In a men's group there is often the opposite problem – that the group is not energetic enough, because of the reluctance to enter into gender issues. The most 'successful' men's groups (in terms of the energy level) have been those which ignore gender issues altogether.

It seems to be very hard for men to get into gender issues without becoming competitive about them. Mirror, mirror on the wall, who is the most nonsexist of all? But if competition is rigorously avoided, the energy level seems to go down or even go out. Avoiding competition about being politically correct becomes just another way of being politically correct. 'Our group is less competitive than your group.'

THE MALE EGO

Men do this in pairs. Each pair of men has a large piece of paper and a number of felt pens or other artistic equipment. They have to sit on opposite sides of the piece of paper and produce a picture between them. This brings out the problems of the male ego much better than any verbal discussion, because the evidence is right there and cannot be denied.

Men's groups can be very positive places, where men can come away feeling better about themselves and better about relating to women in today's society. But if this is to happen we cannot avoid working on deep issues of oppression and domination. This is a major political task of our time. The kinds of exercises to be found scattered through this chapter can be very helpful, but they need to be followed up by sensitive exploration of the issues raised in them if their positive promise is to be fulfilled. The deep confrontation which is sometimes involved needs to be carried out with care and love.

MY OWN WORK

Since about 1972 I have been working with men in groups, specifically on issues of male consciousness in a patriarchal society, or what Eisler and Loye (1990) are now calling, perhaps more helpfully, a dominator model of society. If humanity is to survive, we have to move away from a dominator society towards a partnership society, such as has existed at various times in the past, but now with a much better chance of being understood and being successful. In Chapter 9 we saw the necessary underpinning which is needed if such a society is to come into being.

This is difficult work, because it involves encouraging men to face the oppressor in themselves, as well as the hurt child, the inner person with feelings, the inner female and so forth. So it is rather like working on racism and other uncomfortable topics of that kind (e.g. Jones and Harris 1971). This is why we have to call it initiation, because it is like a rite of passage: out of a patriarchal set of assumptions into a new way of thinking, feeling and acting.

MAN+WOMAN CONVERSATION

Each man in the group puts a cushion or chair in front of his cushion or chair. He imagines that on this is sitting his partner, or a woman with whom he has problems, or has had problems in the past. He talks to her, simply letting anything be said that comes forth, without censorship. Statements, questions, demands, anything is suitable. This goes on until a natural pause is reached.

Then the man switches over, and sits on the other cushion or chair. Now he is the woman, and responds to what the man has said, either replying to the questions asked or whatever in a direct way, or perhaps raising new or different points which have not been mentioned by the original speaker. This again goes on until a natural pause is reached.

Then the man comes back to the original point, and carries on the dialogue, then going back and forth between the two positions until some natural ending point is reached. It is OK for emotions to appear and to be expressed.

This might take about ten minutes in all.

Then the participants discuss what emerged in pairs or threes.

The type of work I have been doing is group work, specifically experiential group work. In this kind of work, I set an exercise for a group of men, and when they have completed it, we work through the feelings aroused by it in a spontaneous and unstructured way, trying to do justice to the feelings which emerge.

For example, I might say: 'Please find a partner, and when you have done so, look into your partner's eyes for one minute, without saying anything.' Some men will find this quite easy, others will be unable to do it at all, others again will find various feelings arising, which may be stronger or weaker. For a few men, this is a very threatening exercise, which makes them feel weak, and which they can then avoid in various ways: for example, one man might say 'I couldn't look directly into the eyes, so I looked instead at the eyebrows, and I found that easier.' We will then explore the implications of this.

As I have gone through the years, and have worked with different types of men in different contexts, I have come to believe that this work can be done in terms of three different positions.

The first is the conscious position, where we are going into matters like how men treat women, how men relate to other men, how men talk about women with other men, and so on.

The second is the unconscious position, where we discover possibly surprising things about how men relate to their mothers or fathers, how internal conflicts arise and how they function, how the dominance model gets into the bones, so to speak.

The third is the transpersonal position, where we go into the question of the anima, the shadow and other archetypes, and also such things as rituals of death and rebirth, of initiation. What is our myth, our legend, our fairy story about men and women? The discoveries here are again often surprising or disturbing. They may or may not include meeting with god-forms, such as the Horned God and the Great Goddess. Actual experiences of wells, of standing stones, of tree circles and so forth can come in.

Let us look at each of these in turn, and see if we can come to terms with the phenomena which arise in each of these positions.

Position 1: conscious

Once the male chauvinist assumptions are challenged, they quite quickly give way in the group setting, and change can come about reasonably fast. One of the exercises I do to explore this is called *The Disappearance*. Here I tell the group of men: 'Two hours ago all the women in the world disappeared. There are no women any more. And this includes girl children and babies, foetuses and embryos and ova kept for research purposes, and so on.' And I just leave them to discuss that scenario for one hour, an hour and a half, or two hours, depending on the length of the workshop. This is a powerful exercise, because the men can see for themselves how they talk and behave: it is not a question of telling them.

Usually what happens is that they talk a great deal about sex: how can they possibly get on without it; will marauding bands of men from other countries have to be dealt with; how can women be replaced somehow by biological research? Sometimes the men form themselves into a committee and have definite offices. This can all be discussed in the light of the idea of male chauvinism.

Sexism is deeply engrained, and hard to get at. It often requires a real change in the whole attitude structure of the person before it can shift. So this is more long-term work. Sexism is often based on low self-esteem, so that the man in question is able to boost himself up by putting women down, or so it seems to him. So the whole pattern of low self-esteem has to change before sexism can go, and this is a long-term therapeutic operation.

However, all these things are kept in place by social assumptions about the male ego and how it should be. It is often stated in articles and books that the male ego needs a lot of support and boosting (and this job is of course mainly done by women) in order to keep it functioning at all. This seems a bit suspect. One of the most striking statements I came across in the early days of the men's movement was a quotation from Keith Paton (later Mothersson) in a newsletter which said 'The healthy male ego is oppressive and wrong'. The exercise given above is useful in exploring this issue. But something even simpler may have a good effect:

THUMB ENCOUNTER

In pairs, so find a partner. Lock the fingers of your right hand into the fingers of your partner's right hand, bending the hand slightly so that the knuckles intertwine. The thumbs will then be upright and free and facing one another. They should be within reach of each other, quite close. Then imagine that you are your thumb and that you must meet your partner. The same goes for your partner, at the same time. Your thumb represents your personality. Be aware of what kind of interaction you have. [Give at least two minutes for this.]
Discuss what happened.

We have to work on this level quite consistently to achieve any real change, because the social reinforcement of sexism is always there. This is also the reason why group work is much more effective than individual psychotherapy in dealing with sexism – the real presence of other men working on the same issues makes it clear that this is a social, not just an individual problem.

Position 2: unconscious

One can go only so far by simply working on the conscious level. Ultimately it is necessary, in any real attempt at change of dominance patterns, to go to the unconscious level. One of the key things here, of course, is the original family pattern from which the man emerged.

How the man related to his father as a child is crucial. What kind of a model of masculinity did the father represent? All kinds of positive and negative messages come from this early relationship.

Feelings about the father may often be closely related to sexuality. Perhaps the father was too sexual, or not sexual enough. Often the father's sexuality is quite mysterious, because of the absence (physical or mental) of the father from the family. Coming to terms with this may be a very important step in discovering one's own sexuality.

Similarly, a man's relationships with women are very strongly influenced, at an unconscious level, by how he related to his mother as a child. Did he love her? Did she love him? These are surprisingly often very loaded questions. They may carry a big charge, and be quite salient in the man's development.

One of the key exercises in this area is to ask the man to get in touch with his inner female. This is almost invariably a revealing and opening-up experience, which can bring some very important insights. This can be done through a guided fantasy, but I usually prefer to do it like this:

A CONTRASEX EXERCISE

Breathing, grounding and centring.

Now find a space where you can have a cushion or a chair in front of you. Cushion facing another cushion or chair facing another chair.

Sit on one and face the other. Close your eyes if you find that helpful. Now find in yourself the opposite sex. See if you can concentrate on finding a woman inside yourself, a woman in every physical sense, and in every psychological sense. See if you can allow yourself to be this woman. Really experience what it is like to be a woman. But it must not be a woman you know in the outside world. It has to be a woman from inside you. Really be that woman.

And then put that woman on the other seat. Imagine her as completely as you can. Get as full an image or impression as you can. How is she dressed? What age is she? What expression does she have on her face? What is her hair like? How is she breathing? And then start to speak to that woman. What would you like to ask her? What would you like to tell her? What would you like to demand from her? Perhaps think of times in the past when you have been aware of her.

And when you have done that, and got some sense of how it goes, switch over and be that woman. And start to speak as that woman. What does that woman say? What do you say as that woman? Let her talk to you, respond to what you said to her. Have a dialogue with that woman. Get to know her, relate to her, find out how things go with her. Visualise her, concretise her, be with her. Go back and forth as you may need to. You have ten minutes for that.

Discuss in groups of three or four.

This can be done in a very shallow way, or in a very deep way: it depends on all sorts of factors which it will be. But such an exercise should not be offered by anyone who is not a therapist or counsellor, or has a great deal of that kind of experience in groups, because of the depth of feeling which can sometimes come up with this exercise.

This is of course not the only exercise which can be done at the unconscious level; we also work on dreams, use guided fantasy, encourage regression to earlier ages, use certain kinds of massage to stimulate early memories, bring in art work and so forth. One useful exercise is this:

T-SHIRT EXERCISE

Ask each man to write down the slogan or motto he would most like to have on the front of his T-shirt. Allow about two minutes for this.

Then ask him to write down the slogan or motto or message he thinks he might have on the back of his T-shirt, expressing the other side of his personality.

Discuss in the whole group or in small groups.

This exercise may bring out the unconscious side of the person, or the shadow side, or simply another subpersonality, but in any case it makes the point that men are not simply just one massive ego.

Position 3: transpersonal

Another way of seeing the deeper relationship with women comes from the collective unconscious. Such an archetype as the anima is highly relevant to the whole way in which the man perceives women. The anima is the woman inside the man. Very often the details of her appearance or character are derived from the mother, but this is not a mother complex, this is a deep archetype.

Also found in this area are the rituals of initiation. All real change in the personality takes the form of initiation into a different state. Very often this initiation takes the form of death and rebirth. The ritual of wounding and healing mentioned earlier is one such.

Group work lends itself to ritual, and new rituals seem to arise quite spontaneously in many groups. But they can also be devised consciously, as in the following example of a ritual which was used by Sue Mickleburgh and me in a workshop we did for a conference on Sexuality and Spirituality on the island of Lanzarote in May 1987.

SEXUALITY AND SPIRITUALITY

As people arrived, there was music playing, earthy and simple. We divided the participants into two groups, twenty men and thirty women. Sue took the female group, and I the male group. The female group occupied the main space with Sue, and the male group went outside with me.

The female group

The women were told that what they were going to do was to create a powerful space, full of energy – female, goddess-type energy – and hold on to it, even when the men re-entered the group. The first thing they did was to form a circle and introduce themselves by saying their names and, at the same time, performing a movement or gesture which expressed how they were feeling, or wanted to feel.

Then came a series of breathing exercises. Breathing unites body, feelings, thought and spirit by operating on all four of those levels.

Then Sue asked the women to hold their arms in front of them, with the palms of their hands about two inches apart, and gave instructions for a ball of energy to appear and grow between them. Then they slowly lowered their hands down to their sides and joined hands. They stayed silent and still for a while, holding hands and feeling the energy being transmitted around the circle. Sue then explained that they were going to use this energy, in a joyful way, to remind themselves where it had come from and to give thanks for it.

They danced around in a circle, still holding hands, singing 'The earth is our Mother, we must take care of her, the earth is our Mother, we must take care of her'. As they went round and round the singing got louder and louder and there was a feeling of energy and joy.

The joining

They stopped, and the men quietly entered the circle, stooping low to get underneath their linked hands. As they entered in this way their bent bodies and hunched shoulders seemed symbolic of the saddened and chastened men of the world realising how much pain and suffering they had caused women and feeling humbly grateful that they were still, after all the bad things they had done, accepted and welcomed into a joyful place where the strength and power of the women was quite different from anything they had ever experienced.

As they did so, the women faced into the centre of the circle, and extended their arms and hands into the centre, raising them as they breathed in and lowering them as they breathed out. They breathed in unison, making a constant wave of female energy directed toward the centre of the circle.

The important thing now was for the women to keep the atmosphere as it had been before the men entered the circle, and not to seek to comfort them and give away everything they had spent time raising. The men were in the circle, lying on the floor, seeming very miserable, and the women were standing tall and proud giving them attention in a strong and loving way. Slowly the men started to make contact with each other, and after a while the women linked hands again and danced around in the circle. Some of the men joined in the dancing and soon everyone was dancing.

The male group

When the men were outside I told them about the whole question of initiation, and explained that it was like death and rebirth.

'There will be three steps in this initiation. The first step is to give up everything that makes us male – to divest ourselves, one by one, of each thing. The second step is to go into the Goddess space and feel what it is like to be surrounded by female energy, not keeping it out and not defending ourselves against it, but accepting it and relating to it. And the third thing is to go deeply into ourselves and find the deeper masculinity within the Goddess space.' There was then some explanation of the Orphic Mysteries, and some discussion of this. I went on to explain the ritual itself.

'You are going to pass through ten gateways, and at each one you will give up something masculine. See if you can allow yourself to experience what life would be like without this thing. And remember that this is cumulative – once you lose something it is gone, and so you lose first one thing, and then two things, and then three things, and so on, until they are all gone.' [Pause]

'Now. Take one step forward, through the first gateway. Here you lose the male attitude to emotions and feelings. This is the attitude which says that emotions and feelings are rather a nuisance, they only get in the way of what is really important, they are irrational and timewasting.' [Here there is a pause of two minutes. This does not sound very long, but in fact it does seem a very long time. This two-minute pause is kept throughout the ritual, between each of the gateways.]

'Now take one step forward, through the second gateway. Here you lose the male attitude to children. This is the attitude which says that children are not very interesting unless they can talk sensibly about things and enter into proper conversations. Before this they are messy and inconvenient, or perhaps sometimes cute and adorable, but not really to be taken seriously.' [Pause]

'Take one step forward, through the third gateway. Here you lose the male attitude to work. This is the one which says that work is the most important thing in life, and that it must take precedence over everything else. If anything else conflicts with work, the work comes first. Be aware of what it is like not to have any more the male attitude to feelings and emotions, or the male attitude to children, or the male attitude to work – try to make it real to yourself.' [Pause]

'Then take one step forward, through the fourth gateway. Here you give up the male attitude to relationships. This is the one which says that relationships should take care of themselves; I do my part, the other person

219

does their part. It is something like a contract; each person carries out what they have agreed to do. And that is really all there is to it.' [Pause]

'One step forward again, through the fifth gateway. Here you surrender the male attitude to women. This says that women are there to be used. They may be used to cook or keep house, they may be used to look up to or have sex with, they may be used to look good on one's arm or play hostess to one's friends and contacts, but the key is to use them well, and never to be used by them. One must be in charge at all times, or run the risk of looking weak and foolish. Be aware of what it feels like not to have this any more.' [Pause]

'Now another step forward, through the sixth gateway. Here you lose the male attitude to science and technology. This is the one which says that science and technology are the answer to everything. Everything that is now unknown and uncontrolled can one day be known and controlled through science and technology, and that would be a very good thing. These things have been successful in the past and will only be more and more successful in the future.' [Pause]

'One step forward, now going through the seventh gateway. Here you give up the male ego. The male ego continually needs to be stroked and looked after and protected; it inflates and deflates very easily, and it is important to keep this under control. It continually thinks of itself as being very important and very worthwhile. It very easily becomes impatient. It is very keen on appearing masculine and desperately afraid of been seen as feminine. It likes showing off, but it hates and can't bear being criticised. Now is the time to let go of this, and really allow yourself to feel what this is like.' [Pause]

'One step forward, through the eighth gateway now. This is where you have to give up your male body hair and beard. All those types of body hair which are typically masculine, including bald heads too. Imagine having nothing to declare you masculine in the way of hair. When we get to these last three, there is sometimes a tendency to laugh or giggle. See if you can do it without laughing, just feeling it directly, and breathing through it if necessary.' [Pause]

'One step forward, now going through the ninth gateway. Here you have to give up your testicles. This is the act of castration, which the priests of Attis always used to do as a sacrifice to the Great Goddess. No testicles, no testes, no balls now. Feel what that is like.' [Pause]

'One last step forward, and now this is the tenth and last gateway. Here you lose your penis, your phallus is gone now. The last masculine possession goes too. See if you can stay with that experience, of having nothing left at all.'

Now here we have to pause until the Goddess space is fully prepared. It was only a matter of three or four minutes before we could go in, waiting for the cue which I knew was going to come. But the men did not know how long it was going to be, and the sun had now set, and the wind was beginning to get cold, so that the weather echoed very well the feeling of loss and deprivation.

The joining

Now the men were asked to blindfold themselves or shut their eyes, and hold hands in line. I led the way, and bent down to go under the arms of the women in the circle. All the men bent down as they came in, and we circled in around the inside of the women's circle until all the men were in. They lay on the ground at first, taking in the fact of being in a circle of female energy. I encouraged them to take it in, not to resist it or compete with it. I reminded them that their task now was to get in touch with their deeper and truer masculinity, as we had discussed earlier, along the lines of my book *The Horned God*.

Then I encouraged them nonverbally to make contact with other men, just stroking their hands and joining hands. Some of them made closer contact, in twos and threes, others just stayed in contact as they were. This felt much better.

Then I encouraged them, nonverbally again, to stand up together. When they were all standing up, I started the music. This music was South American dance music, again rather folky and unfamiliar. They began to move in response to the music, and so did the women.

The final phase

The next phase started spontaneously; we gave no lead at all as to what should happen, apart from starting the music. The women started to dance round in their circle, and the men danced their way into an inner circle. Then all at once the men began to turn outwards, so that the two circles were facing one another. As the music became louder, the circles became more irregular, and eventually broke apart, and people were dancing on their own or forming and reforming small groups of dancers all over the room. This dancing went on for quite a while.

We had thought that people might like to talk in small groups about the experience at this point, but the energy was much too high for that.

We asked people to sit in a circle, and brought out the bread and wine we had ready. We got people to pass it from one to another: as they passed on the wine they said 'May your spirit be strong', and as they passed on the bread they said – 'May you have sustenance'. (These phrases come from the Wicca tradition.) Someone had found a candle and put it in the centre of the seated circle. It was just getting dark and the little light shone brightly for us. We grounded the energy we had raised. We parted with many expressions of feeling. The workshop came to an end.

Next day several people came up to us and said how much they had got out of it. One man shaved off his beard, which was an unintended side effect! The organiser told us later that he had had some glowing reports about our workshop. We felt that we had learned a great deal.

SOME QUESTIONS

But of course this raises a great many questions. A woman who had read an account of the workshop said she felt uneasy about the negativity of the approach to men. One or two men have said the same thing: couldn't I be more positive, more celebratory?

I have experienced a number of efforts for men to discover themselves on their own, in men's groups of various kinds – consciousness-raising groups, therapy groups and spiritual groups. I have not been impressed with the results. So often the group, no matter how it started and with what intentions the men got together, slides into some kind of warm self-congratulation or some kind of cold break-up. I referred to some of the reasons why that might be in *The Horned God*. Reports of the Bly groups in the USA reveal much the same picture. Such groups can be very moving experiences for the men, but they do not seem to help much in changing the patriarchal set-up between men and women, and that is what interests me. The best clues I have got about the latter has been from disciplines like paganism and Tantra, where the relationship between the male and the female is directly referred to. Here is a quotation from Arthur Avalon's *Shakti and Shakta*:

A glorious feature of the Śākta faith is the *honour which it pays to women*. And this is natural for those who worship the Great Mother, whose representative (Vigraha) all earthly women are. . . . 'Women are Devas; women are life itself', as an old Hymn in the *Sarvollasa* has it. It is because Woman is a Vigraha of the Ambā Devī, Her likeness in flesh and blood, that the Śākta Tantras enjoin the honour and worship of women and girls (Kumārīs), and forbid all harm to them such as the Sati rite, enjoining that not even a female animal is to be sacrificed. With the same solicitude for women, the *Mahānirvāna* prescribes that even if a man speaks rudely (Durvācyam kathayan) to his wife, he must fast for a whole day, and enjoins the education of daughters before their marriage. The Moslem Author of the Dabistan (ii. 154, ed. 1843) says 'The Āgama favours both sexes equally. Men and women equally compose mankind. This sect hold women in great esteem and call them Śaktis, and to ill-treat a Śakti, that is, a woman, is a crime.' The Śākta Tantras again *allow of women being Guru*, or Spiritual Director, a reverence which the West has not (with rare exceptions) yet given them. Initiation by a Mother bears eightfold fruit. . . . A high worship therefore which can be offered to the Mother today consists in getting rid of abuses which have neither the authority of ancient Sāstra, nor of modern social science and to honour, cherish, educate and advance women (Śakti).

(Avalon 1978: 172)

There is a lot more, but you can see the drift. This seems to me very compatible with Western paganism, as promulgated for example by Starhawk (1989) or Sjöö and Mor (1987). Some people have related the Shakti directly to therapy, saying that the Shakti eats falsities. This is quite OK if that is what the man wants, but if he resists, the Shakti starts to look very frightening. She is frightening only to those who oppose her.

Coming now to the question of how this applies to the psychology of masculinity as worked out in men's groups, it is as if there are at least three models of maleness and how to work with it. First of all, there is the standard phony social model, where the male has to be a proper man, and not effeminate or cowardly. Here it is OK to be male as long as one stays within the bounds of socially stereotyped masculinity. If one strays outside it in the macho direction, that may be a cause for punishment or treatment, but basically it is acceptable or winked at. If one strays outside it in the feminine direction, however, that is much more suspect and condemnable. We need not say too much about this model – it is too familiar. It is well worked out and defended in that book (Baumli 1985) about the so-called 'Free Men' in the USA.

Second, there is what one might call the monistic model, which is usual in personal growth and the kind of psychotherapy I normally do, where we say that the man has to go down into his depths, finding perhaps first a bad layer of self-putdowns, and then a layer of pain, and then a layer of deeper truth which is OK. It is OK to be male, and just a question of finding the deeper, truer version of it. Here is an exercise based on the idea of layers:

THE ORPHEUS EXERCISE

Write down the numbers I to I0 in a column downwards on the left of the page.

Then write down opposite each one something that you personally associate with being a man, until you have ten of them written down. It can be very biological things like having testicles, or social things like shaving your face, or more personal things like having premature ejaculation. Try and stick to fairly obvious things, rather than trying to be subtle and unusual.

Now look at number I0 on your list and imagine you haven't got it. 'It's not there. It's gone. It doesn't exist. Nothing comes in its place. It's just absent. You don't have to bother with it any more. Just imagine what that is like. What that means, what that feels like. How does it feel to you not to have it?' [The items in quotes are to be used every time, not necessarily in just that order, and not necessarily every one, but most of them each time.]

Now number 9. What is it like not to have number I0 or number 9? They have both gone now . . . [Carry on with 8, 7, 6, 5, 4.]

223

When we get to the top three, sometimes people start giggling. See if you can just observe your desire to giggle, rather than giving in to it. See if you can take these last three quite seriously.

Now number 3 has gone . . . Now number 2 has gone as well . . . Now number I has gone . . .

What does it feel like now to have none of these things? Just stay with that feeling for a moment. There is no need to do anything about it, just be aware of it. [Pause two minutes.]

And now you can have one back. Which will be the first one to have back? [Pause] And what will be the second one? Write down on your sheet the order in which you have them back. [Pause till this is done.]

Now share your reactions to this exercise in pairs or threes. [Allow about ten minutes for this.]

It can be seen how this idea of layers can be a very powerful and useful one, but it is not the only possibility.

Third, there is what one might call a dialectical model, which is much more rarely used by group leaders, where we say that the first 'bad' layer is found to be harmful only because separated from female energy, female power. Connected up in a proper relationship with that energy and that power, the 'bad' transforms into a deeper truth which is OK. One familiar symbol for this is the Yin-Yang diagram, where the white area has a black spot at its centre, and the black area has a white spot at the centre, indicating that opposites interpenetrate each other.

Now there are one or two ways of talking about masculinity which are quite compatible with this dialectical model. I heard it said in one workshop that the male was like an electron circling the female nucleus, and that this was the healthy state; to split that atom could be destructive. This is a very similar point to the one I have been trying to make. I have also heard it said that what was most vulnerable and precious in the person could actually be seen as the vital centre of the person. Again this seems quite compatible with what I am saying here. But very often in groups the leader seems to be adhering to the monistic model, asking people simply to own and to rejoice in their own masculinity.

Now it seems to me that these three approaches are not necessarily contradictory. I think they correspond to three different types of work in this area. This is laid out at length in Chapter 7.

THREE TYPES OF WORK

The first type, which uses the model of adjustment to social reality, is the position of most of the psychotherapy which is generally available. The highest aim is to be able to play one's role in society properly.

The second type, which takes the monistic approach, is the position of personal growth. Here one is interested in the personal unconscious, in the healing of the splits (such as mind/body, left/right, intellect/emotion, topdog/

underdog, but in particular here the split between the male and the female), and generally in the integration of the person as a social and psychological being. We get the first initiation, contacting the real self.

The third type, which uses the dialectical approach, is the position of spirituality and the transpersonal. It says that the male and the female must be related through the *hieros gamos* (the sacred marriage) if the male is not to be destructive. This is not about healing the split between the male and the female, but about seeing these things as spiritual realities. This is the second initiation.

Another way of putting this, which I now think is more useful for some purposes, is to see the three layers as circular (Figure 13.1).

In this way of seeing it, we go from the conscious to the unconscious, and from the unconscious to the spiritual transpersonal, and from the transpersonal back to the conscious, and so on round and round in a spiral of growth. In alchemy we talk about the *Circulatio*, where we go back to a previous stage or go back and forth between stages. See also Jill Purce's (1974) book on *The mystic spiral*. The advantage of seeing it in this way is to underline the point which Starhawk (1979) makes, that it is only the pagan view of the transpersonal which has a political significance in making the male safe for the world, because it is only in paganism that the male is in the right relationship with the female. This entails using what I have just been calling the dialectical model of the male.

This would be to take male-in-relation as safe and to be the focus of attention, and male-out-of-relation to be dangerous or suspect. I feel that the monistic can all too easily become the autistic, and that the autonomous can all too easily become the overweening – as in the story of Inanna and Dumuzi, as told by Perera (1981). I hope that this discussion will make it clearer what the reasons

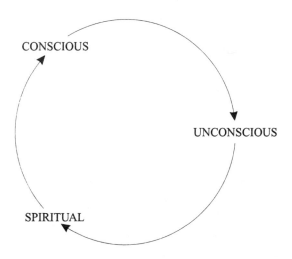

Figure 13.1 Conscious – unconscious – spiritual

are for envisioning the ritual in this way. It very firmly grasps the third position, and works entirely from there.

THE SHAKTI

If we really want to understand death and rebirth, we have to be prepared to go into a further transpersonal area, the realm of the god forms. The Horned God is the consort of the Great Goddess, and can form an ideal image of how the male can relate to the female.

This goes into an area of religion proper. It is only here, I believe, that men can realise that the question of female power is crucial to their own development. This takes us back to politics. Politics is about power, and we have to understand about female power before we can shift male power from its present dangerous position.

Men are very often afraid of female power, I have discovered, and find it hard to come to terms with it. But one way to come to terms with female power is to worship it. It was an exciting day for me when I came across the seven-page entry for Kali-Ma (one name for the Shakti) in Barbara Walker (1983) and found that it said things like this:

> Kali was the basic archetypal image of the birth-and-death Mother, simultaneously womb and tomb, giver of life and devourer of her children: the same image portrayed in a thousand ancient religions. . . .
>
> Kali stood for Existence, which meant Becoming because all her world was an eternal living flux from which all things rose and disappeared again, in endless cycles.
>
> The Nirvana Tantra treated the claims of male gods with contempt:
> *From a part only of Kalika, the primordial Shakti, arises Brahma, from a part only arises Vishnu, and from a part only arises Shiva. O fair-eyed Devi, just as rivers and lakes are unable to traverse a vast sea, so Brahma and other gods lose their separate existence on entering the uncrossable and infinite being of Great Kali. Compared with the vast sea of the being of Kali, the existence of Brahma and the other gods is nothing but such a little water as is contained in the hollow made by a cow's hoof. Just as it is impossible for a hollow made by a cow's hoof to form a notion of the unfathomable depths of a sea, so it is impossible for Brahma and other gods to have a knowledge of the nature of Kali.*
>
> The Yogini Tantra said of Kali, 'Whatever power anything possesses, that is the Goddess.' Shakti, 'Power', was one of her important names. Without her, neither man nor god could act at all. . . .
>
> As a Mother, Kali was called Treasure-House of Compassion (*karuna*), Giver of Life to the world, the Life of all lives. Contrary to the west's idea of her as a purely destructive Goddess, she was the fount of every kind of love, which flowed into the world only through her agents on earth,

women. Thus it was said a male worshipper of Kali 'bows down at the feet of women', regarding them as his rightful teachers.

(Barbara Walker 1983: 488–491)

This was extraordinary stuff for me to read, because it overturned all the ideas I had had up to that time about Kali, who I had thought about if at all as a thoroughly destructive and nasty entity. Our modern consciousness has split apart the benevolent and the destructive aspects of Kali: as Sjöö and Mor (1987) succinctly put it: 'Paradox is split into dualism, an act characteristic of patriarchical consciousness.' Soon after reading this I saw a film called *Indiana Jones and the Temple of Doom*, which underlined all the old errors about Kali, and even added some new ones: for example, the threat to the heroine of being sacrificed to Kali. Kali never had female sacrifices of any kind, not even female animals. Applying this to therapy, we can say that Kali-Shakti questions the ego, and asks if it is ready to die. As a wrathful mother, she strips us of everything we do not need. But just because we don't need it, she remains the good mother. Kail-Shakti eats everything that is devoid of life: and this makes her blacker. She takes away all our illusions.

THE LORD OF THE DANCE

Now the consort to Kali is Shiva, and I read on avidly to find out what Barbara Walker said about him. Here is some of it:

Shiva was called Lord of Yoga, i.e., of the 'yoke' that bound him to the Goddess. . . . Among Shiva's many other titles were Great Lord, Lord of the Dance, Lord of Cattle (Pasupati), Beneficent One (Sankara), Lord who is Half Woman (Ardhanarisvara), God with the Moon in His Hair (Candrasekhara), He Who Belongs to the Triple Goddess, He Who Gives and Takes Away, Consort of the Goddess Uma, Condemned One, Destroyer, Howler. . . .

Tantric yogis insisted that their supreme Shiva was the only god and all other gods were only inferior imitations of him. He was certainly older than the Vedic heaven-gods. . . . As Lord of the Dance, Shiva represented one of Hinduism's most subtle concepts. . . . Shiva performed this dance in a place called Chidambaram, the 'Centre of the Universe'; but the location of this place is within the human heart . . . therefore the god is located within the core of man's own self. . . .

Shiva was seldom depicted alone, for his power depended on his union with Kali, his feminine energy, without whom he could not act. The puzzling vision of Shiva as Shava the corpse, under the Goddess's feet, illustrated the 'doctrine that Shiva without his Shakti can do and is, so far as the manifested is concerned, nothing.' Yet joined to the Goddess, he became the Bindu or spark of creation. Every human orgasm was believed to share in this creative experience as 'an infinitesimally small fragment

227

and faint reflection of the creative act in which Shiva and Shakti join to produce the Bindu which is the seed of the universe.'

(Barbara Walker 1983: 935–936)

Again I found this was exciting stuff. It seemed to offer a mythological account which made perfect sense of the dialectical relationship which I had found to be so important. When I came to investigate, I found that the relationship between Shiva and Kali-Shakti in the Eastern religion was paralleled in the relationship between the Great Goddess and the Horned God in the Western traditions.

This is now spelled out in a masterly work from Janet and Stewart Farrar. Here we can see how the Horned God Cernunnos or Herne in the pagan traditions of our own area has all the characteristics we have found in the East.

> He is usually portrayed with horns and accompanied by animals. He usually either wears or has looped on his horns the torc (circular necklet) of Celtic nobility. Often, as on the Gundestrup Cauldron, he holds a serpent with a ram's head or horns.
>
> (Farrar and Farrar 1989: 97)

This is exactly how he is also portrayed in the Mohenjo-Daro representation of Shiva Pasupati, Lord of the Animals. The serpent is the representative of female underworld wisdom in myth and legend world-wide. The ram's head indicates that this is a specifically masculine version of serpent wisdom. It says that the relationship between the male and the female is particularly close and particularly important for the Horned God.

The Horned God, like the Great Goddess, has many names: they include Dionysus, Pan, Dumuzi, Tammuz, Osiris, Orpheus, Adonis, Attis, Mithra, Quetzalcoatl, Hu, Dis, Hades and Hermes, among others. We shall see later that Dionysus, Hades and Hermes have particular significance for us. All these can be studied with advantage. The Farrars suggest a useful ritual for getting in touch with him in his guise of the stag.

SOME FURTHER ISSUES

At the end of this examination, we have come up with some disturbing news for men. They have to re-evaluate their assumptions radically if they are to come to terms with a more adequate vision of how males and females can relate. And it is not easy for men to do this. One sophisticated and knowledgeable man wrote to me, after reading some of this material, and said that it looked to him as if I were saying that women should be given precedence in all matters. This felt to him as if I were saying that he should agree to be hurt or wounded by women, and 'to lie down and be prepared to be run over by every passing steamroller'.

I replied by saying that unless men agree to be wounded nothing much is going to change. Any man who says 'I refuse to be wounded – this thing can be tackled by intelligence and good will and positive thinking' is highly suspect to me. Suspect because feminism is in a way all about hurt, and unless men actually feel some kind of hurt, rather than sympathising with it in a patronising way, they are not going to experience the message of feminism on any real kind of human level. We have to go through the pain of initiation. This reminds us perhaps of the wise words of Michael Meade about wounding, which we came across in Chapter 9 (p. 134).

Many men seem to get the message of feminism only as far as their heads, which means that they get the words but not the music. If we are going to get the response anywhere near adequate, we have to accept that we are hurt too, we do actually feel something ourselves. The refusal to lie down under every passing steamroller is the refusal to be broken. The 'healthy male ego' has to learn how to be *broken* by feminism. This is not an easy lesson or an easy option – it is hard and has to be hard, because of the resistance which gets in the way. But unless this lesson is learned, men are going to continue to play the 60/40 game.

The 60/40 game was first identified in the early days of the anti-sexist men's movement by Keith Paton (later Keith Mothersson). This is where a man living with a feminist admits that she is most often right about feminist issues, particularly when she confronts him on his own actions. He sees that she has more insight, more feeling, more motive in such things. But in his head this gets translated into a kind of proportion or percentage. She cannot be right all the time; no one can be right all the time. So maybe she is right 90 per cent of the time, or 80 per cent, or 70 per cent, or 60 per cent. Of course, this means that every issue still has to be argued and fought out, because this might be one of the admittedly minority cases where he is right.

And all the other cases the same (funnily enough) so you don't give an inch. The 60/40 game is a heap of *shit*. You know it but you won't *break*. You insist on fragmenting your POWER, your BLOODYMINDEDNESS, into a hundred little issues on each of which (once safely parcelled out) *you* are prepared to argue rationally, it's just that she gets so worked up.

(Paton 1973)

I think this rings as true today as it did then. And this goes with my belief that the male as such is suspect. Men are continually coming up with apparently reasonable notions such as that they are not there to be run over by every passing steamroller, and then using them to avoid even the most obvious changes in their behaviour. Men can be incredibly awful, as can be seen many times in this book. Whenever I hear men talking about sexual politics, I cringe, because what they are saying is generally so dreadful. If it is not dreadful in the direction of getting off the hook and avoiding all the issues, it can be dreadful in the direction of making the challenge of feminism so bad and so demanding that no one can live up to it, and so we retreat into guilt and inaction. This is one of the points which Lynne Segal (1990) has made so powerfully in her excellent book.

229

PENIS EXERCISE

Put a cushion or chair in front of you. Imagine that on that cushion or chair is sitting your penis. Talk to it. Make a statement, or ask a question, or make a demand, anything at all which occurs to you. Carry on talking to your penis until you have said everything you want to say.

Then when you have come to an end, switch over, sit on the cushion or the other chair, and be your penis, which by some miracle can talk back to you. What do you say as your penis? Carry on talking back until the penis has said everything it wants or needs to say.

Then go back to your starting point, and carry on the dialogue. Go back and forth until you have said everything you want to say on both sides. You have about ten minutes for this.

When you have finished, find one or two other men and talk to them about what you discovered. [Allow about ten minutes for this.]

The precise point of all my work is to go fully into the guilt and despair, but not to rest there. In this it is rather like the Joanna Macy (1983) approach to nuclear war. Being a man is like being the pilot who dropped the bomb on Hiroshima. Perhaps more for me, who cheered the dropping of the bomb on the two grounds that it was a marvellous step forward in the mastery of Nature and would also get me back home from India and out of the Army that much quicker, than for those who are too young to have had such an experience. Believing something so terrible is important, but equally important is not being paralysed by that belief. These are the two steps. I think the only real, genuinely well-based and grounded kind of hope is the hope which comes on the other side of despair, and which actually grows out of the despair. I spit on the phoney hope which believes that all is basically OK, and that all we have to do is to celebrate the excellence of men and the marvellousness of women.

If any man says to me that 'We do *sometimes* need to protect ourselves', my answer is that obviously we need to protect ourselves from being killed or having our houses burned down, or something irreparable like that – I am not urging some absurd abandonment of all our interests. As we saw in Chapter 4, there is a stage in life when a young man is building up his ego and needs to protect it in the stage before maturity, as a sapling might need a rigid post to protect it in the early days of growth. But when we have reached maturity, what we do not need to protect, and what it is very important not to protect, is our ego. It is the ego which we are protecting whenever we indulge in the 60/40 game. If any true initiation is to take place, the male ego has to be broken. It can then come into existence again on a deeper level, as Mahrer (1989a) has told us, where it is in right relationship with the female, and does not need the self-protection which was so important before. A man can be strong and vulnerable at the same time: they are not opposites, they are all part of the same thing. It is the openness, the nondefensiveness, which is so important and so hard to learn.

NUDE EXERCISE

Each man undresses in turn while the other men remain dressed. He then describes his body, explaining how he feels positively or negatively about each part of it. It is important to make sure that this goes slowly enough so that any relevant feelings can be accessed and expressed.

The whole group then talks about what happened, and what they felt like when the other men were undressed.

If any man says to me that 'Men have to come to their *own* understanding', of course I agree. Some of women's formulations, while excellent for them, just cannot be used in the same form by men. For example, women can totally exclude any contact with men, for short or long periods, and this may be a useful stage in their own development; but men do not have this option – we have to remain in contact with at least one man! Although John Stoltenberg (1989) denied that, and entitled his book *Refusing to be a man*, that is not really a solution that is open to us.

COMMUNICATION EXERCISE

When conversing, men often interrupt one another, or have difficulty getting in. The following conventions, taken from the work of Aaron Kipnis, may be found useful:

- Holding up one finger means, 'I have a comment to make on this topic.'
- Two fingers mean, 'I have a comment that is tangential to this subject.'
- Three mean, 'I wish to introduce a new topic.'
- Four mean, 'I have a question.'
- Five indicate, 'I want a moment of silence.'
- Ten mean, 'Pass the power along to another speaker . . . now.'

If any man says to me 'We can't prescribe for other men', of course I have to agree. I hold to the general ethical belief that 'you can't lay your trip on someone else', which I learned in the LSD culture of the 1960s. But I have also become very impatient with the avoidance practised by so many men in relation to feminism. So I prefer to say things in a rather challenging way that sounds rather pushy and prescriptive – someone said 'scolding' – just to arouse some response. Then when I get the response, I can come back with some more detailed examination of the answers. In this book I have tried to avoid this for the most part, but have not perhaps always succeeded. I certainly do not think I have all the answers. But I do think I am raising most of the questions.

SECRETS

Each man is given a piece of paper and a pencil. He is then asked to write down, in capital letters, a secret which he would not like the other men in the group to know. It should be worded in such a way as not to give away his identity (age, nationality, individual peculiarities, etc.). He is then asked to fold the paper into four. All the pieces of paper are put into a hat, or box, or other container.

Members of the group then take it in turns to pull out one piece of paper and read it out loud. As each man does so, he reads out the secret as if it were written by him, and then tells the group what it feels like to have such a secret. In other words, he takes on the secret as if it were his own.

When all group members have done this, the whole group discusses the exercise and what it felt like, and how they feel now about their own original secret.

If any man says to me 'You sound very self-righteous', I am worried and think it deserves some examination. Self-righteousness is 'righteousness for which one gives oneself credit'. Righteousness is 'Justice, uprightness, rectitude; conformity of life to the requirements of the divine or moral law; virtue, integrity'. I do not know why stating the obvious about patriarchy should be self-righteous. For example, when Bob Geldof told some of the United Nations people that they were a bunch of hypocrites, he seemed to me righteous but not self-righteous. I really do not know how to say some of the things I want to say without taking the risk of seeming self-righteous to some people. I suppose Bob Geldof seemed self-righteous to some people.

MOTHER EXERCISE

It is often found that men feel guilty about their mothers. They have somehow taken responsibility for their mother's happiness, and feel like failures because she is still unhappy. One exercise which has been found to be useful in such cases is for each man to write a letter to her in which he simply resigns from the job at which he could not succeed. It is not necessary to mail the letter. It is usually enough for *him* to know that he has resigned. It is important that this exercise be not done prematurely: it is necessary for each man to have already gained a clear understanding of how he had been inducted into the role, and that his mother's depression had nothing to do with him. Letter writing of this kind can be used for other people too.

It seems to me that in a million ways you, and I, and all of us, support and maintain the system that dropped the bomb. This is just a sober recognition of the way in which we all subscribe, in our daily purchases, in our taxpaying, in our media consumption, in our work, in our leisure, to the horror world. If I counted up, in the course of one day, the number of actions of mine which supported patriarchy and the number which opposed or questioned it, the first number would be larger than the second number. And I suppose the same would be true of you. So that is one way we drop the bomb on Hiroshima. (As I am writing this the fifty-year anniversary of that day is just being remembered.) To the extent that we perpetuate the linear thinking and competitive attitude that we were brought up with, that would be another way in which we drop the bomb all over again: I myself feel that I have dealt with quite a lot of that at a deep level, and I assume that some readers at least would feel the same, but I wonder if push came to shove whether we have eliminated it all?

I believe that it is in group work that all these issues are most effectively tackled. In the kind of group I have been outlining we can be initiated into being the new breed of man the world needs so much.

233

Part IX

COAGULATIO

If salt as the white earth has something to do with the coagulatio process, then that process must also be a process producing bitterness – those two go together. And that helps to explain why coagulatio – the body, things pertaining to the body – has had such a bad name in the current aeon. In order to be something real and definite, to have a body and have a real incarnated existence, one must expose oneself to the bitterness of salt that accompanies that material existence.

(Edinger 1995: 138)

14

TRAINING FOR MALE
THERAPY

We come now to the application of all that we have discovered to the work of therapy. This is the nitty-gritty, the requirements we shall look for in supervision, the hard stuff.

In a way, training for working with men is no different from training to work with any other special group. But some issues do become more salient and therefore need special attention. Let us go through a series of basic issues which arise in all training and see how they look in this light:

1 Establish contact with the client
2 Operate referral procedures
3 Establish working relationship with the client
4 Operate within agreed codes of practice
5 Monitor and evaluate own work
6 Identify, monitor and review progress with the client
7 Use supervision

ESTABLISH CONTACT WITH THE CLIENT

The student grasps the essentials of the client's presenting problem. Can identify main features and contributing factors. Can utilise theoretical material in understanding or explaining any problem. Can relate assessment of problem to own abilities and understanding and limitations.

Persistence is demonstrated in a thorough exploration of the client's situation and a willingness to be open to aspects which may contradict the student's prevailing theory or ideology.

Here the particular issue which applies to men is one we have mentioned several times: the sensitivity which men have to going into therapy at all. This is a key issue, and the whole therapy may depend on how this is handled at the beginning. Equally important is the tendency of men to want a quick solution. It may require some preliminary laying of groundwork before therapy can start on an agreed basis. Stephen Larsen (1990) has quite an eloquent way of putting this, which fits with the general stance of this book:

The client may have no conscious model of what is happening, but is driven by anxiety, emotions that seem to get out of control, or by a situation – often a relationship problem – that is tearing one apart. Because of the stoicism about tender or painful feelings that is enjoined on them by our society, men, especially, are not always eager to enter therapy (but the psyche will often gear up to the threshold of stoicism, using that scourge we call a symptom). The frequent oblivion of the conscious ego to what is happening strikingly underlines the purposefulness of the unconscious in provoking these confrontations.

(Larsen 1990: 33)

Never forget that the client's professed goals are just as neurotic as anything else about him, and should not be given any more standing than any of his other statements.

OPERATE REFERRAL PROCEDURES

The student recognises the context of accountability to the organisation. (Clients should not be taken on if they are beyond the competence of the student.) Has sound judgement and is not about to engage in 'fools rush in' situations. Can use supervision to help in determining when referral is necessary. Is aware of situations where serious consequences are possible, and is unwilling to work outside prudent limits.

The student can complete the relevant forms and go back to the office with an unsuitable candidate, having worked through the problem in supervision.

For further material on this issue, see Appendix. This is a much less contentious issue. Men are used to rejection and usually have developed defences which enable them to handle it well. To get a 'No' from a therapist is not much more problematic than to get a 'Yes'.

ESTABLISH WORKING RELATIONSHIP WITH THE CLIENT

The student listens well, shows good understanding of non-verbal communication. Can set up rapport with client, and use appropriate interventions well timed. Clients generally respond to the approaches of the student despite their possible initial ambivalence, defensiveness or resistance.

The student is sensitive to the ambivalence of clients and is aware of the implications of low-cost therapy, where this is offered. The student can 'reach out' to clients, has patience and can tolerate rejection. The student is careful to make a proper contract with each client as appropriate.

In response to the desire of male clients for a masculine approach, it may well be desirable to spend some time at the beginning of the relationship setting up a contract, so that both sides know what to expect. This hardly ever does any harm in any case, and some organisations demand it for all clients. Men also tend to like other active strategies, such as the use of lists and diagrams.

There is an interesting point here which Aaron Kipnis brings out, and which I have not seen elsewhere, applying particularly to men.

Men's bodies are used to hunting side by side, an ancient habit. Perhaps women's bodies also have the ancient habit of facing one another and talking while weaving and grinding grain. In any case, men often experience their intimacy more shoulder to shoulder. For men, being face to face often implies conflict or competition with the other team.

(Kipnis 1991: 197)

Most therapy these days is conducted with the therapist facing the client, one-to-one. Women are generally comfortable with this arrangement. But many men are more likely to face the one person in a room they dislike, orienting themselves toward a potential conflict, whereas women are more likely to turn toward someone they like most, a potential relationship.

(Kipnis 1991: 265)

I am not sure about this, but it is certainly something which could be considered. Some of these simple pieces of body language are much more influential than might be expected. To the extent that it is true, it simply underlines the general advice always given to sit at right angles to the client, so that one can easily look at him or look away. The language of furniture is very important, too (Rowan 1992d).

OPERATE WITHIN AGREED CODES OF PRACTICE

The student shows awareness of importance of values, beliefs and attitudes on part of therapist and client. Recognises significance of power and authority in familial, group and therapist/client relationships. Shows commitment to providing an equally valid service to all clients.

The student has an informed approach to issues related to the possible conflict between normative values in culture or subculture and individuals' rights to determine their own lives. The student avoids creating unnecessary or excessive dependency, consistently avoids imposing own feelings and opinions on the client, and enhances rather than reduces clients' autonomy over their affairs. The student recognises the client's right to damage as well as to improve well-being and can deal with 'cries for help' without being smothering or rejecting.

239

The student demonstrates a serious concern for the boundaries of time and confidentiality and uses supervision well as a check on ethical and other standard-keeping. Contacts with clients are regular and in accordance with contract. Appropriate dependency needs are met. Courtesy is conveyed without loss of appropriate authority.

The student sees the current training as a beginning and not a completion, takes opportunities that are available to pursue issues of interest, and is already anticipating future training and career needs.

We have seen all the way through this book the importance of these themes in working with men. 'Normative values in culture or subculture' in our case is a question of patriarchy and hegemonic masculinity, and this question is all pervasive.

On the other hand, autonomy is not such a problem for men. When they feel, through the process of therapy, a greater sense of autonomy, they welcome it without question. But it is connectedness which is much more of a problem with many men. The whole question of intimacy can be very fraught with danger, as we have seen.

The question of boundaries is particularly important in relation to a man's job. Many men regard work as their primary responsibility, and cancel sessions at the drop of a hat if any work issue is involved. Therapists need to be very clear that long-term therapy is a life-changing process, and requires a heavy investment in time and money if it is to be anything like successful. Every time a session is cancelled it needs to be examined in the next session, to explore the issues involved, which may involve some element of compulsive action. Cancelled sessions due to work pressure must always be paid for, even if they are advertised in advance. This whole area of the priority of work and the priority of personal life is a very live one which needs to be kept in mind the whole time.

MONITOR AND EVALUATE OWN WORK

The student understands importance of managing own time effectively – punctuality, ability to meet deadlines, etc.

The student shows capacity for warmth and concern in relationship with clients and demonstrates commitment to persevere with therapy despite setbacks. The student does not become sentimental or over-identified with clients and is able to recognise dislike of some qualities in clients.

The student responds to new ideas and new knowledge thoughtfully and critically, and any defensiveness is temporary. The student demonstrates a capacity for changes in attitudes where appropriate, makes use of sources in addition to the regular seminars and supervision, and demonstrates at least average speed in acquiring knowledge, implementing it and integrating it.

The student is aware that use of self is one of the most important resources in therapy, makes positive use of personal experience as tool for learning, and is equally aware of impact of clients' experiences on therapist. The student shows ability to respond flexibly and openly to those with different standards and value systems.

The student imaginatively innovates in at least some areas of work. Records and discussions reflect an input of relevant ideas even if they have not been fully integrated in the work itself. The student tries out interventions based on a theoretical approach not previouly used – e.g. behavioural programme, family therapy or groupwork – and can test out different ways of practising within a particular theoretical frame.

Nothing much here to remark on, except to say that of course because of the use of self which is mentioned, one's own work as a therapist on one's own prejudices in this area is very important. In particular, a straight therapist must always be aware of the dangers of missing material pertinent to homosexuality, because heterosexual men so easily overlook such issues.

The imaginative innovation mentioned is also important. In this book we have emphasised again and again the importance of the alchemical vision, of the mythic imagination. Stephen Larsen again makes a good point when he says:

To see mythically, then, is not just to fantasize richly or to dwell only on classic myths and fables. The mythically awake imagination would rather see through the ordinary-seeming surface of everyday life to discover the 'secret cause,' the mythic, archetypal patterns beneath.

(Larsen 1990: 50)

As he says, we are surrounded by a forest of symbols, and if we are awake to this we can draw on our own creative imagination in working with clients, and speak to them on this level as well as on the other, more conventional levels.

IDENTIFY, MONITOR AND REVIEW PROGRESS WITH THE CLIENT

The student is aware of a range of intervention options, can produce logical reasons for choices made, and has some confidence in defending them. Can explain nature and purpose of interventions in supervision.

The student wants to be productive while recognising that it is not always achieved in a readily recognisable way, and is sensitive to possible unexpected side-effects of interventions. The student is able to respond to transferential feelings, including negative ones, and can discuss own countertransference in supervision. Strong feelings are accepted. There are indications that some clients are sustained by the student's efforts. There is evidence of client's enhanced motivation to solve problems.

The student demonstrates ability to terminate work with clients in appropriate ways. Most work with clients is sustained to a planned termination. The student expects anticipatory mourning as a feature of ending with some clients and does not avoid the distress for some clients and for self. The student copes with ambivalence and appreciates the possible re-awakening for clients of previous separation anxiety. There is no evidence of abandoned clients.

Countertransference is of course always important, and to be looked out for. In particular, if a therapist has a 'favourite client', this needs looking at for the countertransferential qualities which may be involved. Brammer, Shostrom and Abrego (1989) have a good discussion of this in their excellent Chapter 7.

There is a sort of Catch-22 situation which can sometimes arise, where the client insists on advice, and then resists it if given. In this situation, if therapists give advice it is no good, but if they withhold advice, they are indecisive or incompetent. The therapist has to be careful not to get caught in this sort of dilemma. All the therapist needs to do is to reflect back to the client what is going on here.

Premature termination is particularly likely with men, because of their desire to escape from a situation which is so threatening, and for this reason the keeping of proper boundaries is very important. This makes it easier to insist on a meeting to discuss such premature termination.

USE OF SUPERVISION

The student attends supervision sessions promptly and reliably; hands in written work, and prepares tapes or other agreed work in advance. Participates willingly in discussion. Questions when unsure. Uses material from reading, colleague debate, etc., as input. Makes use of support and advice given. Beginning to initiate discussion. Becoming less reactive, can accept and use constructive criticism.

The student attends sessions with agreed tasks prepared beforehand. There is some challenge to the supervisor's views with theoretical and intuitive backing. The student is thoughtful, spontaneous, honest and generally positive in the sessions. The supervisor relationship is stimulating; challenges are handled with confidence and mutual goodwill. The student is able to accept help constructively despite the potential authority and dependency conflicts implicit in adult learning.

The therapist who tries to do without supervision is a fool, or is only pretending to be a therapist. There are some traditions which say that supervision is unnecessary, but they are wrong. Nor will it do to say that one has an internal supervisor. It somehow turns out, all too often, that the internal supervisor turns a blind eye to the very worst infractions of good practice. Of course, in training there is always supervision, but this does need to continue after the training is over.

Part X

SUBLIMATIO

To make insights practical, they must be grounded in daily life. Sublimatio is an extraction process. It is the process of extracting the transpersonal, objective meaning from your purely subjective, reactionary responses to life's crises. The revelations of the archetypal psyche release you from your personal ego attitudes. . . . A higher view is equivalent to a broader perspective that concentrates less on minute detail and more on scope. Therefore, morality is a product of sublimatio, an elevation of consciousness. As the psychic value and meaning of concrete sitations is extracted, a view independent of personal preferences emerges.

(R. Miller and I. Miller 1994: 89)

15

THERAPIST
CONSCIOUSNESS

Now we are seeing things very differently. We have been through our initiation, we have seen the nitty-gritty of how to proceed, and it is time now to rise to a higher level and take a more wide-ranging view.

TRAINING ISSUES RAISED THROUGHOUT

What comes out of all this for the therapist who wants to do a good job? There seem to me to be several points worth bringing out in an attempt to sum up.

1 Patriarchy is an oppressive system, which narrows men just as it puts down women. If therapists are not aware of this, they may unwittingly reinforce the very problems they are trying to wrestle with. For example, in the case history in Chapter 3, I made it clear that the client had a choice between staying with his mother or finding a woman of his own. It was his choice, not something I was urging one way or the other. Compulsory heterosexuality is no better than any other kind of compulsion.
2 Hegemonic masculinity is a part of this system, and imposes an impossible burden on men, one which restricts them and does them harm. For example, it shortens their lives. The young man who says 'Live fast, die young, leave a handsome corpse' thinks he has made a great discovery of freedom, when all he has done is to fall for the major myth of masculinity.
3 There are many masculinities, rather than just one, and men are happier when they can be their own shape, rather than fitting into someone else's idea of how they should be. This is hard to believe at first, and men are all too prone to the belief that there is a blueprint somewhere of masculine perfection.
4 Every 'should' is worth examining, and every time the word 'natural' is used, see if the word 'compulsive' would also fit. One of the ways men try to justify behaviour that is not working is by saying it is natural.
5 Therapy is a place where a man can find out his own shape and experiment with it to see how it works. It is therefore doubly important with men for the therapist to be nondefensive.

245

6 Group work can be particularly valuable in challenging existing gender expectations, because in a group all the issues come out very naturally. But many men become extraordinarily passive in a group, and may need some stimulation from the group leader in order to get moving.

7 There are implications for how men can develop in a more integrated way. Table 9.1 can be used to check how things are going (see p. 147).

8 Therapists must be aware of their own biases if they are to work with men successfully.

9 Some of men's problems can be solved only by bringing in their partners and treating these problems as a joint issue in the relationship.

10 Connectedness and interdependence often feel strange and unfamiliar to men, and they may need a lot of encouragement to explore such issues.

11 Intimacy is hard for men, and they may often mean something different by it than women expect. To explore such issues is often well worth while.

12 The world of work is particularly difficult for men, even though it is often their main field of interest. It often reinforces all the qualities which they are busy questioning in therapy. It is important to be clear that we are not asking men to be uncompetitive, but simply to be aware that competitiveness is a choice, not a compulsion. Co-creation is another choice.

13 Therapy is difficult for men, because it goes against the grain to admit that one may be vulnerable or needy. Such issues may need to be brought up by the therapist, because the client may be too far away from seeing them.

14 The approach adopted in this book lays great stress on the mythic imagination, and the soul of men.

Let Robert Avens just remind us of what this is all about:

> Soul or imagination is not concerned either with mere matter or with pure spirit; to use a portmanteau term, it is a psychosomatic activity, which, like a rainbow, links these extremes harmoniously together and produces a 'new level of being', a 'third', which is none other than the soul itself. The soul creates itself by imagining itself and it exists only while it imagines. The truth and reality of the soul is created and exists in the created. Imagination is a self-originating, autonomous occurrence, sheer presencing, a 'something' which as a Buddhist would say, is 'just so'. In the strict sense of the word, it is a colourful experience.
>
> (Avens 1982: 64)

One of the things we have always to remember is that this is not remote from the experience of men. It is nearer than near. If we can have the courage and the enterprise to assume that it does make sense, we can be astonished at how easy it is to introduce this kind of thinking.

LEARNING ABOUT INTIMACY

We have seen that intimacy is one of the big problems for men. Ian Harris, in his big piece of research on men, says:

> Over time the 'control' message has a negative correlation with 'nurturer', which suggests that the male desire for power keeps them from achieving intimacy.
>
> (Harris 1995: 110)

If this is true, then one of the most important things which a man can learn in the process of therapy is that he can become intimate with another human being without losing his self and without being engulfed. In the safety of the structured therapeutic setting, with its clear limits and boundaries, it becomes possible to try out this feeling side of self with someone who understands the struggle from his own experience and understanding of intimacy. This is an important part of the process of initiation.

POWER AND COMPETITION

For a male to enter therapy and abdicate power to another man, with whom he is usually expected to be competitive, is very stressful. If, of course, he is experiencing extreme emotional discomfort, at which time alleviating the pain is his primary concern, this cost may be payable. The power dynamics may become an issue, however, as the pain diminishes. The power issues tend to dissipate with an explanation that he is in charge of defining the direction of the therapy and for educating the therapist about who he is. This is the underlying message of all good therapy, and it is sometimes worth while to spell it out explicitly.

VULNERABILITY

Vulnerability, weakness and childishness all sound very similar to many men, and so it may not be easy for a man to become vulnerable to the child subpersonality in himself, which fears being hurt or abandoned by anyone he is beginning to trust and need. To admit such a thing can be a profound threat for a male who has been told he should be independent, and protect others, all his life. Sometimes this child self comes to the surface at critical times in the therapy, and this may bring about sudden termination, renewed efforts to control the interaction, or a sabotaging of the therapy in any number of ways. On the other hand, it may signal a new level of trust and a new phase in the therapy. Awareness of this possibility is essential for the therapist who wants to do a good job.

SEX ROLES

Therapists must move beyond limiting sex roles in order for their clients to do so. If a therapist gives continual messages to the client that he at least is open and male, this in itself gives a role model of noncompetitiveness and nondefensiveness. If the therapist makes it clear that co-creation is the name of the game, the client is likely to get the message more easily. The question of gender roles is going to come up again and again in one form or another.

THERAPIST RESPONSIBILITY

This does not mean that any therapist can work with any client. Continuing to work with any client one fears and does not like is neither ethical nor humane. An honest disclosure regarding the therapist's inability to provide what the client may need and suggesting an appropriate referral may be the best service the client can receive. Fear of a client prevents any real possibility of openness and understanding. The Appendix has a whole list of things to look for, but simple dislike and mistrust are also important.

THE NEW MALE MANIFESTO

It may be useful at this point to have a look at the manifesto which Aaron Kipnis (1991) drew up with some friends of his, and see if we agree with it or want to modify it. It goes like this [my own comments are in square brackets]:

1 Men are beautiful. Masculinity is life-affirming and life-supporting. Male sexuality generates life. The male body needs and deserves to be nurtured and protected. [A bit one-sided, but manifestos are like that. Men are beautiful, and ugly, and fascinating, and boring, and mature, and childish, and positive, and negative . . .]
2 A man's value is not measured by what he produces. We are not merely our professions. We need to be loved for who we are. We make money to support life. Our real challenge, and the adventure that makes life full, is making soul. [Again a bit partial, but worth stating as a counterbalance to the usual doctrine.]
3 Men are not flawed by nature. We become destructive when our masculinity is damaged. Violence springs from desperation and fear rather than from authentic manhood. [That is certainly worth saying.]
4 A man doesn't have to live up to any narrow, societal image of manhood. There are many ancient images of men as healers, protectors, lovers, and partners with women, men, and nature. This is how we are in our depths: celebrators of life, ethical and strong. [This is where I believe the Horned God, the Green Man, Shiva, the Serpent Warrior, come in as exemplars.]
5 Men do not need to become more like women in order to reconnect with

soul. Women can help by giving men room to change, grow, and rediscover masculine depth. Women also support men's healing by seeking out and affirming the good in them. [Some very important points here; there is persistent confusion about 'developing our female side' and so forth, which this book has tried to clarify.]

6 Masculinity does not require the denial of deep feeling. Men have the right to express all their feelings. In our society this takes courage and the support of others. We start to die when we are afraid to say or act upon what we feel. [Not quite right here; male expression of feelings can be quite frightening at times, and quite dominant at others. It is not a question of giving carte blanche to men to cultivate their feelings at the expense of others, but rather a question of expanding the range of our feelings in appropriate ways.]

7 Men are not only competitors. Men are also brothers. It is natural for us to cooperate and support each other. We find strength and healing through telling the truth to one another – man to man. [This misses the point about co-creation as a third choice, which this book has been trying to make, but it is worth saying.]

8 Men deserve the same rights as women for custody of children, economic support, government aid, education, health care, and protection from abuse. Fathers are equal to mothers in ability to raise children. Fatherhood is honourable. [On slightly dangerous territory here: it sounds all right at first, but it ignores the points about power which we have been trying to make here, and assumes a level playing field.]

9 Men and women can be equal partners. As men learn to treat women more fairly they also want women to work toward a vision of partnership that does not require men to become less than who they authentically are. [Similar reservations here: we can't be equal in a culture of inequality, and until the culture changes equality may be impossible. It is not just an individual matter.]

10 Sometimes we have the right to be wrong, irresponsible, unpredictable, silly, inconsistent, afraid, indecisive, experimental, insecure, visionary, lustful, lazy, fat, bald, old, playful, fierce, irreverent, magical, wild, impractical, unconventional, and other things we're not supposed to be in a culture that circumscribes our lives with rigid roles. [I agree.]

(Kipnis 1991: 93)

Part XI

RUBEDO

Know that no body is more precious and pure than the sun, and that no dyeing poison is generated without the sun and its shadow. . . . He who hath dyed the poison of the sages with the sun and its shadow hath attained to the greatest secret. And know that our silver when it has become red is termed gold.

(Turba Philosophorum, quoted in Fabricius 1994: 194)

16

INTEGRATION AND
ACTUALISATION

We have now reached the end of the road. The *Rubedo* is the final stage in alchemy. We started with the black of the *Nigredo*, worked through the white of the *Albedo*, and have ended up with the *Rubedo*, the red-gold. Does that mean that we are now permanently happy, permanently satisfied, absolutely smug?

At the end of the road it is important not to give the impression that all is sweetness and light. Men are complex creatures, and vulnerability does not go away simply because it is recognised and allowed. Suffering is not something just to be overcome and left behind – it is part of what makes us human. If nothing could hurt us at the end of the process we should not be human beings.

INITIATION

For all the talk about gods and goddesses, the aim is not to be something beyond the human or above the human. To think this is to be oppressive, either to oneself or to others. What we have been talking about is a human initiation, not an inhuman one.

> Life systems evolve flexibility and intelligence, not by closing off from the environment and erecting walls of defence, but by opening ever wider to the currents of matter-energy and information. It is in this interaction that life systems grow, integrating and differentiating. Here power, far from being identified with invulnerability, requires just the opposite – openness, vulnerability, and readiness to change.
>
> (Macy 1995: 256)

Nevertheless, initiation at its best always involves ecstasy, and we have noticed various points at which ecstasy may arise: contacting the real self; contacting the god or goddess; opening to the nondual nature of reality. To deny ecstasy is also to deny important human capacities.

In alchemy these things are recognised, which is one reason why we have

253

found it useful to tread the alchemical path. We do not just end up with the sun, in the quotation above, but with the sun and its shadow. It is important, too, to recognise that the sun is not just a masculine symbol. Janet McCrickard has written a book about Sun goddesses and Moon gods:

> I found Sun-goddesses everywhere – from Australia to the Baltic, from Siberia to Southern India, from Ireland to Japan, from Russia to Malaya, in every era and in every kind of culture, from aboriginal hunter-gatherers to settled farmers.
>
> (McCrickard 1990: xviii)

She points out that Jungians and alchemists are very bad at recognising this, sticking firmly to the view that the sun is male and the moon female. But she wants to say that this is wrong – and interestingly enough one of her chapters is entitled 'Shakti power of the sun's light'.

> In Hindu thought the Sun is the fiery principle of life, its active initiating force – here represented by *Shakti*, the female divine power – while the Moon is the primeval cold, watery and passive element – represented in this Tantric rite as *Shiva*, the masculine divine power. Women may now find it easier to see why the goddess Kali, the violent and destructive shakti-power, dances upon the corpse of her husband under her feet, for he is the lunar partner who is constantly destroyed and regenerated by the terrible aspect of the feminine Sun – just as the phallus itself, like the Moon, is 'destroyed' and 'regenerated' by the power of feminine 'heat'. This is a new way of looking at sexual symbolism – new, at any rate, for Westerners who are so used to thinking of the supposedly hot, active, solar masculine and the cold, passive lunar feminine.
>
> (McCrickard 1990: 181)

All I am trying to do here is to say that being a man is never going to be something simple and easy to understand, any more than being a woman is. All our symbols are open to change and challenge, all our assumptions are up for grabs, all our taken-for-granted simplicities have to come up for scrutiny.

PARADOX

Even the celebrated resistance to therapy exhibited by men has another side to it. Resistance is a powerful bond. By resistance I mean that phenomenon by which someone comes for therapy and then tries as hard as possible not to get anywhere. We often think of it as something negative, like refusing to talk at all, or refusing to come on time, or keeping on cancelling appointments. But it can take a huge variety of forms. Agreeing with everything the therapist says is a form of resistance. It gets the client off the hook as well as anything else.

Cooperating too much is a form of resistance. There can be session after session where the client follows every suggestion of the therapist, conscientiously and thoroughly, without ever getting personally involved or genuinely committed. Prolonged dependence on the therapist is a form of resistance. As soon as the therapy looks like coming to an end, a new flurry of symptoms may be brought forth.

Getting interested in the philosophy of therapy is a form of resistance. There can be interesting discussions which serve to postpone the real action.

Asking for more time is a form of resistance. It is a way of taking charge of the session and making the therapist into an ally who will be loyal and true.

Some therapists talk about there being no such thing as resistance, and say or imply that a truly flexible therapist would never find any resistance. But resistance is the way in which we keep our secrets: it is one of the most revealing things about us. The conflict which it engenders forms a strong connection between therapist and client. Therapy is about wrestling with the angel, and sometimes this can be done by the therapist and the client joining together in the struggle. But sometimes the therapist is the angel, and has to be struggled with, through the resistance. To acc-ent-uate the positive and e-lim-i-nate the negative is not on in therapy. As James Hillman has so wisely said:

Suffering is necessary for increased awareness and the development of personality. . . . If malfunctioning and suffering are viewed only pathologically, the physician prevents himself from sensing his own wound. . . . The purpose of training analysis is not merely to heal the personality of the analyst, but to open his wounds from which his compassion will flow.

(Hillman 1990: 132)

So at the end of the road we have burned away the falsities, voluntarised the compulsion, hacked off the shackles, and now – now we are ordinary. Now we just have to live as men on this earth, connecting with women and children and each other as best we can.

AUTONOMY

Even the precious idea of autonomy, so common to all types of therapy, comes into question. It has been pointed out that:

From a feminist viewpoint, a construction of reality that hierarchically orders the world order under the control of autonomous individuals is evidence of the male domination of cultural meaning systems.

(Gergen 1995: 364)

All through this book we have been criticising hierarchical systems, but this idea, that autonomous individuals very naturally start up new hierarchical systems, has to be watched. In a patriarchal society, it is hard even to think about non-hierarchical organisation. Yet if we entertain the idea of a heterarchy instead, we remember such things as the game of paper–stone–scissors, where paper wraps stone, stone blunts scissors and scissors cut paper. This is perfectly orderly and rule-bound, but it is not hierarchical.

This also applies within the person. To think that at the end of the road we should end up with total control, total order, is to construct a totalitarian ego. Much better to allow that there might be subpersonalities – alternative centres of control within the person, which may come into operation at different times in different circumstances. At the lowest level of development, these might take over in neurotic ways, but even after full initiation there might be alternative centres of colour and light, adding to the interest and depth of the character. I have explored this idea in detail elsewhere (Rowan 1990).

CONNECTEDNESS

'Growth is always within a dialectical relationship in a dilemma which is never fully resolved.' That is what Rollo May said once. What is a dialectical relationship? It is a relationship characterised by engagement and commitment, where growth happens through conflict. Sometimes the conflict is inside the person, between different subpersonalities of the person; sometimes it is between therapist and client. The essence of it is that whatever conflicts arise are worked through and dealt with as thoroughly as need be.

By saying that the dilemma is never resolved, Rollo May is giving the basic existential warning that something settled and final is not to be had among human beings. We start on the existential edge, and we finish on the existential edge. Hopefully we have grown somewhat between start and finish. Engagement and commitment lead to higher levels of paradox, not to an end or a cure.

Diversity is of value, not just because it gives us a richness which we need for our own depth, but because it links us with the struggles over the whole position of women and the whole biosphere.

> The marginalization of women and destruction of biodiversity go hand in hand. Loss of diversity is the price paid in the patriarchal model of progress which pushes inexorably toward monocultures, uniformity and homogeneity. . . . Diversity is the basis of women's politics and the politics of ecology.
>
> (Mies and Shiva 1993: 164–165)

Conflict is there to be worked through and learned from, not something to be avoided. Looked at in the right light, it is part of a dialectical dance, which brings down powerful energy. It is a dance which never ends, because it is a holy dance: it is the dance of Shiva and Shakti, which brings creation and destruction at one end and the same time. The place where Shiva dances his dance with Shakti is within the human heart, and the human heart can include the world.

Why should the dilemma ever be resolved? Why should the dance ever end? How are we ever going to leave the existential edge?

This is the only kind of connectedness which will be truly satisfying – a connectedness which takes diversity and conflict seriously as an essential part of the deal.

THE SERPENT WARRIOR

Many people today are putting forward the notion that the warrior is some kind of ideal for men. We hear of peaceful warriors, creative warriors, spiritual warriors, inner warriors, shadow warriors, sadistic warriors, rainbow warriors, and so on and so forth. I would like to float the idea of the Serpent Warrior.

In my own work, developed with Jocelyn Chaplin at the Serpent Institute, I have found that the concept of Goddess spirituality has a great deal to offer. This means that we respect the principles of rhythm as the dance of life energies interweaves in or out of opposites and polarities throughout nature and human life. Sometimes this is called the feminine principle, but we also stress the importance of the male polarity and of male sexuality as an essential part of goddess spirituality.

One of the things involved here is a reclaiming of very ancient pre-Christian pagan symbols and rituals that embody more of the 'feminine' principle. The serpent is one of these symbols, representing wisdom, transformation, connections between the worlds and even the spiralling shape of the primal earth and human energies themselves.

This rhythmic and fundamentally erotic model of life is contrasted with patriarchal relationships based on dominance and submission. It celebrates difference and interconnectedness through dance and sometimes struggle. It is not rigidly hierarchical and is in a constant state of change. It represents both male and female inner powerfulness rather than 'power-over'. The emphasis is on partnership, social equality and justice as well as individual well-being.

The vision that we arrived at was to see therapy and counselling as a kind of initiation process. The kind of initiation we are talking about is a process of symbolic death and rebirth, leading to a new phase of life or a new existence as a different kind of woman or man. Each individual starts at a different point in this process and may need different styles of therapy at different times. Some need to develop a well-functioning ego before they can begin to question it. Some need to work through problems to do with their sexual identity in a patriarchal society. Some have to clean up their karma before they can go on. Some need a counsellor, while others need a guide.

This means that a proper training along these lines has to cover a much broader range than was thought necessary in the past. For example, we have to use non-possessive warmth, but also to understand the world of myths and symbols.

One of the major symbols which we discovered was the labyrinth. As therapists we are privileged witnesses to other people's stories and can help them follow their threads through their own journeys in and out of the labyrinths of self-discovery. Psychotherapy can indeed be thought of as a seven-stage journey into and out of the labyrinth, as we saw in Chapter 8. It starts with an emphasis on mothering, trust and childhood, and goes on to deal with separation from the mother and difference. This may lead to the exploration of life myths and stories, which may in turn enable the client to face the loss of illumination and ambivalence at the centre. Then there is the return to the world with new awareness and assertiveness, learning to dance to our own rhythms. Finally we deal with endings and new beginnings.

> To the ancients, the cosmic serpent – the spirit of earth and water – was everywhere known as the energy source of life: of healing and oracular powers, fertility and maternal blessing.
>
> (Sjöö and Mor 1987: 251)

So the serpent became for us a symbol of this journey, of this path through the labyrinth. And it was good for men too, because of its basic ambivalence and dual nature:

> Finally, the snake came to symbolize the phallus, male sexual energy, which was understood to be originally contained within the Goddess – born from her, and returning to her again, when at the end of each world cycle (expansion-contraction) she curls up in dark sleep. . . . But these are not aggressive or misogynistic phallic images; rather, they seem to represent the phallus *serving* the Goddess, women, and the life processes of all.
>
> (Sjöö and Mor 1987: 61)

This then seems a rich source of imagery for the whole process of psychotherapy and counselling. Michael Meade (1993) has a good discussion of the myth of Gilgamesh, but Stephen Larsen brings out something which Meade does not emphasise in quite the same way:

> While he [Gilgamesh] bathes in a stream for renewal, the serpent, who more than once has served as nemesis to heroes, creeps out of the water, attracted by the herb's fragrance, and eats it, thereby learning immortality's secret: death and rebirth, the sloughing of the skin, the art of perpetual self-transformation.
>
> (Larsen 1990: 102)

As we have seen many times in this book, death and rebirth is at the heart of initiation, and at the heart of therapy. But the serpent also leads us to study Dionysus, because Dionysus was the god who reconciled the male and female energies in his own body. And the serpent was one of his symbols.

> With the help of Dionysos an analyst is better able to get caught by the drama of the patient, to enter madness and be torn apart, to let the woman in him show, to admit his animal shape and be impelled by the brute drives of power, of raw laughter, of sexual passion, and the thirst for more and more. Dionysos offers involvement in suffering, and the mark of the hero-

healer here would be that ability to undergo in oneself *the trials of emotion* and through these emotions find an identification with the same powers in the other.

(Hillman 1990: 124)

Hillman has a great deal to say about Dionysus, and Hades (Lord of the underworld where our dreams come from) and Hermes, who goes back and forth between the worlds. The Serpent Warrior has most to learn from Dionysus. The whole world of dreams is a very powerful one in therapy, leading us to the heart of the matter, as Hillman (1979) has forcefully reminded us. Dreams take us into the chthonic realm, which means the realm of the earth. Some of the most powerful gods and goddesses of ancient times were associated with the underworld, the earth realm, and not with some high heaven. Stephen Larsen tells us:

> For the Greeks the deep unconscious was the chthonic realm. Its lord was Hades-Dionysus-Pluto. ('Hades and Dionysus are the same,' said Heraclitus, Frag. 15.) The gateway to the underworld is sexuality, intoxication and self-abandonment. Yet the chthonic realm is that creative deep from which dreams (*oneiros*) arise; Pluto, the euphemistic name for Hades, means 'wealth', which the underworld lord was said both to possess and to bestow. The modern dreamer above is invited to the ancient *nekyia*, the underworld journey, as a mode of self-discovery – and thus personal enrichment – invoked by heroes (Aeneas, Odysseus and Dante) throughout the ages.
>
> (Larsen 1990: 123)

Though Dionysus is male, and phallic, there is no misogyny in his structure of consciousness because it is not divided from its own femininity. Dionysus is man and woman in one person. Dionysus was bisexual in the first place. If we want to get rid of homophobia and heterosexism, we can learn about this from Dionysus.

One of the names for Dionysus was 'The Undivided', and one of his main representations was as a child. The child refers to a view of reality which is not divided. Like a child asked which sweet he prefers, he asks for both. He must declare that truth is both/and, not either/or. A Dionysian perspective toward therapy, says James Hillman (1978), would not exclude the child for the sake of maturity, since the child is the synthesis itself. The childish may not be put away, but shall be retained within consciousness for the sake of 'both/and'.

This is so important, because men so easily think in terms of winning or losing, right or wrong, true or false. And if we seriously want to study how to avoid the either/or and how to go for the both/and in our daily life and work, we can study Mary Parker Follett, in the wonderful book on her approach (Graham 1995).

In Dionysus, borders *join* that which we usually believe to be separated by borders. The riotous Dionysus has but one wife, Ariadne. Dionysus presents us with borderline phenomena, so that we cannot tell whether he is mad or sane, wild or sombre, sexual or psychic, male or female, conscious or unconscious. Stephen Larsen again:

Snakes are among the most primary and powerful of symbolic animals; they lend themselves to multiple representations. Freud's favourite was of the phallus, but why not also the spinal cord – our more 'instinctual' part of the central nervous system – or the digestive tract, which expands to swallow? Snakes live in hidden places in the earth or in water. They carry poisons, also potentially usable as medicines. Their legendary serpentine movement we now know as an elementary form of energy, the sine wave. Most important for the archaic world – as in the tale of Gilgamesh – was their ability to shed their skin, which became a primary and perennial symbol of transformation.

(Larsen 1990: 160)

The serpent goes back and forth like Hermes between the worlds, linking and connecting them. It inhabits the margins, and is quite unabashed to do so. Kerenyi (1976) says that wherever Dionysus appears, the border also is manifested. He rules the borderlands of our psychic geography. If the Serpent Warrior can adopt him as exemplar, we are in new territory.

GOING ON

But perhaps we should come down to the ordinary at last. Many of us are not ready to adopt Dionysus, or any other pagan god or goddess, as our teacher or inspiration. Some people go into the wilderness on a vision quest, to discover what they may discover. Someone who has done this, Steven Harper, has come back to tell us what we might do instead:

Over the year I have found myself, more often than not, recommending gardening to workshop participants who seek ways of staying connected outside of the wilderness environment. When practiced in a sustainable way, gardening and farming are activities in which people and wild nature intermesh and begin to coevolve. Gardening yields deep insights into how we can physically, mentally and spiritually find creative balance between wild nature and human nature. Gardening immerses us in a basic natural cycle that directly sustains our life. We get our hands dirty and our bodies sweaty. Gardening can be the physical embodiment of symbiosis and coevolution, the 'ground' in which we practice what we have learned in wilderness. We give to the Earth as well as receiving.

(Harper 1995: 198)

And so perhaps in the end we come back to the earth. Even the window-boxes of our urban flats can be a connection with something greater and deeper than our everyday selves.

So let us come to an end with Joseph Campbell's words, written half a century ago, which sums up something of what this has been about:

And where we had thought to find an abomination, we shall find a god; where we had thought to slay another, we shall slay ourselves; where we had thought to travel outward we shall come to the centre of our own existence; where we had thought to be alone, we shall be with all the world.

(Campbell 1949: 25)

APPENDIX

SHOULD I TAKE ON THIS CLIENT?

A practitioner should not expect to be able to take on everyone who applies. Very often in training there is a preliminary interview by a staff member before a client is referred, but even at this stage there may be some people who are taken on in other ways. Some considerations:

1 *The nature and severity of the client's symptoms* For example, prolonged delusional thinking may be a sign of psychosis, and people suffering in this way usually need residential facilities, rather than once or twice a week therapy. Or outbursts of uncontrolled anxiety or hostility again require quite secure environmental situations before a practitioner should be asked to deal with them.

2 *Length and persistence of symptoms* The longer something has been going on the longer it is going to take to deal with it. "Am I ready to take on a client who may require constant attention for five years?" There is a responsibility not to bite off more than one can chew. One of the terrible things about some institutional set-ups is that personnel are transferred without any consideration of the possible effects on clients.

3 *The nature of the predisposing and precipitating experiences* If a client has had a series of severe traumas over a short period there may be a need for sessions much more frequently than you can in practice offer. It may be better to refer the client to someone who can offer this. Do not be panicked into firefighting if you have not been trained as a firefighter.

4 *Past stability and defensive functioning* Has the person shown the ability to handle deep feelings in the past, or is there a history of breakdown, self-mutilation, attempted suicide or the like? You are going to be asking the person to explore their inner life, and you want to be reasonably sure that this is not simply asking for trouble. Again residential facilities may be required.

5 *Resistance to therapy* If in the first interview there is a lot of blocking of your attempts to open up significant areas, this may be because they are generally resistant to therapy, or it may be that they are resistant to you and your approach. Either way, it is not a good bet. It may also be that they are not ready to do therapy at the moment, but would be later. However, as we

have seen all through this book, men are under a good deal of pressure to resist therapy, due to their conditioning, and a certain amount of this is to be expected.

6 *The person's network* Does the person have friends, relatives, colleagues, etc., around and available? It is more acceptable to take on a difficult client who has such support than one who does not.

7 *Extent and adequacy of the practitioner's training* Generally speaking, although there can be exceptions to this, it is unwise to take on someone who has had more experience of therapy than you. There are games which can be played in therapy; if the client knows more of them than you do, the therapy may go off the rails. You can refer such a client to someone more experienced.

8 *The problems of the practitioner* Often the practitioner is unable to handle feelings because the client's feelings touch upon sore spots of his or her own. If this is so, it may be better to refer the client on. Empathy can turn into sympathy, and sympathy into collusion to avoid what needs to be faced.

9 *The amount of time available* It is better not to take on long-term clients if you know you will be leaving the country or the neighbourhood, or retiring, etc., within a relatively short period of time. (See also 2 above.)

10 *Institutional policy* If you are working for an agency or other organisation, they may have rules as to which clients you may take on, or how deep you are to go with them. These have to be observed, and you should think about whether you are willing to abide by such rules when you take on such a job.

BIBLIOGRAPHY

Abrams, Jeremiah (ed.) (1991) *Reclaiming the inner child*, Mandala, London.

Adams, J. S. (1965) 'Inequity in social exchange' in L. Berkowitz (ed.) *Advances in experimental social psychology, Vol. 2*, Academic Press, New York.

Adcock, Cynthia (1982) 'Fear of "Other": The common root of sexism and militarism' in P. McAllister (ed.) *Reweaving the web of life*, New Society Publishers, Philadelphia, PA.

Albery, Nicholas (1985) *How to feel reborn?*, Regeneration Press, London.

Allen, Jo Ann and Gordon, Sylvia (1990) 'Creating a framework for change' in R. L. Meth and R. S. Pasick (eds) *Men in therapy*, Guilford Press, New York.

Anthony, Carl (1955) 'Ecopsychology and the deconstruction of whiteness' in T. Roszak, M. E. Gomes and A. D. Kanner (eds) *Ecopsychology*, Sierra Club, San Francisco.

Anthony, Richard, Ecker, Bruce and Wilber, Ken (eds) (1987) *Spiritual choices: The problem of recognising authentic paths to inner transformation*, Paragon House, New York.

Appley, D. G. and Winder, A. E. (1977) 'An evolving definition of collaboration and some implications for the world of work' *Journal of Applied Behavioural Science* 13/3 279–291.

Assagioli, Roberto (1975) *Psychosynthesis*, Turnstone Books, London.

Ausubel, D. P. (1954) *Theory and problems of adolescent development*, Grune & Stratton, New York.

Avalon, Arthur (1978) *Shakti and Shakta*, Dover, New York.

Avens, Robert (1982) *Imaginal body: Para-Jungian reflections on soul, imagination and death*, University Press of America, Washington, DC.

Baillargeon, R., Spelke, E. and Wasserman, S. (1985) 'Object permanence in five-month-old infants' *Cognition* 20 191–208.

Bandler, Richard and Grinder, John (1979) *Frogs into princes*, Real People Press, Moab, UT.

Barkham, Michael (1992) 'Research on integrative and eclectic therapy' in Windy Dryden (ed.) *Integrative and eclectic therapy: A handbook*, Open University Press, Milton Keynes.

Bateson, Gregory (1972) *Steps to an ecology of mind*, Ballantine, New York.

Baumli, Francis (ed.) (1985) *Men freeing men*, New Atlantis Press, Jersey City, NJ.

Bernard, J. (1981) 'The good provider role: Its rise and fall' *American Psychologist* 36 1–12.

Beutler, L. E., Crago, M. and Arizmendi, I. G. (1986) 'Therapist variables in psychotherapy process and outcome' in S. L. Garfield and A. E. Bergin (eds) *Handbook of psychotherapy and behaviour change* (3rd edn), John Wiley, New York.

Birren J. E. (1970) 'Toward an experimental psychology of ageing' *American Psychologist* 25.

Bly, Robert (1990) *Iron John: A book about men*, Addison-Wesley, Reading.

BIBLIOGRAPHY

Boadella, David (1987) *Lifestreams*, Routledge, London.

Boadella, David and Smith, David (1986) *Maps of character*, Abbotsbury Publishers, Abbotsbury.

Bolen, Jean Shinoda (1989) *Gods in everyman*, Harper & Row, San Francisco.

Bowen, M. (1978) *Family therapy in clinical practice*, Jason Aronson, New York.

Bower, Tom (1977) *A primer of infant development*, W. H. Freeman, San Francisco.

Bradshaw, John (1988a) *Bradshaw on the family*, Health Communications, Deerfield Beach, FL.

Bradshaw, John (1988b) *Healing the shame that binds you*, Health Communications, Deerfield Beach, FL.

Bradshaw, John (1991) *Homecoming*, Piatkus, London.

Bragdon, Emma (1990) *The call of spiritual emergency*, Harper & Row, San Francisco.

Brammer, Lawrence M., Shostrom, Everett L. and Abrego, Philip J. (1989) *Therapeutic psychology: Fundamentals of counselling and psychotherapy*, Prentice-Hall, Englewood Cliffs, NJ.

Brannon, R. (1976) 'The male sex role: Our culture's blueprint for manhood, what it's done for us lately' in D. David and R. Brannon (eds) *The forty-nine per cent majority: The male sex role*, Addison-Wesley, Reading.

Brod, Harry (ed.) (1987) *The making of masculinities*, Allen & Unwin, Boston, MA.

Bromley, D. B. (1988) *Human ageing*, Penguin, Harmondsworth.

Brown, Laura S. (1992) 'While waiting for the revolution: The case for a lesbian feminist psychotherapy' *Feminism and Psychology* 2/2 239–253.

Browne, Kevin (1994) 'Child sexual abuse' in J. Archer (ed.) *Male violence*, Routledge, London.

Brownmiller, Susan (1976) *Against our will: Men, women and rape*, Penguin, Harmondsworth.

Buber, Martin (1975) *Tales of the Hasidim*, Schocken, New York.

Bushnell, I. W. R. (1987) 'Neonatal recognition of the mother's face', Paper presented at the Annual Conference of the Developmental Psychology Section of the BPS, York.

Butler, R. N. and Lewis, M. I. (1982) *Ageing and mental health: Positive psychosocial approaches (3rd edn)*, C. V. Mosby, St Louis, MO.

Butterworth, G. (1981) 'The origins of auditory-visual perception and visual proprioception in human development' in R. D. Walk and H. L. Pick (eds) *Intersensory perception and sensory integration*, Plenum Press, New York.

Campbell, Joseph (1949) *The hero with a thousand faces*, Princeton University Press, Princeton, NJ.

Campbell, Joseph (1988) *Historical atlas of world mythology: Vol. 1 – The way of the animal powers – Part 2: Mythologies of the great hunt*, Harper & Row, New York.

Chamberlain, David (1988) *Babies remember birth*, Ballantine, New York.

Chambless, Dianne L. and Goldstein, Alan J. (1979) 'Behavioral psychotherapy' in R. J. Corsini (ed.) *Current psychotherapies*, F. E. Peacock, Itasca, IL.

Chaplin, Jocelyn (1988) *Feminist counselling in action*, Sage, London.

Cherniss, Cary (1980) *Staff burnout*, Sage, Beverly Hills, CA.

Chickering, J. (1969) *Education and identity*, Jossey-Bass, San Francisco.

Chown, S. M. and Heron, H. (1965) 'Psychological aspects of ageing in man' in P. R. Farnsworth (ed.) *Annual Review of Psychology*.

Clarkson, M. G., Clifton, R. K., Swain, I. U. and Perris, E. E. (1989) 'Stimulus duration and repetition rate influence newborns' head orientation towards sound' *Developmental Psychology* 22 683–705.

Clarkson, Petruska (1989) *Gestalt counselling in action*, Sage, London.

Clarkson, Petruska (1992) 'A multiplicity of psychotherapeutic relationships' in *On psychotherapy*, Whurr, London.

BIBLIOGRAPHY

Clarkson, Petruska (1993) *Transactional analysis psychotherapy*, Routledge, London.

Clatterbaugh, Kenneth (1986) *Contemporary perspectives on masculinity*, Westview Press, Boulder, CO.

Clifford, Jenny (1990) 'Adlerian therapy' in W. Dryden (ed.) *Individual therapy: A handbook*, Open University Press, Milton Keynes.

Connell, Robert W. (1987) *Gender and power*, Polity Press, Cambridge.

Corey, Gerald (1991) *Theory and practice of counselling and psychotherapy (4th edn)*, Brooks/Cole, Pacific Grove, CA.

Craig, Grace J. (1992) *Human development: 6th edition*, Prentice-Hall, Englewood Cliffs, NJ.

Cumming, E. and Henry, W. E. (1961) *Growing old: The process of disengagement*, Basic Books, New York.

Daly, Mary (1973) *Beyond God the Father: Toward a philosophy of women's liberation*, Beacon Press, Boston, MA.

Delafield, G. L. (1979) 'Social comparisons and pay' in G. M. Stephenson and C. J. Brotherton (eds) *Industrial relations: A social psychological approach*, John Wiley, Chichester.

Devall, B. and Sessions, G. (1985) *Deep ecology: Living as if nature mattered*, Gibbs Smith, Layton, UT.

Diamond, Jed (1987) 'Counselling male substance abusers' in M. Scher, M. Stevens, G. Good and G. A. Eichenfield (eds) *Handbook of counselling and psychotherapy with men*, Sage, Newbury Park, CA.

Douglas, Anne (1989) 'The limits of cognitive-behaviour therapy: Can it be integrated with psychodynamic therapy?' *British Journal of Psychotherapy* 5/3 390–401.

Douglas, Tom (1976) *Group work practice*, Tavistock, London.

Dryden, Windy (ed.) (1984) *Individual therapy in Britain*, Open University Press, Milton Keynes.

Dryden, Windy (ed.) (1987) *Key cases in psychotherapy*, Croom Helm, London.

Dryden, Windy (1992) 'Therapists and the whole person: An interview with John Rowan' in W. Dryden (ed.) *The Dryden interviews*, Whurr, London.

Dryden, Windy and Golden, William (eds) (1986) *Cognitive-behavioural approaches to psychotherapy*, Harper & Row, London.

Dryden, W. and Norcross, J. C. (1990) *Eclecticism and integration in counselling and psychotherapy*, Gale Centre Publications, Loughton, Essex.

Duke, Marshall P. and Nowicki, Stephen (1986) *Abnormal psychology: A new look*, Holt, Rinehart & Winston, New York.

Dziurawiec, S. and Ellis, H. D. (1986) 'Neonates' attention to face-like stimuli: Goren, Sarty and Wu (1975) revisited', Paper presented at the Annual Conference of the Developmental Psychology Section of the BPS, Exeter.

Edelwich, Jerry (with Archie Brodsky) (1980) *Burnout*, Human Sciences Press, New York.

Edinger, Edward F. (1978) 'Psychotherapy and alchemy (1)' *Quadrant* 11/1.

Edinger, Edward F. (1985) *Anatomy of the psyche: Alchemical symbolism in psychotherapy*, Open Court, La Salle, IL.

Edinger, Edward F. (1995) *The mysterium lectures*, Inner City Books, Toronto.

Eisler, Riane (1987) *The chalice and the blade*, Harper, San Francisco.

Eisler, Riane and Loye, David (1990) *The partnership way*, Harper, San Francisco.

Eliade, Mircea (1964) *Shamanism*, Pantheon, New York.

Ellenberger, Henri (1970) *The discovery of the unconscious*, Basic Books, New York.

Elliott, Jim (1976) *The theory and practice of encounter group leadership*, Explorations Institute, Berkeley, CA.

Ellis, Albert and Yeager, R. (1990) *Why some therapies don't work: The dangers of transpersonal psychology*, Prometheus Books, Buffalo, NY.

266

Emery, F. E. and Trist, E. L. (1965) 'The causal texture of organisational environments' *Human Relations* 18 1–10.

Emmons, M. L. (1978) *The inner source*, Impact, San Luis Obispo, CA.

Engen, T., Lipsitt, L. P. and Kaye, H. (1963) 'Olfactory responses and adaptation in the human neonate' *Journal of Comparative Physiology and Psychology* 56 73–77.

Erickson, Beth M. (1993) *Helping men change: The role of the female therapist*, Sage, Newbury Park, CA.

Erikson, Eric H. (1966) *Identity: Youth and crisis*, W. W. Norton, New York.

Ernst, Sheila and Goodison, Lucy (1981) *In our own hands*, The Women's Press, London.

Erskine, Richard G. and Moursund, Janet P. (1988) *Integrative psychotherapy in action*, Sage, Newbury Park, CA.

Evison, Rose and Horobin, Richard (1988) 'Co-counselling' in J. Rowan and W. Dryden (eds) *Innovative therapy in Britain*, Open University Press, Milton Keynes.

Eysenck, H. J. (1952) 'The effects of psychotherapy: An evaluation' *Journal of Consulting Psychology* 16 319–324.

Eysenck, H. J. (1992) 'The outcome problem in psychotherapy' in W. Dryden and C. Feltham (eds) *Psychotherapy and its discontents*, Open University Press, Milton Keynes.

Fabricius, Johannes (1994) *Alchemy: The medieval alchemists and their royal art*, Diamond Books, London.

Farrar, Janet and Farrar, Stewart (1989) *The witches' god*, Robert Hale, London.

Farrell, Warren (1990) *Why men are the way they are*, Bantam, New York.

Farrell, Warren (1993) *The myth of male power*, Simon & Schuster, New York.

Feinstein, David and Krippner, Stanley (1988) *Personal mythology*, Tarcher, Los Angeles.

Ferrucci, Piero (1982) *What we may be*, Turnstone Press, Wellingborough.

Fine, Reuben (1988) *Troubled men*, Jossey-Bass, San Francisco.

Fodor, I. G. (1987) 'Moving beyond cognitive behavior therapy: Integrating gestalt therapy to facilitate personal and inter-personal awareness' in N. S. Jacobson (ed.) *Psychotherapists in clinical practice*, Guilford Press, New York.

Fogel, Alan (1993) *Developing through relationships*, Harvester Wheatsheaf, Hemel Hempstead.

Fonagy, Peter (1989) 'On the integration of cognitive-behaviour therapy with psycho-analysis' *British Journal of Psychotherapy* 5/4 557–563.

Fordyce, J. K. and Weil, R. (1971) *Managing with people*, Addison-Wesley, Reading.

France, Ann (1988) *Consuming psychotherapy*, Free Association Books, London.

Freundlich, David (1974) 'Countertransference in individual and group therapy' *Primal Experience Monograph*, Centre for the Whole Person, New York.

Frye, Marilyn (1983) *The politics of reality: Essays in feminist theory*, Crossing Press, Trumansburg, NY.

Fukuyama, Y. (1961) 'The major dimensions of church membership' *Review of Religious Research* 2.

Ganley, Anne L. (1988) 'Feminist therapy with male clients' in M. A. Dutton-Douglas and L. E. A. Walker (eds) *Feminist psychotherapies: Integration of therapeutic and feminist systems*, Ablex, Norwood, NJ.

Garfield, S. L. (1992) 'Response to Eysenck' in W. Dryden and C. Feltham (eds) *Psychotherapy and its discontents*, Open University Press, Milton Keynes.

Garfield, S. L. and Bergin, A. E. (eds) (1986) *Handbook of psychotherapy and behaviour change (3rd edn)*, John Wiley, New York.

Garfinkel, Perry (1992) *In a man's world*, Ten Speed Press, Berkeley, CA.

Gergen, Mary (1995) 'Postmodern, post-Cartesian positionings on the subject of psychology' *Theory and Psychology* 5/3 361–368.

Gilbert, Lucia Albino (1987) 'Women and men together but equal: Issues for men in dual-career marriages' in M. Scher, M. Stevens, G. Good and G. A. Eichenfield (eds) *Handbook of counselling and psychotherapy with men*, Sage, Newbury Park, CA.

Glouberman, Dina (1989) *Life choices and life changes through imagework*, Mandala, London.

Goffman, Erving (1961) *Asylums*, Doubleday, New York.

Goldberg, A. (1973) 'Psychotherapy of narcissistic injury' *Archives of General Psychiatry* 28 722–726.

Gomes, Mary E. and Kanner, Allen D. (1995) 'The rape of the well-maidens' in T. Roszak, M. E. Gomes and A. D. Kanner (eds) *Ecopsychology*, Sierra Club, San Francisco.

Good, Glenn and May, Ronald (1987) 'Developmental issues, environmental influences, and the nature of therapy with college men' in M. Scher, M. Stevens, G. Good and G. A. Eichenfield (eds) *Handbook of counselling and psychotherapy with men*, Sage, Newbury Park, CA.

Goodrich, T., Rampage, C., Ellman, B. and Halstead, K. (1988) *Feminist family therapy: A casebook*, Norton, New York.

Goren, C., Sarty, M. and Wu, P. (1975) 'Visual following and pattern discrimination of face-like stimuli by newborn infants' *Pediatrics* 56 544–549.

Graham, Pauline (1995) *Mary Parker Follett: Prophet of management*, Harvard Business School Press, Boston, MA.

Gray, Elizabeth Dodson (1982) *Patriarchy as a conceptual trap*, Roundtable Press, Wellesley, VA.

Gray, John (1992) *Men are from Mars, women are from Venus*, HarperCollins, New York.

Green, Hannah (1964) *I never promised you a rose garden*, Gollancz, London.

Greenberg, L. G. (1981) 'Advances in clinical intervention research: A decade review' *Canadian Psychology* 22/1 25–34.

Greenberg, Leslie S. and Pinsof, William M. (eds) (1986) *The psychotherapeutic process: A research handbook*, Guilford Press, New York.

Greene, Liz (1988) 'Alchemical symbolism in the horoscope' in L. Greene and H. Sasportas, *Dynamics of the unconscious*, Arkana, London.

Greenson, R. R. (1968) 'Dis-identifying from mother: Its special importance for the boy' *International Journal of Psycho-Analysis* 49 370.

Grof, C. and Grof, S. (1990) *The stormy search for the self*, Tarcher, Los Angeles.

Grof, Stanislav (1979) *Realms of the human unconscious*, Souvenir Press, London.

Grof, Stanislav (1985) *Beyond the brain*, State University of New York Press, Albany, NY.

Grof, Stanislav (1988) *The adventure of self-discovery*, State University of New York Press, Albany, NY.

Grof, Stanislav (1992) *The holotropic mind*, Harper, San Francisco.

Grof, S. and Grof, C. (1989) *Spiritual emergency*, Tarcher, Los Angeles.

Haigh, Gerald (1968) 'The residential basic encounter group' in H. A. Otto and J. Mann (eds) *Ways of growth*, Grossman, New York.

Haley, Jay (1976) *Problem solving therapy*, Jossey-Bass, San Francisco.

Hamisch, Carol (1969) 'The personal in political' in Redstockings (ed.) (1975) *Revolution*, Random House, New York.

Hampden-Turner, Charles (1976) *Sane asylum*, William Morrow, New York.

Hanna, Fred J., Giordano, Francesca, Dupuy, Paula and Puhakka, Kaisa (1995) 'Agency and transcendence: The experience of therapeutic change' *The Humanistic Psychologist* 23/2 141–160.

Hargreaves, David J. and Colley, Ann M. (1986) *The psychology of sex roles*, Harper & Row, London.

Harper, Steven (1995) 'The way of wilderness' in T. Roszak, M. E. Gomes and A. D. Kanner (eds) *Ecopsychology*, Sierra Club, San Francisco.

Harris, Ian M. (1995) *Messages men hear: Constructing masculinities*, Taylor & Francis, London.

Harrison, James (1987) 'Counselling gay men' in M. Scher, M. Stevens, G. Good and G. A. Eichenfield (eds) *Handbook of counselling and psychotherapy with men*, Sage, Newbury Park, CA.

Harrison, James (1995) 'Roles, identities and sexual orientation: Homosexuality, heterosexuality and bisexuality' in R. F. Levant and W. S. Pollack (eds) *A new psychology of men*, Basic Books, New York.

Harrison, James, Chin, James and Ficarrotto, Thomas (1989) 'Warning: Masculinity may be dangerous to your health' in M. Kimmel and M. A. Messner (eds) *Men's lives*, Macmillan, New York.

Havighurst, R. J. (1953) *Human development and education*, Longmans Green, London.

Herink, Richie (ed.) (1980) *The psychotherapy handbook*, New American Library, New York.

Heron, John (1977) *Catharsis in human development*, University of Surrey, Guildford.

Heron, John (1988) *Cosmic psychology*, Endymion Press, London.

Hillman, James (1975) *Revisioning psychology*, Harper & Row, New York.

Hillman, James (1978) *The myth of analysis*, Harper & Row, New York.

Hillman, James (1979) *The dream and the underworld*, Harper & Row, New York.

Hillman, James (1983) *Archetypal psychology*, Spring, Dallas, TX.

Hillman, James (1990) *Suicide and the soul*, Spring, Dallas, TX.

Hillman, James (1991) 'The yellowing of the work' in M. A. Mattoon (ed.) *Paris 89*, Daimon Verlag, Einsiedeln.

Hillman, James (1993) 'Alchemical blue and the unio mentalis' *Spring 54* June.

Hillman, James and Ventura, Michael (1992) *We've had a hundred years of psychotherapy and the world's getting worse*, HarperCollins, New York.

Hite, Shere (1981) *The Hite report on male sexuality*, Macdonald, London.

Hogan, Daniel (1979) *The regulation of psychotherapists (4 vols)*, Ballinger, Cambridge, MA.

Holland, Sue (1990) 'Psychotherapy, oppression, and social action: Gender, race and class in black women's depression', in R. J. Pevelberg and A. C. Miller (eds) *Gender and power in families*, Routledge, London.

Homans, George C. (1961) *Social behaviour: Its elementary forms*, Routledge, London.

Hopkins, J. (1984) *Deity yoga*, Wisdom Publications, London.

Hudson, Liam and Jacot, Bernardine (1993) *The way men think: Intellect, intimacy and the erotic imagination*, Yale University Press, London.

Humphries, Martin (1985) 'Gay machismo' in A. Metcalf and M. Humphries (eds) *The sexuality of men*, Pluto Press, London.

Jaffe, Aniela (ed.) (1979) *C. G. Jung: Word and image*, Princeton University Press, Princeton, NJ.

Jaffe, Dennis T. and Scott, Cynthia D. (1984) *From burnout to balance*, McGraw-Hill, New York.

James, Jenny (1985) *Male sexuality: The Atlantis position*, Caliban Books, London.

Janov, Arthur (1983) *Imprints: The lifelong effects of the birth experience*, Coward-Mccann, New York.

Jastrab, Joseph (1994) *Sacred manhood, Sacred earth: A vision quest into the wilderness of a man's heart*, HarperCollins, New York.

Joba, Cynthia, Maynard, Herman Bryant, Jr, and Ray, Michael (1993) 'Competition, cooperation and co-creation: Insights from the World Business Academy' in M. Ray and A. Rinzler (eds) *The new paradigm in business*, Tarcher, Los Angeles.

Jones, F. and Harris, M. W. (1971) 'The development of interrracial awareness in small groups' in L. Blank, G. B. Gottsegen and M. G. Gottsegen (eds) *Confrontation: Encounters in self and interpersonal awareness*, Collier-Macmillan, New York.

Jourard, Sidney (1974) 'Some lethal aspects of the male role' in J. H. Pleck and J. Sawyer (eds) *Men and masculinity*, Prentice-Hall, Englewood Cliffs, NJ.

Jukes, Adam (1993) *Why men hate women*, Free Association Press, London.

Jung, Carl G. (1968) *The archetypes and the collective unconscious – CW9, i* (2nd edn), Routledge, London.

Jung, Carl G. (1969) *Psychology and religion: West and East – CW11* (2nd edn), Routledge, London.

Jung, Carl G. (1980) *Psychology and alchemy (2nd edn)*, Routledge, London.

Kappeler, Susanne (1986) *The pornography of representation*, Polity Press, Cambridge.

Karle, Hellmut W. A. and Boys, Jennifer H. (1987) *Hypnotherapy: A practical handbook*, Free Association Books, London.

Katcharian, Leon, *et al.* (1990) *Grounding of the US tankship* Exxon Valdez *on Bligh Reef, Prince Williams Sound, near Valdez, Alaska, March 24, 1989* (Washington, DC: NTSB/MAR-90/04): 166–167.

Keating, M. B., McKenzie, B. E. and Day, R. H. (1986) 'Spatial localization in infancy: Position constancy in a square and circular room with and without a landmark' *Child Development* 57 115–124.

Keen, Sam (1991) *Fire in the belly*, Bantam Books, New York.

Keller, Catherine (1986) *From a broken web: Separation, sexism and self*, Beacon Press, Boston, MA.

Kerckhoff, A. C. (1964) 'Husband–wife expectations and reactions to retirement' *Journal of Gerontology* 19.

Kerenyi, Carl (1976) *Dionysos: Archetypal image of indestructible life*, Princeton University Press, Princeton, NJ.

Kernberg, Otto (1975) *Borderline conditions and pathological narcissism*, Jason Aronson, New York.

Kipnis, Aaron (1991) *Knights without armour: A practical guide for men in quest of masculine soul*, Tarcher, Los Angeles.

Kirschenbaum, H. and Henderson, V. L. (eds) (1990) *The Carl Rogers reader*, Constable, London.

Kitzinger, Sheila (1985) *Woman's experience of sex*, Penguin, Harmondsworth.

Klein, Kenny (1993) *The flowering rod: Men, sex and spirituality*, Delphi Press, Oak Park, Queensland.

Klimo, Jon (1988) *Channeling*, Aquarius, Wellingborough.

Kohlberg, Lawrence (1981) *Essays on moral development Vol. 1*, Harper & Row, San Francisco.

Kohlberg, Lawrence (1984) *The psychology of moral development*, Harper & Row, San Francisco.

Kohut, H. (1971) *The analysis of the self: A systematic approach to the psychoanalytic treatment of narcissistic personality disorders*, International Universities Press, New York.

Kokopeli, Bruce and Lakey, George (1982) 'Masculinity and violence' *Peace News* 20 May 1977. Reprinted in Pam McAllister (ed.) *Reweaving the web of life: Feminism and nonviolence*, New Society Publishers, Philadelphia, PA.

Kopp, Sheldon (1977) *Back to one*, Science and Behaviour, Palo Alto, CA.

Kovel, Joel (1978) *A complete guide to psychotherapy*, Penguin, Harmondsworth.

Krugman, Steven (1995) 'Male development and the transformation of shame' in R. F. Levant and W. S. Pollack (eds) *A new psychology of men*, Basic Books, New York.

Kupers, Terry A. (1993) *Revisioning men's lives: Gender, intimacy and power*, Guilford Press, New York.

Kutash, I. L. and Wolf, A. (eds) (1986) *Psychotherapists' casebook*, Jossey-Bass, San Francisco.

Laing, Ronald D. (1983) *The voice of experience*, Penguin, Harmondsworth.

BIBLIOGRAPHY

Lake, Frank (1980) *Constricted confusion*, Clinical Theology Association, Oxford.
Larsen, Stephen (1990) *The mythic imagination: Your quest for meaning through personal mythology*, Bantam, New York.
Lazarus, A. A. (1989) *The practice of multimodal therapy*, Johns Hopkins University Press, Baltimore, MD.
Lederer, Laura (ed.) (1980) *Take back the night*, William Morrow, New York.
Lee, John (1991) *At my father's wedding*, Bantam, New York.
Leslie, A. M. (1984) 'Infant perception of a manual pick-up event' *British Journal of Developmental Psychology* 2 19–32.
Levant, Ronald F. and Pollack, William S. (eds) (1995) *A new psychology of men*, Basic Books, New York.
Levinson, D. J. (1978) *The seasons of a man's life*, Knopf, New York.
Lincoln, Y. S. and Guba, E. G. (1985) *Naturalistic inquiry*, Sage, Beverly Hills, CA.
Lipsitt, L. (1969) 'Learning capacities of the human infant' in R. J. Robinson (ed.) *Brain and early behaviour*, Academic Press, London.
Lister, L. (1991) 'Men and grief: A review of research', *Smith College Studies in Social Work* 61/3.
Loevinger, Jane (1976) *Ego development*, Jossey-Bass, San Francisco.
Lomas, Peter (1987) *The limits of interpretation*, Penguin, Harmondsworth.
Long, Pauline and Coghill, Mary (1977) *Is it worthwhile working in a mixed group?*, Beyond Patriarchy Publications, London.
Lorber, Judith (1994) *Paradoxes of gender*, Yale University Press, New Haven, CT.
Love, Patricia (1990) *The chosen child syndrome*, Piatkus, London.
Lowen, Alexander (1976) *Bioenergetics*, Coventure, London.
Lukoff, David and Everest, Howard C. (1985) 'The myths in mental illness' *Journal of Transpersonal Psychology* 17/2 123–153.
McCrickard, Janet (1990) *Eclipse of the sun*, Gothic Image, Glastonbury.
Macfarlane, A. (1975) 'Olfaction in the development of social preferences in the human neonate' in *Parent–Infant Interaction* (CIBA Foundation Symposium 33) Elsevier, Amsterdam.
Mack, John E. (1955) 'The politics of species arrogance' in T. Roszak, M. E. Gomes and A. D. Kanner (eds) *Ecopsychology*, Sierra Club, San Francisco.
McNeilly, Cheryl L. and Howard, Kenneth I. (1991) 'The effects of psychotherapy: A reevaluation based on dosage' *Psychotherapy Research* 1/1 74–78.
Macy, Joanna (1983) *Despair and personal power in the nuclear age*, New Society Publishers, Philadelphia, PA.
Macy, Joanna (1995) 'Working through environmental despair' in T. Roszak, M. E. Gomes and A. D. Kanner (eds) *Ecopsychology*, Sierra Club, San Francisco.
Madison, Peter (1969) *Personality development in college*, Addison-Wesley, Reading.
Mahrer, Alvin R. (1985) *Psychotherapeutic change*, W. W. Norton, New York.
Mahrer, Alvin R. (1986) *Therapeutic experiencing*, W. W. Norton, New York.
Mahrer, Alvin R. (1989a) *Experiencing*, University of Ottawa Press, Ottawa.
Mahrer, Alvin R. (1989b) *The integration of psychotherapies*, Human Sciences Press, New York.
Malinak, D. P., Hoyt, M. F. and Patterson, V. (1979) 'Adults' reactions to the death of a parent: A preliminary study' *American Journal of Psychiatry* 136 1152–1156.
Manor, Oded (1984) *Family work in action*, Tavistock, London.
Marina, Ninoska (1982) 'Restructuring of cognitive-affective structure: A central point of change after psychotherapy' Brunel, unpublished doctoral dissertation.
Marineau, Rene F. (1989) *Jacob Levy Moreno 1889–1974*, Routledge, London.
Martin, C. L. (1989) 'Children's use of gender-related information in making social judgements' *Developmental Psychology* 25/1 80–88.

Martin, C. L. (1990) 'Attitudes and expectations about children with nontraditional and traditional gender roles' *Sex Roles* 22/3+4 151.

Maslow, A. H. (1987) *Motivation and personality (3rd edn)*, Harper & Row, New York.

Masson, Jeffrey (1990) *Against therapy*, Fontana, London.

Matteson, David R. (1987) 'Counselling bisexual men' in M. Scher, M. Stevens, G. Good and G. A. Eichenfield (eds) *Handbook of counselling and psychotherapy with men*, Sage, Newbury Park, CA.

May, Rollo (1991) *The cry for myth*, W. W. Norton, New York.

Mays, J. B. (1969) *The young pretenders*, Sphere, London.

Meade, Michael (1993) *Men and the water of life: Initiation and the tempering of men*, Harper, San Francisco.

Meltzoff, A. N. and Moore, M. K. (1983) 'The origins of imitation in infancy: Paradigm, phenomena and theories' in L. P. Lipsitt (ed.) *Advances in infancy research vol. 2*, Ablex, Norwood, NJ.

Meth, Richard I. and Pasick, Robert S. (eds) (1990) *Men in therapy*, Guilford Press, New York.

Metzner, Ralph (1986) *Opening to inner light*, Tarcher, Los Angeles.

Mies, Maria and Shiva, Vandana (1993) *Ecofeminism*, Zed Books, London.

Miller, Richard and Miller, Iona (1994) *The modern alchemist: A guide to personal transformation*, Phanes Press, Grand Rapids, MI.

Miller, Stuart (1983) *Men and friendship*, Gateway Books, Bath.

Mintz, Elizabeth E. (1972) *Marathon groups: Reality and symbol*, Avon, New York.

Mintz, Elizabeth E. (1983) *The psychic thread: Paranormal and transpersonal aspects of psychotherapy*, Human Sciences Press, New York.

Minuchin, Salvatore (1974) *Families and family therapy*, Tavistock, London.

Mitchell, Juliet (1974) *Psychoanalysis and feminism*, Pantheon Books, New York.

Mitler, Merrill M., Carskadon, Mary A., Czeisler, Charles A., *et al.* (1988) 'Catastrophes, sleep, and public policy: Consensus report', Association of Professional Sleep Societies, Committee on Catastrophes, Sleep, and Public Policy, *Sleep*, vol. 11, no. 1 (New York, Raven Press) pp. 100–109.

Moore, Robert and Gillette, Douglas (1990) *King, Warrior, Magician, Lover*, Harper, San Francisco.

Moore, Thomas (1992) *Care of the soul*, Judy Piatkus, London.

Moss, Donald M. (1981) 'Transformation of self and world in Johannes Tauler's mysticism' in R. S. Valle and R. von Eckartsberg (eds) *The metaphors of consciousness*, Plenum Press, New York.

Mowbray, Richard (1995) *The case against psychotherapy registration*, Transmarginal Press, London.

Mullender, Audrey and Ward, Dave (1991) *Self-directed groupwork*, Whiting & Birch, London.

Neugarten, B. L. (1963) 'Personality and the ageing process' in R. H. Williams, C. Tibbitts and W. Donahue (eds) *Processes of ageing, Vol. 1*, Atherton Press.

Newman, B. M. (1982) 'Mid-life development' in B. Wolman (ed.) *Handbook of developmental psychology*, Prentice-Hall, Englewood Cliffs, NJ.

Norcross, J. C. and Prochaska, J. O. (1983) 'Clinicians' theoretical orientations: selection, utilization and efficacy' *Professional psychology* 14 197–208.

Nowicki, S. (1983) *Village of St Joseph: An integrative approach*, Emory University, Atlanta, GA.

O'Connor, Terrance (1995) 'Therapy for a dying planet' in T. Roszak, M. E. Gomes and A. D. Kanner (eds) *Ecopsychology*, Sierra Club, San Francisco.

Olivier, Christiane (1989) *Jocasta's children*, Routledge, London.

Osherson, Samuel (1986) *Finding our fathers: How a man's life is shaped by his relationship with his father*, Fawcett Columbine, New York.

BIBLIOGRAPHY

Osterweiss, M., Solomon, F. and Green, M. (eds) (1984) *Bereavement: Reactions, consequences and care*, National Academy Press, Washington, DC.
Pagels, Elaine H. (1979) *The gnostic gospels*, Random House, New York.
Palmer, Barry (1979) 'Learning and the group experience' in W. G. Lawrence (ed.) *Exploring individual and organisational boundaries*, John Wiley, Chichester.
Palmer, Barry (1992) 'Ambiguity and paradox in group relations conferences' in M. Pines (ed.) *Bion and group psychotherapy*, Routledge, London.
Papousek, H. (1969) 'Individual variability in learned responses in human infants' in R. J. Robinson (ed.) *Brain and early behaviour*, Academic Press, London.
Parkes, C. M. and Weiss, R. S. (1983) *Recovery from bereavement*, Basic Books, New York.
Pasick, Robert S. (1990) 'Friendship between men' in R. L. Meth and R. S. Pasick (eds) *Men in therapy*, Guilford Press, New York.
Pasick, Robert S., Gordon, Sylvia and Meth, Richard L. (1990) 'Helping men understand themselves' in R. L. Meth and R. S. Pasick (eds) *Men in therapy*, Guilford Press, New York.
Paul, Nancy C. (1985) 'Increasing organisational effectiveness: A training model for developing women' *Management Education and Development* 16/2 211–222.
Pedler, Mike and Boydell, Tom (1981) 'What is self-development' in T. Boydell and M. Pedler (eds) *Management self-development*, Gower, Farnborough.
Peine, H. and Howarth, R. (1975) *Children and parents: Everyday problems of behaviour*, Penguin, Harmondsworth.
Perera, Sylvia Brinton (1981) *Descent to the Goddess*, Inner City Books, Toronto.
Perkins, Rachel (1991) 'Therapy for lesbians?: The case against' *Feminism and Psychology* 1/3 325–338.
Perkins, Rachel (1992) 'Waiting for the revolution – or working for it?: A reply to Laura Brown and Katherine Sender' *Feminism and Psychology* 2/2 258–261.
Perls, Fritz (1969) *Gestalt therapy verbatim*, Real People Press.
Person, Ethel Spector (1993) 'Male sexuality and power' in Robert A. Glick and Steven P. Roose (eds) *Rage, Power and Aggression*, Yale University Press, New Haven, CT.
Pesso, Albert (1973) *Experience in action: A psychomotor psychology*, New York University Press, New York.
Peters, Larry G. (1989) 'Shamanism: Phenomenology of a spiritual discipline' *Journal of Transpersonal Psychology* 21/2 115–137.
Pines, Malcolm (ed.) (1992) *Bion and group psychotherapy*, Routledge, London.
Pitcher, Evelyn Goodenough and Schultz, Lynn Hickey (1983) *Boys and girls at play: The development of sex roles*, Praeger, New York.
Pittman, Frank (1993) *Man enough: Fathers, sons and the search for masculinity*, Perigee, New York.
Pleck, Joseph H. (1981) *The myth of masculinity*, MIT Press, Cambridge, MA.
Pleck, Joseph H. (1987) 'The theory of male sex-role identity: Its rise and fall, 1936 to the present' in H. Brod (ed.) *The making of masculinities*, Allen & Unwin, Boston, MA.
Pleck, Joseph H. (1989) 'Men's power with women, other men, and society: A men's movement analysis' in M. S. Kimmel and M. A. Messner (eds) *Men's lives*, Macmillan, New York.
Pleck, Joseph H. (1995) 'The gender role strain paradigm: An update' in R. F. Levant and W. S. Pollack (eds) *A new psychology of men*, Basic Books, New York.
Pogrebin, L. C. (1987) *Among friends*, McGraw-Hill, New York.
Purce, Jill (1974) *The mystic spiral*, Thames & Hudson, London.
Purcell, P. and Stewart, L. (1990) 'Dick and Jane in 1989' *Sex Roles* 22/3+4 177–185.
Radin, N. (1982) 'Primary caregiving and role-sharing fathers of preschoolers' in M. E. Lamb (ed.) *Nontraditional families*, Erlbaum, Hillsdale, NJ.

273

BIBLIOGRAPHY

Rands, T. A. (1984) *Grief, dying and death*, Research Press, Champaign, IL.

Rawson, Philip (1973) *The art of Tantra*, New York Graphic Society, Greenwich, NY.

Reason, Peter and Rowan, John (1981) *Human inquiry: A sourcebook of new paradigm research*, John Wiley, Chichester.

Red Therapy (1978) *Red therapy*, Red Therapy, London.

Reich, Wilhelm (1990) *Character analysis (3rd edn)*, Noonday Press, New York.

Reichard, S., Livson, F. and Peterson, P. G. (1962) *Ageing and personality: A study of eighty-seven old men*, Wiley, New York.

Reuveni, R. (1979) *Networking families in crisis*, Human Science Press, New York.

Rinpoche, Sogyal (1992) *The Tibetan book of living and dying*, Rider, London.

Roberts, John (1994) 'Prisoners of grief: Some thoughts on men and bereavement' *Counselling* 5/3 220–221.

Rochat, P. (1987) 'Mouthing and grasping in neonates: Evidence for early detection of what hard or soft substances afford for action' *Infant Behaviour and Development* 10 435–449.

Rogers, Carl R. (1942) *Counselling and psychotherapy*, Houghton Mifflin, Boston, MA.

Rogers, Carl R. (1970) *On encounter*, Penguin, Harmondsworth.

Roose, Kris (1991) 'An integrative model in psychotherapy training', Paper presented at the Society for the Exploration of Psychotherapy Integration (SEPI) congress in London in July 1991.

Rossi, Ernest L. (ed.) (1980) *The nature of hypnosis and suggestion*, Irvington, New York.

Roszak, Betty (1995) 'The spirit of the goddess' in T. Roszak, M. E. Gomes and A. D. Kanner (eds) *Ecopsychology*, Sierra Club, San Francisco.

Roszak, Theodore (1995) 'Where Psyche meets Gaia' in T. Roszak, M. E. Gomes and A. D. Kanner (eds) *Ecopsychology*, Sierra Club, San Francisco.

Roszak, Theodore, Gomes, Mary E. and Kanner, Allen D. (eds) (1995) *Ecopsychology*, Sierra Club, San Francisco.

Rowan, John (1973) *The social individual*, Davis-Poynter, London.

Rowan, John (1983) *The reality game*, Routledge, London.

Rowan, John (1987) *The Horned God: Feminism and men as wounding and healing*, Routledge & Kegan Paul, London.

Rowan, John (1988) *Ordinary ecstasy (2nd edn)*, Routledge, London.

Rowan, John (1990) *Subpersonalities*, Routledge, London.

Rowan, John (1992a) 'Spiritual experiences in primal integration' in J. Rowan (ed.) *Breakthroughs and integration in psychotherapy*, Whurr, London.

Rowan, John (1992b) 'A growth episode' in J. Rowan (ed.) *Breakthroughs and integration in psychotherapy*, Whurr, London.

Rowan, John (1992c) 'Holistic listening' in J. Rowan (ed.) *Breakthroughs and integration in psychotherapy*, Whurr, London.

Rowan, John (1992d) 'Counselling and the psychology of furniture' in J. Rowan (ed.) *Breakthroughs and integration in psychotherapy*, Whurr, London.

Rowan, John (1993a) *The transpersonal in psychotherapy and counselling*, Routledge, London.

Rowan, John (1993b) *Discover your subpersonalities*, Routledge, London.

Rowan, John (1994) 'Do therapists ever cure clients?' *Self and Society* 22/5 4–5.

Sagi, A. (1982) 'Antecedents and consequences of various degrees of paternal involvement in child rearing: The Israeli project' in M. E. Lamb (ed.) *Nontraditional families*, Erlbaum, Hillsdale, NJ.

Samuels, Andrew (1989) *The plural psyche*, Routledge, London.

Samuels, Andrew (1993) *The political psyche*, Routledge, London.

Satir, Virginia (1988) *The new peoplemaking*, Science and Behaviour, Mountain View, CA.

Sattel, Jack W. (1989) 'The inexpressive male: Tragedy or sexual politics?' in M. Kimmel and M. A. Messner (eds) *Men's lives*, Macmillan, New York.

Scheeringa, M. S., Zeanah, C. H., Drell, M. S. and Larrien, J. A. (1995) 'Two approaches to the diagnosis of posttraumatic stress disorder in infancy and early childhood' *American Academy of Child and Adolescent Psychiatry* 34/2 191–200.

Schutz, Will (1973) *Elements of encounter*, Joy Press, Big Sur, CA.

Schutz, Will (1981) 'Holistic education' in R. Corsini (ed.) *Innovative psychotherapies*, John Wiley, New York.

Schutz, Will (1984) *The truth option*, Ten Speed Press, Berkeley, CA.

Schutz, Will (1989) *Joy: Twenty years later*, Ten Speed Press, Berkeley, CA.

Schwartz, Robert M. (1993) 'The idea of balance and integrative psychotherapy' *Journal of Psychotherapy Integration* 3/2 159–181.

Segal, Lynne (1990) *Slow motion: Changing masculinities, changing men*, Virago Press, London.

Senge, Peter M. (1990) 'Catalyzing systems thinking within organisations' in F. Massarik (ed.) *Advances in organization development, Vol. 1*, Ablex, Norwood, NJ.

Shaffer, John B. P. and Galinsky, M. David (1989) *Models of group therapy*, Prentice-Hall, Englewood Cliffs, NJ.

Shapiro, D. A. and Shapiro, D. (1982) 'Meta-analysis of comparative outcome studies: A replication and refinement' *Psychological Bulletin* 92 581–604.

Sherrod, Drury (1987) 'The bonds of men' in H. Brod (ed.) *The making of masculinities*, Allen & Unwin, Winchester.

Signorielli, N. (1989) 'Television and conceptions about sex roles: Maintaining conventionality and the status quo' *Sex Roles* 21/5+6 341–350.

Sjöö, Monica and Mor, Barbara (1987) *The great cosmic mother: Rediscovering the religion of the earth*, Harper & Row, San Francisco.

Slater, A. M., Morison, V. and Rose, D. (1983) 'Perception of shape by the new-born baby' *British Journal of Developmental Psychology* 1 135–142.

Smail, David (1987) *Taking care: An alternative to therapy*, J. M. Dent and Sons, London.

Smith, Jack C., Mercy, James A. and Conn, Judith M. (1988) 'Marital status and the risk of suicide' *American Journal of Public Health* 78/1 79.

Smith, M. L., Glass, G. V. and Miller, T. J. (1980) *The benefits of psychotherapy*, Johns Hopkins University Press, Baltimore, MD.

Southgate, John (1983) *Inner and outer group dynamics*, Polytechnic of North London.

Southgate, John and Whiting, Liz (eds) (1987) *Journal of the Institute for Self-Analysis* 1/1.

Spelke, E. S. (1982) 'Perceptual knowledge of objects in infancy' in J. Mehler, M. Garrett and E. Walker (eds) *Perspectives on mental representation*, Erlbaum, Hillsdale, NJ.

Spinelli, Ernesto (1989) *The interpreted world*, Sage, London.

Spinelli, Ernesto (1994) *Demystifying therapy*, Constable, London.

Starhawk (1982) *Dreaming the dark*, Harper, San Francisco.

Starhawk (1989) *The spiral dance (2nd edn)*, Harper, San Francisco.

Starhawk (1990) *Truth or dare*, Harper & Row, San Francisco.

Stern, Daniel N. (1985) *The interpersonal world of the infant*, Basic Books, New York.

Stevens, Barry and Rogers, Carl (eds) (1967) *Person to person: The problem of being human*, Real People Press, Moab, UT.

Stoltenberg, John (1989) *Refusing to be a man*, Fontana, London.

Stone, M. (1985) 'Shellshock and the psychologists' in W. F. Bynum, R. Porter and M. Shepherd (eds) *The anatomy of madness, Vol. 2*, Tavistock, London.

Sutherland, Stuart (1992) 'What goes wrong in the care and treatment of the mentally ill' in W. Dryden and C. Feltham (eds) *Psychotherapy and its discontents*, Open University Press, Milton Keynes.

BIBLIOGRAPHY

Swenson, Clifford H. (1973) *Introduction to interpersonal relationships*, Scott Foresman.

Tanner, J. M. (1978) *Fetus into man: Physical growth from conception to maturity*, Harvard University Press, Cambridge, MA.

Thompson, M. (ed.) (1987) *Gay spirit: Myth and meaning*, St Martins Press, New York.

Tobin, Stephan (1991) 'A comparison of psychoanalytic self psychology and Carl Rogers' person-centred therapy' *Journal of Humanistic Psychology* 31/1 9–33.

Turner, Angela K. (1994) 'Genetic and hormonal influences on male violence' in J. Archer (ed.) *Male violence*, Routledge, London.

Tyler, A. (1986) 'The abusing father' in M. E. Lamb (ed.) *The father's role: Applied prospectives*, Wiley, New York.

Underhill, Evelyn (1961) *Mysticism*, Dutton, New York.

Vaillant, G. E. (1978) *Adaptation to life: How the best and the brightest came of age*, Little, Brown, Boston, MA.

Vaughan, Frances (1985) *The inward arc*, New Science Library, Boston, MA.

Verny, Tom (1982) *The secret life of the unborn child*, Sphere, London.

Wachtel, P. L. (1977) *Psychoanalysis and behaviour therapy: Toward an integration*, Basic Books, New York.

Wachtel, P. L. (ed.) (1982) *Resistance: Psychodynamic and behavioural approaches*, Plenum Press, New York.

Waldron, Ingrid (1976) 'Why do women live longer than men?' *Social science and medicine* 10 349–362.

Walker, Alice (1983) *In search of our mothers' gardens*, Harcourt Brace Jovanovich, New York.

Walker, Barbara G. (1983) *The women's encyclopaedia of myths and secrets*, Harper & Row, San Francisco.

Wallis, Ray (1985) 'Betwixt therapy and salvation: The changing forms of the human potential movement', in R. K. Jones (ed.) *Sickness and sectarianism*, Gower, Aldershot.

Walsh, Roger (1993) 'The transpersonal movement: A history and state of the art', *Journal of Transpersonal Psychology* 25/2 123–139.

Waterhouse, Ruth L. (1993) '"Wild women don't have the blues": A feminist critique of "person-centred" counselling and therapy' *Feminism and Psychology* 3/1 55–71.

Wehr, Demaris (1988) *Jung and feminism*, Routledge, London.

Wertheimer, M. (1961) 'Psycho-motor coordination of auditory-visual space at birth' *Science* 134 1692.

Wibberley, Mike (1988) 'Encounter' in J. Rowan and W. Dryden (eds) *Innovative therapy in Britain*, Open University Press, Milton Keynes.

Wilber, Ken (1980) *The Atman Project*, Quest Books, Wheaton, IL.

Wilber, Ken (1981) *No boundary*, Shambhala, Boston, MA.

Wilber, Ken (1983) 'The pre/trans fallacy' in *Eye to eye: The quest for the new paradigm*, Anchor, Garden City, NY.

Wilber, Ken, Engler, Jack and Brown, Daniel P. (1986) *Transformations of consciousness*, New Science Library, Boston, MA.

Wilson, Michael (1994) 'Spiritual terrain' *Counselling News* 16, December.

Winnicott, Donald (1958) *Collected papers: Through paediatrics to psychoanalysis*, Tavistock, London.

Wyckoff, Hogie (1975) 'Problem-solving groups for women' in C. Steiner *et al.*, (eds) *Readings in radical psychiatry*, Grove Press, New York.

Yablonsky, L. (1965) *Synanon: The tunnel back*, Macmillan, London.

INDEX

277